MW01705782

CLOUD

ESSENTIALS

CompTIA® Authorized Courseware for Exam CLO-001

Kirk Hausman
Susan L. Cook
Telmo Sampaio

WILEY

CLOUD ESSENTIALS

CompTIA® Authorized Courseware for Exam CLO-001

Authorized reprint by Wiley India Pvt. Ltd., 4435-36/7, Ansari Road, Daryaganj,
New Delhi – 110002.

Senior Acquisitions Editor: Jeff Kellum
Development Editor: Kim Wimpsett
Technical Editors: Kunal Mittal and Sourya Biswas
Production Editor: Rebecca Anderson
Copy Editor: Judy Flynn
Editorial Manager: Pete Gaughan
Production Manager: Tim Tate
Vice President and Executive Group Publisher: Richard Swadley
Vice President and Publisher: Neil Edde
Book Designer: Happenstance Type-O-Rama
Proofreader: Dawn Adams
Indexer: Robert Swanson
Project Coordinator, Cover: Katherine Crocker
Cover Designer: Ryan Sneed
Cover Image: © iStockphoto.com / Aleksandar Velasevic

Reprint: 2013

Printed at: *Lalit Printer & Binder, Delhi*

ISBN: 978-81-265-4288-8

Dear Reader,

Thank you for choosing *Cloud Essentials*. This book is part of a family of premium-quality Sybex books, all of which are written by outstanding authors who combine practical experience with a gift for teaching.

Sybex was founded in 1976. More than 30 years later, we're still committed to producing consistently exceptional books. With each of our titles, we're working hard to set a new standard for the industry. From the paper we print on, to the authors we work with, our goal is to bring you the best books available.

I hope you see all that reflected in these pages. I'd be very interested to hear your comments and get your feedback on how we're doing. Feel free to let me know what you think about this or any other Sybex book by sending me an email at `nedde@wiley.com`. If you think you've found a technical error in this book, please visit `http://sybex.custhelp.com`. Customer feedback is critical to our efforts at Sybex.

Best regards,

Neil Edde
Vice President and Publisher
Sybex, an Imprint of Wiley

To my two wonderful children and my bride (who married me even amidst this book's creation).

—Kirk Hausman

To Jonathan and Cassandra.

—Susan Cook

To my half brother Fernando Barros. For being there for me during my teenage years. For listening to me and my problems even when he had his own to take care of. You were an uncle, a friend, and a brother. I love you and will always carry you in my heart. I know you are up there in a cloud somewhere looking down at us. Rest in peace.

—Telmo Sampaio

About the Authors

Kirk Hausman has been an IT professional for more than 20 years, working in state government, health care, and higher education and as an enterprise architect and security consultant. He is the co-author of *IT Architecture for Dummies* (Wiley, 2010) and the upcoming *3D Printing for Dummies* (Wiley, 2013). Kirk teaches information security, digital forensics, and networking, and his research includes social media management, cyberterrorism, additive manufacturing (3D printing), and strategies for developing interest in young learners toward STEM subjects. He has facilitated cloud initiatives using Amazon EC2, Azure, and high-performance computing technologies. Kirk holds a master's degree in information technology and a range of professional certifications, including PMP, CGEIT, CISSP, CISA, CISM, and CRISC. Kirk can be reached via `kkhausman@hotmail.com`.

Susan Cook has been an IT professional for over 15 years and has professional experience in higher education, state government, and financial sectors. Prior to her career in IT, she worked as a compliance auditor and as a licensed private investigator. She is the coauthor of *IT Architecture for Dummies* (Wiley, 2010), and her educational projects include bachelor's level course development in networking and network security. She is currently employed by Texas A&M University and specializes in enterprise risk assessment and compliance. She has master's degrees in information technology and security management and several IT certifications, including ISACA's Certified Information Systems Auditor (CISA) and Certified in Risk and Information Systems Control (CRISC). Susan can be reached at `scook@maelstromrider.com`.

Telmo Sampaio is the chief geek for MCTrainer.NET and TechKnowLogical, specializing in System Center, SharePoint, SQL, and .NET. Telmo wrote his first application in 1984, with the intent of demonstrating physics concepts to his fellow classmates. His passion for technology and teaching made him a self-taught developer from an early age. In 1989 he moved to Wellesley, Massachusetts, when his father was transferred to work in Boston for a year. He kept developing applications to demonstrate science and math concepts and decided to remain in the United States after his family left. In 1990, while still in high school, he was hired by IBM to demonstrate its most powerful CAD application, CATIA, to corporate customers like Boeing. In 1991 he moved back to Brazil and studied systems analysis at PUC/RJ. When Microsoft extended its Microsoft Certification program to Brazil, Telmo was one of the first in the country to become certified. In 1994 he started teaching Microsoft classes. Soon he was managing the largest training center in Latin America, after having worked for Microsoft in Brazil as a technical account manager. To date he has been certified in over 20 different Microsoft products, passing over 80 exams. After moving back to the United States in 2003, Telmo became a contributor to several Microsoft certification exams, an author for official courseware, and a speaker at events such as TechEd, PASS, and MMS.

Acknowledgments

Just as technologies in the cloud involve many different components to provide the final product to the consumer, so too does a book like this require the dedication and focused effort of many whose names are not presented on the cover. I would first like to thank my coauthors, Susan Cook and Telmo Sampaio, but also the many excellent people at Sybex who took my rough material and polished it into a gem for readers: our acquisitions editor, Jeff Kellum; development editor, Kim Wimpsett; production editor, Rebecca Anderson; and the many other editorial reviewers that are simply amazing in what they do. I offer thanks to my good friend and literary agent, Carole Jelen, whose efforts provide me the chance to work with so many amazing people on so many exciting topics.

—Kirk Hausman

It is amazing to me how many people contribute to the creation of a published work. They all deserve thanks, but I'm particularly grateful to a special few at Sybex—Jeff Kellum in his dual role as acquisitions editor and chief cat herder, development editor Kim Wimpsett, and production editor Rebecca Anderson. I would also like to thank my agent, Carole Jelen, and my coauthors, Kirk Hausman and Telmo Sampaio, for all their hard work.

—Susan Cook

I would like to acknowledge the amazing contribution of my best friend and gorgeous wife, Jo Sampaio, who spent countless nights caring for the kids so that I could finish this book. Without her support and understanding I would not be where I am today. My boys, Marco, Rafael and Enzo, for being supportive and giving up a bit of dad time. And my family back home in Brazil, who pretend to understand what I write about.

—Telmo Sampaio

Contents at a Glance

CONTENTS

CompTIA Certification

Qualify for Jobs, Promotions and Increased Compensation

CompTIA. The CompTIA Cloud Essentials specialty certification demonstrates that an individual knows what cloud computing means from a business and technical perspective, as well as, at a high level, what is involved in moving to and governing the cloud.

It Pays to Get Certified

In a digital world, digital literacy is an essential survival skill. Certification proves you have the knowledge and skill to solve business problems in virtually any business environment. Certifications are highly valued credentials that qualify you for jobs, increased compensation, and promotion.

- **Organizations do not have adequate cloud competencies** especially infrastructure and service providers. Excellent job opportunities exist and will grow for knowledgeable cloud professionals.
- **The cloud is a new frontier** that requires astute personnel who understand the strategic impact of cloud computing on an organization.
- Research has shown that **certified IT professionals score better** when tested for their knowledge of foundational principles and skills, and from the employer's perspective, certification provides solid evidence of successful training.
- **Cloud technologies and business needs are moving faster than organizations can adapt.** Therefore staff understanding of cloud computing is key for the initial project planning for cloud solutions, and a safe and well-managed implementation of any cloud project.
- Getting your people up to speed with a fundamental understanding of cloud computing enables the whole organization to speak the same language.

How Certification Helps Your Career

IT Is Everywhere IT is ubiquitous, needed by most organizations. Globally, there are over 600,000 IT job openings.

IT Knowledge and Skills Get Jobs Certifications are essential credentials that qualify you for jobs, increased compensation, and promotion.

Retain Your Job and Salary Make your expertise stand above the rest. Competence is usually retained during times of change.

Want to Change Jobs Certifications qualify you for new opportunities, whether locked into a current job, see limited advancement, or need to change careers.

Stick Out from the Résumé Pile Hiring managers can demand the strongest skill set.

CompTIA Career Pathway

CompTIA offers a number of credentials that form a foundation for your career in technology and allow you to pursue specific areas of concentration. Depending on the path you choose to take, CompTIA certifications help you build upon your skills and knowledge, supporting learning throughout your entire career.

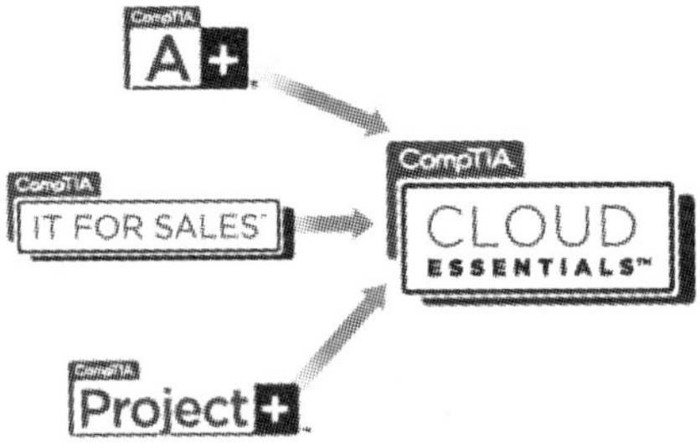

Possible certified candidates for Cloud Essentials among helpdesk staff, project management, sales and service professionals in emerging cloud environments

Steps to Certification

Steps to Getting Certified and Staying Certified	
Review Exam Objectives	Review the certification objectives to make sure you know what is covered in the exam. www.comptia.org/certifications/testprep/examobjectives.aspx
Practice for the Exam	After you have studied for the certification, take a free assessment and sample test to get an idea what type of questions might be on the exam. www.comptia.org/certifications/testprep/practicetests.aspx
Purchase an Exam Voucher	Purchase your exam voucher on the CompTIA Marketplace, which is located at: www.comptiastore.com
Take the Test!	Select a certification exam provider and schedule a time to take your exam. You can find exam providers at the following link: www.comptia.org/certifications/testprep/testingcenters.aspx

Join the Professional Community

Join the IT Pro Community at http://itpro.comptia.org. The free IT Pro online community provides valuable content to students and professionals.

- Career IT job resources
  - Where to start in IT
  - Career assessments
  - Salary trends
  - US job board
- Forums on networking, security, computing, and cutting-edge technologies
- Access to blogs written by industry experts
- Current information on cutting-edge technologies
- Access to various industry resource links and articles related to IT and IT careers

Content Seal of Quality

This courseware bears the seal of **CompTIA Approved Quality Content**. This seal signifies this content covers 100% of the exam objectives and implements important instructional design principles. CompTIA recommends multiple learning tools to help increase coverage of the learning objectives.

Why CompTIA?

Global Recognition CompTIA is recognized globally as the leading IT non-profit trade association and has enormous credibility. Plus, CompTIA's certifications are vendor-neutral and offer proof of foundational knowledge that translates across technologies.

Valued by Hiring Managers Hiring managers value CompTIA certification because it is vendor- and technology-independent validation of your technical skills.

Recommended or Required by Government and Businesses Many government organizations and corporations either recommend or require technical staff to be CompTIA certified. (e.g. Dell, Sharp, Ricoh, the US Department of Defense and many more)

Three CompTIA Certifications ranked in the top 10. In a study by DICE of 17,000 technology professionals, certifications helped command higher salaries at all experience levels.

How to Obtain More Information

Visit CompTIA online—`www.comptia.org` to learn more about getting CompTIA certified.

Contact CompTIA—call 866-835-8020 ext. 5 or email `questions@comptia.org`

Connect—on LinkedIn, Facebook, Twitter, Flickr, and YouTube

Introduction

IT is moving out of the local data center into the cloud, where data and services become easily available via cell phones, tablets, and other mobile devices around the world.

In this book, you will learn the basic concepts of cloud computing as it exists in an international setting, using the criteria specified by professional cloud computing foundation certifications used throughout the United States and worldwide. With the information provided in this book, you will be able to understand the specific terminology and its application in the continued shift into the cloud, where costs are billed like electricity and reflect monthly usage levels rather than the traditional up-front major cost of new servers and storage for a data center rack. Migration into the cloud allows rapid deployment of test applications and then rapid scale-up to meet growing demands without worrying about whether the current network or hardware can keep up.

Who Should Read This Book

Cloud Essentials is for anyone who is interested in understanding the fundamentals of cloud computing from both a technical and a business perspective. This book is suitable whether you are a student using it in an IT class, an entry-level IT professional who needs a better understanding of cloud computing, an IT manager in an organization considering adopting cloud services, or a non-technical manager or executive curious about what cloud services can do for your business.

Although deep technical knowledge and work experience in the IT field are not necessary, it will be helpful if you have a basic understanding of enterprise technologies such as networking and client/server architecture, and those who have worked in and around an IT environment are likely to gain a better understanding of some of the topics being covered.

If you are preparing to take the CompTIA Cloud Essentials certification exam (CLO-001), this book is ideal for you. It will also help those preparing to take the EXIN Cloud Computing Foundation certification exam (EX0-116). You can find more information about the CompTIA Cloud Essentials certification at `http://certification.comptia.org/getCertified/certifications/cloud.aspx` and about the EXIN Cloud Computing Foundation certification exam at `www.exin.com/US/en/exams/&exam=exin-cloud-computing-foundation`.

What Is Covered in This Book

Cloud Essentials is organized to provide you with the knowledge needed to understand the basics of cloud computing and how it may be implemented in a business environment. Each chapter begins with an introduction and a list of topics that correspond to chapter headings. Illustrations, diagrams, and screen captures are included, where appropriate, to enhance your understanding of the topic. At the end of each chapter, in "The Essentials and Beyond," you will find additional exercises that you can work on independently and 10 review questions that will help you prepare for the CompTIA and EXIN exams.

Chapter 1, "What Is Cloud Computing?" Starts by defining cloud computing and identifying the attributes that differentiate cloud services from hosted services. Covers virtualized computing environments and high-performance computing as they relate to cloud services and discusses the client/server relationship in the cloud.

Chapter 2, "Cloud Models" Discusses the four types of cloud deployment models and hosting options. Also identifies the IT-based organizational roles helpful both with transitioning and managing IT operations to the cloud.

Chapter 3, "Service Models" Identifies the various types of cloud service models using the industry standard syntax of *as a Service* and explains how they relate to each other. Examines Software, Platform, and Infrastructure as a Service models in detail and explains their use in a business computing environment.

Chapter 4, "Current Cloud Technologies" Compares traditional computing solutions to cloud services, using currently available cloud offerings as examples. Examines accessing cloud services across networks, relating cloud functions to the OSI model. Discusses how cloud services can empower mobile computing.

Chapter 5, "Cloud Business Value" Starts by identifying the business drivers for cloud computing such as reduced costs and increased efficiency. Covers both direct and indirect costs of cloud computing and what types of organizations are likely to benefit from cloud computing.

Chapter 6, "Cloud Infrastructure Planning" Covers networking requirements and goes into more depth on the OSI model. Identifies several network challenges associated with cloud computing as well as changes to the network infrastructure. Discusses how to leverage automation for resource provisioning, achieving interoperability between services, and introduces cloud computing standards.

Chapter 7, "Strategies for Cloud Adoption" Explores aligning cloud deployment with organizational goals and provides guidance on selecting cloud service vendors. Identifies the impact to business processes and discusses the importance of service-level agreements (SLAs).

Chapter 8, "Applications in the Cloud" Explains the role of standard applications in a business environment and the difference between desktop, distributed, web-based, and cloud applications. Discusses important considerations to developing cloud-ready applications and migrating applications to the cloud.

Chapter 9, "Cloud Service Rollout" Identifies topics of consideration for inclusion into a cloud service rollout plan. Includes the importance of identifying vendor roles and responsibilities and organizational skill requirements, both technical and business related. Follows with a discussion of the transition from a test to a production environment and ends with incident management planning.

Chapter 10, "Cloud Service-Level Management" Provides an overview of the Information Technology Infrastructure Library (ITIL) and discusses how its service management practices apply to cloud computing, particularly service desk operation. Discusses developing and utilizing performance metrics to monitor and improve service.

Chapter 11, "Security in the Cloud" Provides foundational material covering information security and risk management in preparation for identifying cloud-specific security risks and mitigations. Introduces some of the more well-known information security standards appropriate to a business environment.

Chapter 12, "Privacy and Compliance" Discusses legal and privacy risks involved in adopting cloud computing services and provides examples of applicable laws in various jurisdictions. Examines strategies for identity management in the cloud.

Appendix A, "Future of the Cloud" Explores the future of cloud computing through an examination of advanced cloud-specific hardware, ongoing development of smart cities, and increasing automation of traditional data center operations.

Appendix B, "Answers to Review Questions" This appendix includes all of the answers to the review questions found in the section "The Essentials and Beyond" that appears at the end of every chapter.

Appendix C, "CompTIA's Certification Program" Describes CompTIA's certification program and the Cloud Essentials CLO-001 exam. Maps each exam objective to specific chapters and section in this book.

Appendix D, "EXIN's Certification Program" Describes EXIN's certification program and the EXIN Cloud Computing Foundation EX0-116 exam. Maps each exam objective to specific chapters and section in this book.

Glossary Lists the most commonly used words throughout the book.

In addition, we have provided suggested or recommended answers to the additional exercises at the end of each chapter. You can download these at `www.sybex.com/go/cloudessentials`. There you'll also find a bonus appendix, which includes a security case study.

Sybex strives to keep you supplied with the latest tools and information you need for your work. Please check its website at `www.sybex.com/go/cloudessentials`, where we'll post additional content and updates that supplement this book if the need arises. Enter **cloud essentials** in the Search box (or type the book's ISBN, **9781118408735**), and click Go to get to the book's update page.

What Is Cloud Computing?

Cloud computing has become such a buzzword in the industry that it is being used to market many different types of software and network services, not all of which really fit the proper, technical definition of the *cloud*. So, before we examine the use, impact, and security issues of working in the cloud, it is necessary to define what cloud computing really is.

This chapter defines cloud computing, covers the origins of cloud computing, and briefly examines the technologies used in cloud computing to help you understand the role the cloud can play in organizational enterprise planning.

- **Defining cloud computing**
- **Understanding distributed application design**
- **Understanding resource management automation**
- **Understanding virtualized computing environments**
- **Understanding high-performance computing models**
- **Understanding cloud computing technologies**

Defining Cloud Computing

More than a marketing term, *cloud computing* refers to flexible self-service, network-accessible computing resource pools that can be allocated to meet demand. Services are flexible because the resources and processing power available to each can be adjusted on the fly to meet changes in need or based on configuration settings in an administrative interface, without the need for direct IT personnel involvement. These resources are assigned from a larger pool of available capacity (for examples, memory, storage, CPUs) as needed, allowing an organization to spin up a proof-of-concept application, expand that to a full prototype, and then roll it out for full use without having to worry about whether existing hardware, data center space, power, and cooling are capable of handling the load. Cloud computing allows the allocation of resources to be adjusted as needed, creating a hardware-independent framework for future growth and development.

Since the dawn of the networking age, when network diagrams depicted an enterprise and its extended components, the industry standard has been to use a simple cloud icon to identify the public Internet, as shown in Figure 1.1. This cloud represents all of the various types of networking and functions that are necessary to bridge together various parts of the enterprise over the Internet because the specific routing details are subject to change and are outside the enterprise network environment. That's where the term *cloud* originated, and when we discuss migration into the cloud, what we generally mean is applications and services being moved from the organizational or hosting data center to cloud service providers available through the Internet.

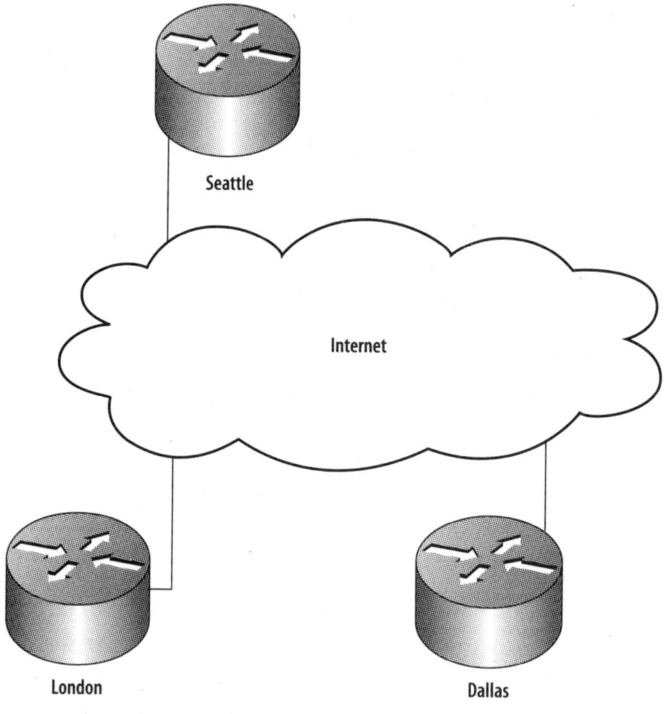

FIGURE 1.1 An example of the cloud symbol in network diagrams

Clouds Hold More than Just Rain

Almost anything can be hosted in the cloud, from databases and applications to complete virtual infrastructures encompassing data storage, networking, and all components of the server environment. The cloud can also host virtualized user desktop environments available from any networked client device, whether or not the client has sufficient local resources to host the virtualized desktop environment and its various applications.

Internet-based offsite-managed hosting services have been around for a while, available through specialty providers such as Rackspace since 1997 and even provided as value additions by local ISPs. However, cloud computing goes beyond simply hosting a website or database service on a machine located in a remote data center, with early cloud services such as Google Gmail and Google Apps showing off the power of cloud computing starting in 2006. Cloud computing solutions have several common characteristics, regardless of their form:

Managed by the provider Cloud computing services are managed by the cloud provider. Once applications and services have been moved to external cloud computing, an organization no longer needs to worry about local data center issues regarding power, space, and cooling, and developers need only know whether their applications will be running on one cloud service platform or another—for example, Amazon Elastic Compute Cloud (EC2) or Microsoft Azure—without having to consider where the services or application resources will be located. Knowledge of individual hardware characteristics and capacity measures is no longer important to the organization, while tech refresh and update becomes a background matter for the cloud provider to manage.

Flexible resource assignment The capacity and resources available to cloud computing services can be increased or decreased, with costs adjusted according to actual consumption. This allows an organization to spin up a new offering with only minimal costs for the resources used and then to meet spikes or cyclic use patterns with increased capacity, paying for only the level of use needed. Traditional data centers must always plan for future growth, and a sudden success for a web-based offering can rapidly overrun available server and network capacity unless data center managers purchase sufficient "spare" resources beforehand. Cloud computing draws resources from a pool as they are needed, based on level of service consumption. This is similar to the way power companies supply power to individual organizations, billing each according to its individual use.

For example, a new cloud application might experience a sudden increase in use following mention on a popular blog and require additional network bandwidth, data storage, server memory, or CPU power to keep up with the sudden increase in demand. Traditional data centers would be limited by hardware constraints, while cloud computing alternatives can simply add CPUs or expand available database file storage up to predefined limits when needed and then shrink back after the storm of access has passed to manage on-demand costs.

Pay Only for What You Need

Instead of buying huge storage arrays just in case of later need, you can start out small and grow your cloud resources only when required. Automatic failover to public cloud services when local resources are insufficient, a practice termed *cloud bursting*, will be discussed in Chapter 2, "Cloud Models," as we review cloud deployment solutions.

Network accessible Cloud services are available via networked devices and technologies, facilitating rapid access by mobile customers and remote office locations. This provides an "anywhere, anytime" service model not possible in traditional data centers, where service downtime and local-area outages in power and networking can impact uptime. Because cloud computing vendors can be located anywhere in the world, they can host organizational services from areas outside of geopolitical turmoil or environmental threats. Before a hurricane, for example, a cloud service provider could transfer operations from Florida to Washington transparently to the service consumer.

Sustainable Because cloud providers can provision resources at need, it is possible to reduce power and cooling requirements during off-peak times, gaining economies of scale well beyond those available to single-tenanted hardware-based data services, which must stay on waiting for later use. The flexibility in cloud hosting location allows providers to shift operations without disruption to consumers. They can move data center activity north during summer months to save on cooling costs or transfer operations to areas with excess power production capability, such as Iceland.

Cloudy Skies Are "Greening" the Data Center

Cloud hosting supports green initiatives through the use of environmental cooling by transferring operations to cooler locations rather than requiring ever-larger refrigerated air systems to meet summer heat increases, reducing an organization's environmental footprint.

Managed through self-service on demand After limits for resource availability are configured within the cloud provider's systems, available resource capacity can be automatically expanded or managed by the client with minimal effort. Bringing up a test server no longer requires access to the physical system, loading software, and configuring networking by hand; instead, the customer need only access their cloud provider and request a new resource allocation using the self-service user interface. As long as the organization's contractual limits on resources allow the addition, it is managed automatically without further technical assistance needed.

Understanding Distributed Application Design

Distributed design is one of the fundamental technologies supporting cloud computing. Early software had to operate on a single powerful system, together with its data and ancillary programs. The development of distributed application designs using a standardized application programming interface (API) model allowed one computer to host an application while others could hold the data and perform secondary tasks.

Once applications could work together to provide the consumer with a single interface, new technologies were developed such as just-in-time (JIT) inventory management. In JIT, a user places an order on a single website where availability is verified before the order is placed, and then the application alerts the warehouse to prepare the item for shipping, the shipper is notified for a pickup, and the accounting software handles payment transactions all behind the scenes. The customer merely selects what they want, sees that it is available, and then receives their receipt with confirmation of delivery date all in one seamless process.

Many CPUs Make Light(er) Work

Services such as eBay depend on distributed processing to integrate real-time bids with item availability and many other factors calculated and managed simultaneously across many systems. No single system could handle the volume of transactions occurring simultaneously as items are placed for bid, bids are submitted, notifications for winning bids are transmitted, and the various other aspects of online real-time auctions are carried out.

In cloud computing environments, even the location and type of hardware supporting a software application can shift from moment to moment as additional capacity is allocated or services are transferred between cloud provider data centers. An organization's services could not adapt to these changes without a flexible link between services, resources, networking, and storage. Theoretically speaking, if an earthquake disrupted California's Internet services, services hosted in the cloud could continue operating without interruption or be rapidly transferred to data centers outside of the affected area.

The cloud is interconnected through standard APIs and XML web service interfaces, allowing developers to rapidly move their applications into the cloud without requiring a completely new set of skills. This improves future planning for technology's constant evolution and update. Issues of technical refresh are no longer based on hardware life cycles but instead are handled by the cloud provider transparently as required. APIs still vary from one cloud provider to another, so applications developed under Amazon's EC2 will not be able to directly transfer to Microsoft's Azure, while Microsoft's own utilities and tools can manage both local and cloud equivalents of its own services. Until cloud technologies mature into a common standard, application development will still retain some aspects of siloed technology/vendor lock-in. We will examine these issues in greater detail in subsequent chapters.

Clouds Virtualize the Application Development Cycle

Application development in the cloud improves business agility to offer new services to customers by making services immediately available with whatever resources turn out to be needed rather than via the traditional model of application development, prototyping, testing, and then rollout to production systems after procurement.

Understanding Resource Management Automation

Another key function underlying the success of cloud computing is the management of resources automatically. When demand nears capacity, the cloud hosting software is able to identify need and respond by adding resources up to predetermined levels based on an organization's contractual limits or limits configured in the management software. This protects application availability while also ensuring that attacks will not overrun an organization's budget.

Clouds Help Deal with Botnets and Distributed Denial-of-Service Attacks

Cloud services protect an organization by simply scaling up resources to meet growing demands during an attack while also ensuring that attacks, such as botnet distributed denial of service attacks, will not overrun an organization's resources. However, this defense comes at a cost for the added resource capacity.

Botnets are collections of individual computers remotely controlled by the "bot herder" to perform tasks as directed. Most bots are standard personal computers located in people's homes and businesses and infected with viruses and remote control software that lets the bot herder issue commands. By commanding all of the individual bots to connect to a target server, the bot herder consumes all of the targeted server's resources trying to handle the attack, preventing legitimate use.

Organizations can configure resource limits so that an attacker cannot generate uncontrollable costs by adding more bots into the attack. Botnets of a million or more controlled systems have been identified and shut down by law enforcement, and these could easily run up the cloud bill for a targeted organization if there were no limits to resource allocation.

In addition to handling periods of high use, cloud computing can automatically reduce resource allocations during off-peak periods. Periodic and cyclical resource requirements have long presented problems for data center managers, who must make sure that equipment has sufficient resources for peak load periods but then must power and cool those systems even when they are minimally utilized. Defensive planning for cloud services includes a new aspect in the strategies planners will need for managing automatic resource provisioning, which we will discuss in greater detail in Chapter 12, "Privacy and Compliance."

CPA firms might see a peak once a year during tax time, while a website featured in the news might need expanded resources only one time ever.

Because cloud resources are managed automatically, an organization can meet increasing need while also saving on costs during periods of reduced need without requiring constant management by human resources. The flexibility of Internet-accessible cloud computing applications will allow a single service to be utilized by many components of an organization's geographically distributed sites. A single call center service could be used around the clock to support users within the local time zone, or a cloud service could transfer its operations to cloud hosting sites based on time of day statutes to provide the lowest latency to consumers in New York, London, and Hong Kong for one shared set of centrally negotiated licensing costs.

Understanding Virtualized Computing Environments

> Because cloud hosting providers use virtualization to expand capacity and to provision new services, automated deployment speeds capacity expansion and tech refresh operations.

Virtualization of storage systems in early storage area networks and of entire computer systems forms the backbone of cloud computing. Because an organization no longer needs to worry about where data is located or what hardware resources are available on a particular server, focus can be turned to business uses of technology rather than on technology itself. Cloud computing also makes extensive use of server virtualization to better utilize cloud hosting servers by allowing multiple systems to run on a more powerful server, as shown in Figure 1.2. This is referred to as *multitenancy* and allows system resources to be fully utilized before another server is brought online, further reducing operating costs and data center cooling requirements.

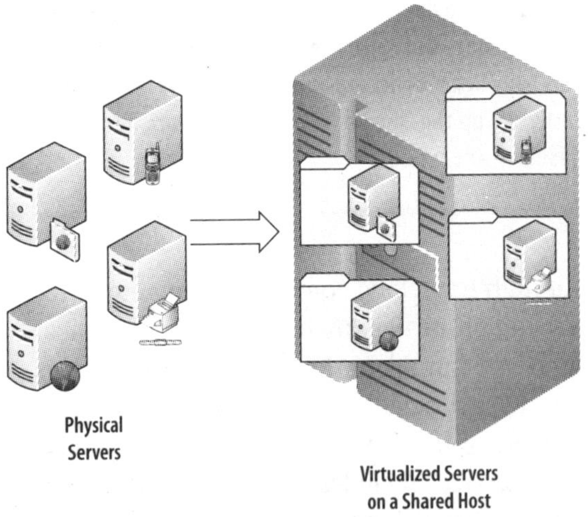

FIGURE 1.2 Virtualizing individual physical systems onto a shared powerful server

Understanding High-Performance Computing Models

Cloud computing also borrows from high-performance computing (HPC) techniques for separating individual procedures into multiple simultaneous processes that are sent out to individual computers, which then complete their portion of the final result. Individual results are combined later to provide the complete final result, as illustrated in the digital animation example of Figure 1.3. The digital animation example shows how a complete animation can be broken down into smaller segments for concurrent rendering and then combined into the final product using grid computing technologies.

High-performance computers are also termed *supercomputers.*

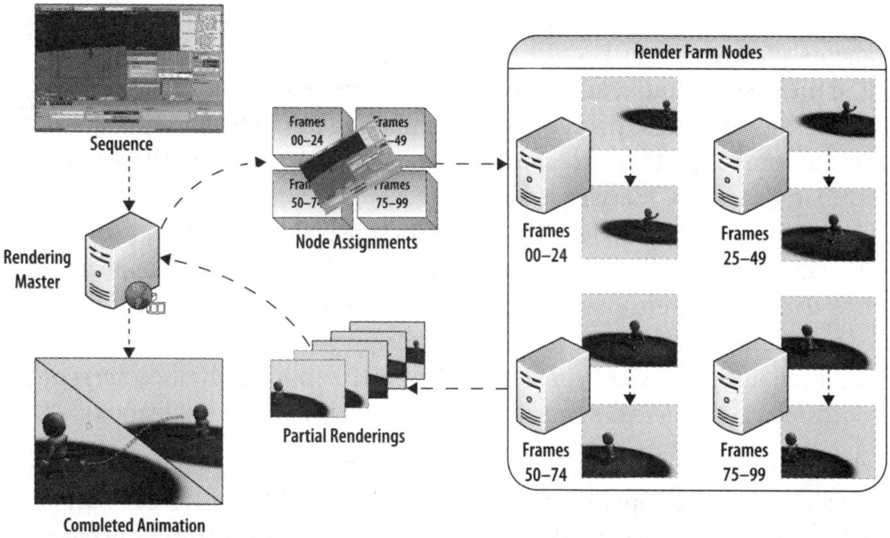

FIGURE 1.3 Rendering a complete video sequence using multiple computers simultaneously

By leveraging high-performance computing models for distributing processes across multiple systems, cloud computing allows more resources to be dedicated to an application than are present on its host server alone. CPU chip manufacturers are developing new technologies that can also dedicate per-core resources to individual processes, like the Intel Many Integrated Core (Intel MIC) CPUs being developed for high-performance and cloud computing environments.

Because HPC and cloud computing models use similar technologies and strategies, they work very well together. Some cloud providers now offer high-performance computing power on demand for data-intensive analytics and modeling, allowing thousands of CPU cores to be made available for research without an organization having to maintain a multimillion-dollar supercomputing data center for itself. In this configuration, cloud computing allows on-demand self-serve access to broad pools of computing power using the same technologies that allow cloud service providers to serve up email, e-business applications, and solutions for many other nonscientific tasks.

Understanding Cloud Computing Technologies

Cloud service models will be reviewed in Chapter 3, addressing the capabilities of each successive layer of "as a Service" cloud offerings.

Cloud computing offers many different levels of services, from individual Software as a Service (SaaS) to Platform as a Service (PaaS) development environments and even Infrastructure as a Service (IaaS) complete solutions resident in the cloud. Some vendors now term even Everything as a Service (XaaS) as an offering, although this is more of a marketing term melding traditional and cloud computing than an established standard. We will cover these models in detail in Chapter 3, "Service Models." Because cloud computing involves the service provider hosting applications and data supplied to end users, various levels of computing "as a Service" can be acquired, from individual applications such as database servers to whole network infrastructures serving up fully featured user desktops to mobile devices anywhere in the world.

Cloud computing services run atop hosting virtualized hardware servers and are accessed via the network, making them available to clients of many types:

Workstations The most common access client in an existing enterprise network will be the traditional thick client workstation system with a CPU, display device, and input devices (keyboard, mouse, trackball). This type of client works equally well in cloud environments, accessing web applications and cloud resources through locally loaded applications and web browsers.

Thin clients Thin clients have only a very basic operating system, display device, and input devices but lack onboard storage for local applications. They depend on remote software running on servers and so work very well with cloud services. Thin clients are not common outside of business organizations where vendors such as Citrix can work with central IT offices to manage the infrastructure necessary for thin clients to be useful. With cloud computing, this may change as more and more functions are shifted into the cloud, and thin clients may soon be found in homes and in place of traditional thick client workstations. A very limited version of the thin client once provided access to mainframe computers through directly connected dedicated terminals lacking all but the most basic of interfaces for human programmers and users, while today's plug computers like Dell's Ophilia™ are designed to pull their operating system and all software from a server or cloud service each time they power up.

Mobile clients Mobile devices from smartphones to tablets and constantly emerging variations are perfect clients for blending with cloud services. These devices have sufficient onboard storage for rich user interface applications but limited CPU power and so rely on remote servers for the "heavy lifting" within data processing and analytics applications. Using wireless networking for remote connections to web services, these low-power devices provide excellent on-the-go clients for the modern workforce.

Servers Traditional data center servers and services can make use of cloud computing resources, which is particularly helpful during migration to cloud alternatives. Deep integration is possible, such as the ability to interoperate on-premise Microsoft Exchange email servers with Azure-based Office 365 equivalents in a manner that is transparent to users and services that rely on email integration. Cloud backups provide another area in which traditional on-premise data centers can take advantage of the economies of scale and automatic resource allocation of cloud services to reduce costs for larger tape silos and expanded backup data storage.

Other cloud services Leveraging XML in much the same way as early service-oriented architecture (SOA) forerunners, elements of cloud computing can consume resources from other cloud services to leverage emerging offerings as they offer value to the organization.

The blending of cloud services is already becoming commonplace in existing enterprise networks. It is possible to find organizations with Salesforce CRM operating alongside Google Apps for user productivity while Azure SQL database applications power business applications running in Amazon S3 cloud services, with Iron Mountain providing cloud backup and recovery—all being accessed using iPads, whose automatic integration with cloud-based Dropbox, Flickr, and social media services improve customer interaction.

The Essentials and Beyond

Cloud computing is already present in today's enterprise networks and offers a utility-like model in which organizations can purchase only the capacity and resources they are using, adjusting to meet changing needs automatically and with only minimal administrative effort. Building atop technologies for distributed, virtualized, and high-performance computing and linked by XML techniques developed for earlier SOA implementation, cloud computing supports the ever-evolving span of mobile technologies and user devices enhancing today's business organizational needs.

Additional Exercises

- Identify familiar cloud-based services.
- Identify client types you use to access cloud services.
- Describe at least three characteristics of cloud computing.

To compare your answer to the author's, please visit `www.sybex.com/go/cloudessentials`.

Review Questions

1. Where does the term *cloud* come from?
   - A. Environmental threats
   - B. Network diagrams
   - C. Exposed networks
   - D. Legacy term for SOA
2. What characteristic of cloud computing reduces administrative costs?
   - A. Self-service or automated resource management
   - B. Placing the cloud data center farther away from local administrators
   - C. Limitation of platform/application development selection (in PaaS environments)
   - D. Paying only for resources actually consumed
3. True or false? Cloud computing is the same as virtualized computing.
   - A. True
   - B. False
4. Which type of client lacks storage for applications?
   - A. Thick
   - B. Thin
   - C. Mobile
   - D. Remote

(Continues)

The Essentials and Beyond *(Continued)*

5. What characteristic of cloud computing reduces data center costs?
   - A. Using energy-efficient technologies in cloud data centers
   - B. Flexibility and sustainability of cloud service models
   - C. Allowing services to be automatically migrated between data center locations as required
   - D. Remote availability for mobile devices
6. Which fundamental technology provides cloud computing with its ability to split up processes across multiple resource pools?
   - A. Distributed application design
   - B. Resource management automation
   - C. Virtualized computing
   - D. High-performance computing
7. What is another term for a flexible pool of computing resources available to network clients and managed by self-service on-demand automated tools?
   - A. Server virtualization
   - B. High-performance computing
   - C. Cloud computing
   - D. Server consolidation
8. True or false? Cloud computing is inherently an ecologically green technology.
   - A. True
   - B. False
9. When a service has been migrated into the cloud, where is it really located?
   - A. In the local data center
   - B. In a partner organization's data center
   - C. At a service provider's virtualized data center
   - D. Almost anywhere
10. What is the term used in system virtualization to reflect more than one operating system or instance running on a single host server?
    - A. Heterogeneous servers
    - B. Homogeneous servers
    - C. Multitenancy
    - D. Colocation

CHAPTER 2

Cloud Models

When planning cloud computing deployments, enterprise architects and network planners need to be able to identify the expectations for control and management based on the type of cloud and its level categorization. Categorization such as Software as a Service (SaaS), Platform as a Service (PaaS), and Infrastructure as a Service (IaaS) will be the topic of Chapter 3, "Service Models."

This chapter covers the models for cloud computing deployment, which relate to strategies for extending virtualization outside of the data center into the cloud.

- **Evolving from virtualization to the cloud**
- **Planning organization roles in the cloud**
- **Identifying cloud deployment models and scope modifiers**
- **Including future cloud models**

Evolving from Virtualization to the Cloud

When we examine the evolution of traditional data center infrastructure into the cloud, the journey starts with server virtualization and moves through privately hosted and hybrid clouds into fully public cloud infrastructures with all elements virtualized. This progression represents an increase in overall virtualization from storage and hardware server machines through successive layers to include all components of the network infrastructure as organizations reduce their onsite data center requirements in place of data and services existing entirely in the cloud. Figure 2.1 shows an example of the steady transformation from physical traditional data centers to increasingly virtualized IT infrastructures existing in the cloud.

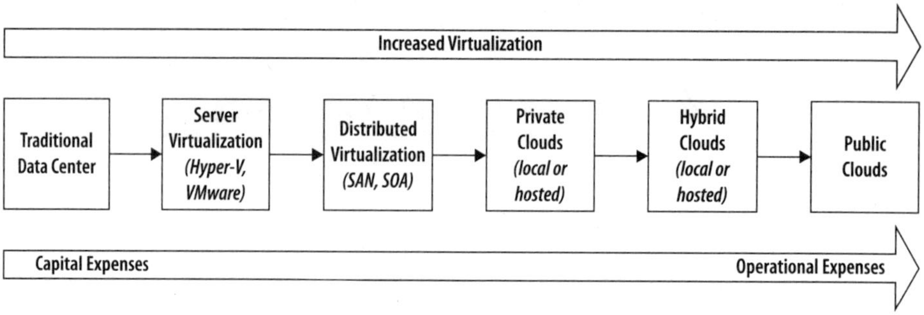

FIGURE 2.1 **Going from physical traditional data centers to increasingly virtualized IT infrastructures in the cloud**

The following are the major steps on the pathway from physical traditional data centers to increasingly virtualized IT infrastructures in the cloud:

Server virtualization Once a relative rarity, today's data centers are rapidly deploying virtualization technologies to allow the consolidation of server resources into smaller numbers of more robust host hardware components able to share resources across multiple virtual machines operating atop the virtualization hypervisor. Server virtualization allows organizations to concentrate their data center resources across a smaller number of physical hosts with a lower percentage of potential resources left idle and consuming power when unused.

Virtualized data centers gain a measure of hardware independence, allowing the organization to purchase best-cost alternatives and avoid vendor lock-in for procurement. This same capability improves the efficiency of disaster recovery and business continuity because a virtualized server can be simply moved to a new host site and brought online to return normal operational capabilities. Costs at this level are managed as capital expenses.

Distributed virtualization By extending the virtualization to include distributed resources using technologies that can transfer operations between automated systems, organizations can increase the flexibility of their server infrastructure and the operational resources available to virtual machines. Some of the technologies that have improved flexibility in distributed virtualization are listed here:

- Virtualization of data storage across distributed storage area network (SAN) infrastructures

- Interoperation of application component services through service-oriented architectural (SOA) integration
- Automatic load-management utilities that can migrate virtualized server instances from one host to another based on total resource load

Costs at this level are managed as mixed capital and operational expenses, providing greater resistance to capacity overruns and server node loss through automated failover and resource capacity leveling.

Private clouds Through the implementation of a local private cloud resident upon hardware located in local data centers but running cloud infrastructural software, organizations can take advantage of the self-service resource allocation and consumption metering for cost recovery billing models. The cloud software provides a standard platform for application development and availability even when the hardware remains heterogeneous in make and model, transforming IT toward a utility business model able to allocate resources based on service performance rather than on projections of planned resource needs.

This is the first true transformation from traditional data center resources to cloud-based alternatives, enhancing the flexibility of resource assignment while still relying on local server resources. Because cloud computing is often discussed in terms of utilities (for example, providing resources based on utility and consumption as the power grid does), this stage of cloud technology aligns with the early 1900s when individual organizations had their own local power plants to provide electrical power. Mild efficiencies of scale can be achieved at this stage, but costs remain both capital and operational because tech refresh comes only from the organization itself.

Hybrid clouds As organizations continue the transition made possible by enhanced virtualization, they can bridge local private clouds with other cloud offerings to create hybrid clouds, extending their resource pool beyond the systems present in local data centers. This allows an organization's services to develop greater capacity for response to peak loads and unanticipated demands. Billing continues to develop along the utility model, allowing load to determine cost as operational expenses and internal billing for cost recovery.

Hybrid clouds allow organizations to retain total control over data resources that are critical, sensitive or transformative to their business operations while transferring less-sensitive operations to more efficient public cloud service providers that can reduce costs through massive economies of scale not possible in a local data center. Capital expenses are reduced because only key services might be retained on the organization's local server resources. This is also the model for mid-transition between local and public cloud services, allowing developers to test applications using local resources with very low latency and locally controlled high-capacity networking.

Public clouds As organizations move to eliminate private cloud components in favor of externally provided public cloud environments, the data center continues to empty and IT expands as a business component with a smaller dedicated server support staff required for daily operations. Capital expenses for IT focus on client access technologies, while applications, services, and infrastructural elements become operational expenses alone. Public clouds operate like public power production systems, bringing industrial-scale cost efficiencies and hosting location flexibility to the organization, following the utility model transformation from building power generation to the distributed power grid available today. Beyond simple cost reduction, public clouds leverage efficiencies of scale and mobility of hosting to facilitate green initiatives aimed at reducing the carbon footprint or power consumption for the same class of organizational information technology services previously managed in isolated local data centers.

Obviously, the trail from servers to virtualized public cloud computing will process at different rates as individual services are transformed and migrated, so the total elimination of data center resources is not a near-term target — it is the end state of today's virtualization taken to its full potential.

Resistance Due to Perceived Loss of Control

Security and control over data continue to play a significant role in plans for cloud computing initiatives. When public cloud resources are brought to the table, opponents are quick to bring up the idea that "if you cannot touch it, you no longer own it." This is a holdover from mainframe computing in many instances, where all technologies were held in secure, closed central data centers. The resistance to cloud technologies remains interesting because offsite hosting and outsourcing have been taking components out of the local data center for some time due to cost advantages. To meet cloud computing initiatives, infrastructure and operations staff must evolve their skill sets along with the organization's transformation to remain viable in the new configuration.

Planning Organizational Roles in the Cloud

When planning for cloud integration in the enterprise, many organizational roles will change while new ones will emerge within the IT business component. Automation has already impacted organizations' IT personnel and created a fear of change as an immediate threat to existing positions. Because clouds provide automation for server and service provisioning, resource allocation, and peak capacity management, they would seem to be threatening all positions within the data center, but in reality, there is a continued need for IT career professionals, who may simply have to develop additional skills in this new environment. What is true is that cloud services will continue to need dedicated professionals, but they might be IT professionals who have developed business skills or business professionals who have developed an understanding of the IT elements required for cloud implementation.

The organizational roles are defined as follows:

Capacity planners Cloud planners will no longer focus simply on the infrastructure components that may need to be purchased during the yearly technical refresh cycle; they must instead understand the performance data and operational thresholds necessary for business services and understand the key assets necessary to meet rising demands. Capacity planners will need to understand the cost associated with resource allocations within the cloud service agreements in order to work with chargeback and cost recovery financial managers. Obviously, these changes will require additional business skills not generally necessary for traditional data center capacity planners; in fact, many organizations may find that it is sometimes easier for existing business financial planners to develop IT planning skills.

Network operation center staff The traditional network operation center (NOC) staff member spends time monitoring the operating envelope of their servers, spending resources and time to acquire and implement data center management utilities like Nagios, shown in Figure 2.2, and Big Brother. Because cloud utilities are present in nonlocal data centers or balanced across multiple systems even when locally managed as a private cloud, NOC staff will have to develop new strategies for monitoring and managing cloud resources, just as they did to facilitate the evolution of virtualization in the data center.

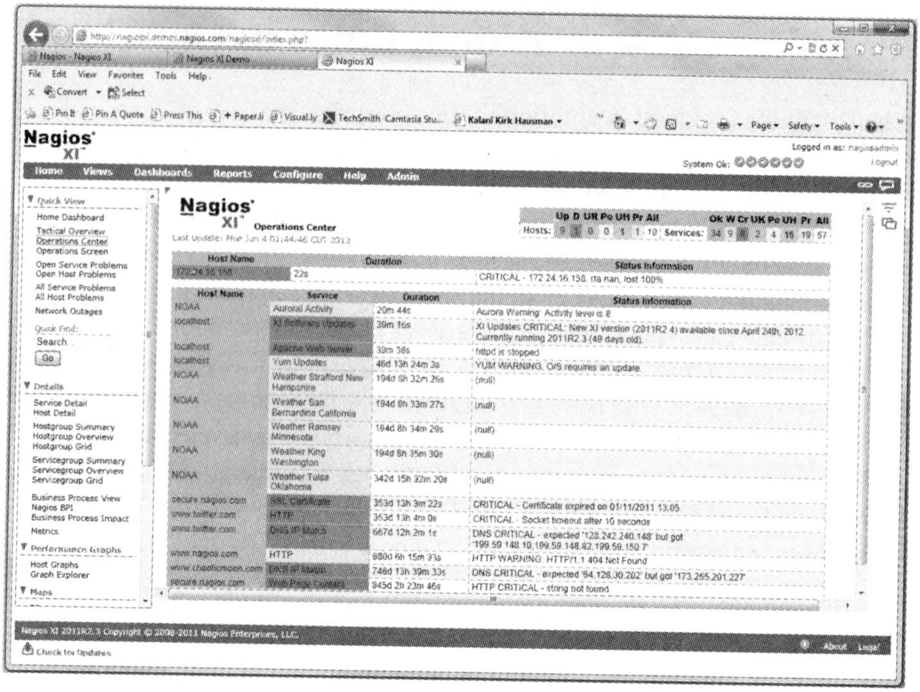

FIGURE 2.2 A view from the Nagios XI monitoring console showing example status data for multiple servers. This view would be used by operational monitoring staff to rapidly identify servers in need of support.

Vendor management staff These organizational staff members will be critical in developing early private cloud environments as well as, during the process, extending resources into hybrid and public cloud service infrastructures. Rather than buying resources once and then handing shortfalls and exceptions later, cloud vendor management personnel will be required to negotiate service-level contracts and then update or extend them to meet changes in service-level requirements over time. This group of staff will also need financial management skills to aid in chargeback and cost-recovery billing based on service resource consumption.

Support desk staff The support desk will continue to provide value, aiding users during the transfer from traditional to cloud computing models while both systems coexist and then providing client access support management of incidents and problems that will continue until technology matures greatly beyond today's systems. Support staff will need to develop greater understanding of networking to identify the source of cloud access issues for remote services.

Beyond transformation of existing positions, cloud computing will also create new requirements unique to the cloud environment; the enterprise architect will obviously have to take cloud technologies into account in their organizational planning, but additional architectural and management roles will focus solely on the cloud:

Cloud architect An expert will be required to handle the reinvention of the enterprise as it migrates into the cloud, with detailed knowledge of the layers necessary for private, hybrid, and public cloud integration. This position will require an understanding of networking and cloud infrastructural software platforms as well as an understanding of business functions that will be migrated into the cloud. An understanding of virtualization, interoperable connections, and database sharding or parallelization will be important when planning applications and software services that will exist in the cloud environment. The lack of maturity in the cloud environment presents a steady set of new issues that will continue to evolve as adoption and legal mandates change to meet the expansion of cloud computing services.

Cloud service manager More a financial manager than a purely technical professional, the cloud service manager will be responsible for financial management, including pricing, service levels, and service classes that will factor into cloud hosting contracts and billing policies for cloud resource consumption. This role will be involved in service retirement or renewal of hosted services, ordering and request procedures, and tracking for the total cost of cloud ownership.

Obviously, there will be many other changes to existing positions and new positions created to meet the need for cloud computing operations.

Identifying Cloud Deployment Models and Scope Modifiers

Existing cloud models derive their designations based on deployment and audience alignment using terms such as *public clouds* and *private clouds*, but the scope of their hosting will allow the four common models to fit emerging cloud implementations as organizations take advantage of local, offsite, and outsourced cloud hosting as each best meets their needs.

Cloud Deployment Models

The National Institute of Standards and Technology (NIST) has published a definition of cloud computing that the CompTIA Cloud Essentials exam uses as its basic categorization for cloud services based on deployment, provisioning, and consumption.

NIST Special Publication 800-145 documents four models for cloud deployments:

Private clouds Provisioned for use by a single user or group of users within an organization, the private cloud is owned, managed, and operated by the organization. Private clouds reside on a private network owned or managed by the organization itself. The private cloud is often the first entry into this technology for the data center, providing flexibility and resource consumption monitoring across cloud hosts located in organizational data centers. Private clouds are often selected when external mandates such as regulations and legislative requirements require a high degree of access accountability, control, and governance.

Community clouds Provisioned for use by a group of related organizations with shared concerns, such as a group of governmental or educational institutions that choose to share a common cloud of services not available to the general public, community clouds may reside as local, private cloud resources for the hosting organization and be accessed remotely as a community cloud by its partner organizations. Partitioned public clouds are examples of community clouds, with public cloud services isolated from general consumption through limitations restricting access to specified network address schemes or other forms of access specification. Community clouds can be use to gain improved reuse and sharing of information resources, such as an online call center application that can be transferred between geographically distributed support staff members to provide 24/7 coverage using the same application technology base.

Public clouds Provisioned for use the general public, public cloud services represent the most thoroughly virtualized cloud infrastructural design, removing data center information resources partially or completely. Public clouds reside on hosting data center resources and are accessed via public Internet connectivity by users located anywhere in the world. Transparent redirection of public cloud services to data centers in variable locations presents concerns for organizations with regulatory or legislative mandates demanding data accountability and governance.

Hybrid clouds Provisioned using components of private, community, or public clouds, the hybrid cloud provides access to two or more infrastructures bridged by standardized technologies or proprietary cloud services. Hybrid clouds are simply a mixture of cloud types, such as a private cloud customer relationship management (CRM) application together with public cloud Google Apps services used to integrate CRM data into an organization's collaboration services.

Bursting at the Seams

Cloud bursting is a hybrid cloud implementation where local private cloud resources are used in support of an application until a spike in demand exceeds local resource limits, at which point the app "bursts" out of the private cloud into designated public cloud resources to manage the overrun. Designated cloud providers must be running a compatible platform to support cloud bursting from the private cloud.

For example, a tax preparation service might experience a tremendous increase in volume when its software is discounted to end users, creating a flood of sudden new clients over a short time and overrunning private cloud capacities available in its organizational data center. If a public cloud alternate set of resources is properly set up, the flood could burst out of the private cloud into the extended public cloud until resource utilization baselines are realigned with data center resources.

Model Scope Modifiers

Beyond the NIST model, organizations may choose to host private, community, or parts of hybrid clouds either on site or outsourced to a hosting provider. This differs from a public cloud in that access remains limited to the appropriate category (private, community, or hybrid) even though the equipment is located beyond the organization's data center. Further resolution of the cloud model is possible through considerations of the hosting and access requirements for the cloud.

Onsite private clouds When the traditional data center is extended to include cloud services on site, the organization's traditional network and IT support will continue to be involved in cloud support. The cloud services will conceal operational details such as workload location and multitenancy on individual host systems, but they can provide enhanced control over resource monitoring and flexibility with dedicated virtualization hosts or physical server hosting scenarios. Costs may be high if new data centers are required or data center conversion is required for the new private cloud, and local resource constraints will still be present if not coupled to external services for cloud bursting.

Sharing the Same Box

Multitenancy **refers to a particular hosting server sharing workloads from multiple clients or services, which are separated only by access policies configured on the cloud server software. Attacks on one service could overwhelm resources available to an unrelated service if multitenancy planning is not imposed to isolate key services.**

Outsourced private clouds All of the traditional outsourcing security issues factor in, such as network bandwidth mandates and the need for transport security between the organization and the outsourcing host data center. All of the same limitations from onsite private clouds are present in outsourced private clouds, save that outsourcing host organizations can typically retain a larger resource pool than is present in the onsite data center and will accomplish tech refresh without intervention by the client organization. Data center costs are reduced for outsourced private cloud implementations, with higher operational costs for the outsourcing itself.

Onsite community clouds When a private cloud is expanded to provide services to a community of related organizations, it is termed a community cloud. The community cloud operates as a private cloud to the hosting organization but as a remote partitioned public cloud to the other organizations in the same community. Allowing only a limited scope of requestors access helps to improve the security of community clouds, but resource limitations and high costs are still retained from the private cloud model. Because the community's networks and resource requirements may vary widely from the hosting organization's standards, they can create variable costs in addition to those of the private cloud model.

Outsourced community clouds Outsourced community clouds carry the same issues as their onsite community cloud counterparts and gain the same advantages as their outsourced private equivalents — data center costs will be lower, but the outsourcing operating expenses may be higher than for self-hosted alternatives.

One change from private community clouds is that all organizations will access the outsourced community cloud as a remote partitioned public cloud because no organization in the community will host the outsourced resources.

Public clouds Public cloud models continue the evolution of virtualization, extending the outsourced community cloud to services available to authorized access from organizational, community, and general public security requestors. All access will be remote, while operational details such as workload location and multitenancy are concealed beyond the organization's monitoring scope.

Public clouds typically carry the lowest up-front costs because they rely on existing data centers, creating very large resource pools. Although these provide a high degree of elasticity, they require management to ensure that rising demands do not generate unexpected cost overruns. Service-level agreements and other contractual agreements also present challenges for the organization when dealing with public cloud services.

Hybrid clouds Hybrid cloud models can bridge any of the previously mentioned models for cloud computing and will include all of the same limitations and advantages of their component models with the additional requirement for standardization and compatibility between onsite, outsourced, and public components (Figure 2.3). Hybrid clouds require more management than the other models but can allow an organization or community the ability to align resources with business requirements to gain the best solution to meet all of their various needs.

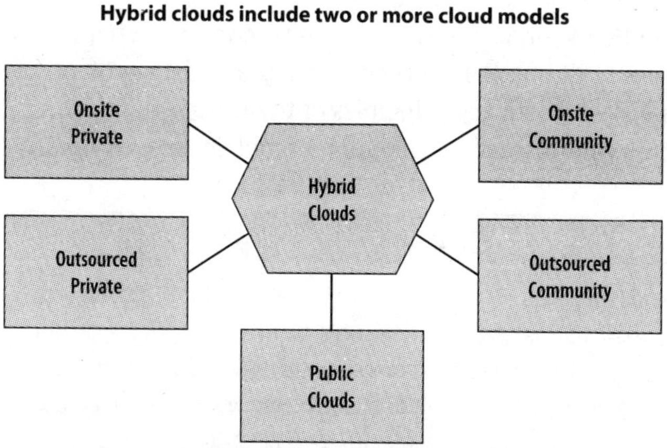

FIGURE 2.3 Hybrid clouds include two or more cloud models and may contain all models in some cases.

Hybrid as a Surface Rather than an Axis

Hybrid clouds might be built as horizontal hybrid models intended to provide services such as multiple avenues of data access or presentation to different access groups, or they may be constructed as vertical hybrid models that bring together all services required for a particular task, such as the database, web interface, payment application, and shipping management applications supporting an e-purchase service. Hybrids can also span both vertical and horizontal hybrid models at once to construct applications layered atop an organization's various needs and products, supporting multiple forms of access and consumption by various groups (private, community, or public).

Including Future Cloud Models

As cloud computing matures, additional models will undoubtedly evolve to meet arising needs. Already, cloud-based services such as disaster recovery and backup are expanding traditional data center and core IT functions into the cloud, but the potential for data loss or exposure remains one of the key elements of concern. Users can often access cloud services like Dropbox entirely within their web browsers, bypassing many controls of information provisions in the enterprise environment.

Because data operations such as workload location and resource pool limits are hidden from common use by cloud infrastructural components, regulatory mandates and legal requirements for accountability and responsibility require additional planning and user training. For example, privacy and data control legislation such as the Safe Harbor privacy principles of the European Union's Directive on Data Protection may impact the adoption of mobile data services.

The Essentials and Beyond

Cloud computing will not completely replace traditional IT service personnel with automation, but it will require retraining of existing personnel and the introduction of new cloud-specific task assignments to extend resources beyond the data center into the cloud. Cloud deployments can be identified based on their provisioned consumers as private, community, or public clouds.

Adding provisions for hosting location allows further resolution of requirements for onsite and outsourced cloud servers. Hybrid clouds bridge two or more of the various other models to create horizontal, vertical, and customized cloud models tailored to the specific requirements of an organization, a community, or the general public audience.

(Continues)

THE ESSENTIALS AND BEYOND *(Continued)*

ADDITIONAL EXERCISES

Identify cloud models based on simplified illustrations of hosting location and audience type.

Describe hybrid cloud advantages including cloud bursting, vertical and horizontal hybrid models, and application development within private clouds before deployment to public cloud production hybrid environments.

To compare your answer to the author's, please visit `www.sybex.com/go/cloudessentials`.

REVIEW QUESTIONS

1. What type of cloud model would enable cloud bursting?

   A. Private
   B. Public
   C. Community
   D. Hybrid

2. Which example of new cloud computing roles will focus more on financial matters than on technical ones?

   A. Vendor management staff
   B. Support desk staff
   C. Cloud architect
   D. Cloud service manager

3. True or false? Adoption of public cloud services requires an organization to first implement server virtualization and private and hybrid clouds.

   A. True
   B. False

4. At what IT infrastructural level are server costs capital expenses rather than operational?

   A. Traditional
   B. Private cloud
   C. Hybrid cloud
   D. Public cloud

5. Which type of cloud computing definitely involves resources in the organization's own data center?

   A. Public
   B. Private
   C. Community
   D. Hybrid

6. Which type of cloud is not specified expressly by NIST?

   A. Private
   B. Community
   C. Partitioned public
   D. Public

7. Which model of cloud computing best mirrors the current electrical utility grid?

   A. Community
   B. Private
   C. Public
   D. Hybrid

(Continues)

The Essentials and Beyond *(Continued)*

8. Which type of cloud is often used when external mandates require a high degree of data governance?

   A. Private
   B. Community
   C. Partitioned public
   D. Public

9. Which type of cloud allows an organization to share its local cloud services with its partners?

   A. Private
   B. Community
   C. Public
   D. Hybrid

10. An organization that blends Google Docs forms and Microsoft's Azure services for data collection and management is using what type of cloud deployment?

    A. Private
    B. Community
    C. Public
    D. Hybrid

CHAPTER 3

Service Models

Cloud services are aligned by their mode of deployment, such as public, private, and hybrid as discussed in Chapter 2, "Cloud Models." Cloud services can also be aligned with their service model, in which each level of service abstraction will be associated with the term *as a Service (aaS)*. Consumers of cloud resources access these "as a Service" resources via their favorite web browser without considering whether they are consuming an application or an entire infrastructure within the cloud.

The three primary models for services in the cloud computing stack are Software as a Service, Platform as a Service, and Infrastructure as a Service. Cloud vendors often describe their products as Backup as a Service (BaaS), Database as a Service (DBaaS), or even Everything as a Service (XaaS) to fit their particular product's function, but these all fit within the three standard models designated by NIST. Chapter 4, "Current Cloud Technologies," presents common examples of various "as a Service" cloud services in greater detail.

- **Categorizing cloud services**
- **Examining Software as a Service**
- **Examining Platform as a Service**
- **Examining Infrastructure as a Service**
- **Identifying emerging cloud Database as a Service capabilities**
- **Defining Everything as a Service**

Categorizing Cloud Services

Cloud resources can be consumed by other cloud services, by traditional electronic devices, and by consumers using common web browsers as the cloud computing client. Cloud providers group their offerings into three primary "aaS" categories according to their level of abstraction, identified by National Institution of Standards and Technology (NIST) by these designations: Software as a Service (SaaS), Platform as a Service (PaaS), and Infrastructure as a Service (IaaS).

The Cloud According to NIST

NIST operates under the US Department of Commerce and has defined many of the key concepts used in cloud computing. As we discussed in Chapter 2, NIST Special Publication 800-145 identifies the four deployment models: public, community, hybrid, and private. It further defines the three standard service models: SaaS, PaaS, and IaaS. These concepts form the basis for CompTIA's Cloud Essentials exam and pervade media discussions of cloud computing.

The service models are often represented in the form of a pyramid like that shown in Figure 3.1 because IaaS provides the most fundamental service category and each successive level includes elements of the lower-level service categories.

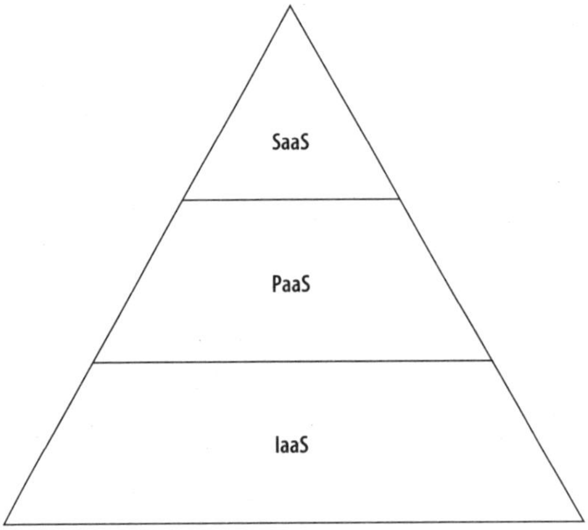

FIGURE 3.1 A common depiction of the cloud service models, depicting their relationship as a hierarchical model with each layer consuming elements of layers lower in the model

Building atop successive layers, providers begin with the most fundamental level of IaaS, which includes familiar elements from traditional settings such as networking and storage and other architectural elements of interest to system administrators and enterprise planners. Application developers will consume services provided by PaaS providers, which also support the hosting infrastructure. Users will consume applications provided by the SaaS level, which itself includes components of both platform and infrastructure services beyond the consumer's visibility. Figure 3.2 aligns these roles using the same model layering.

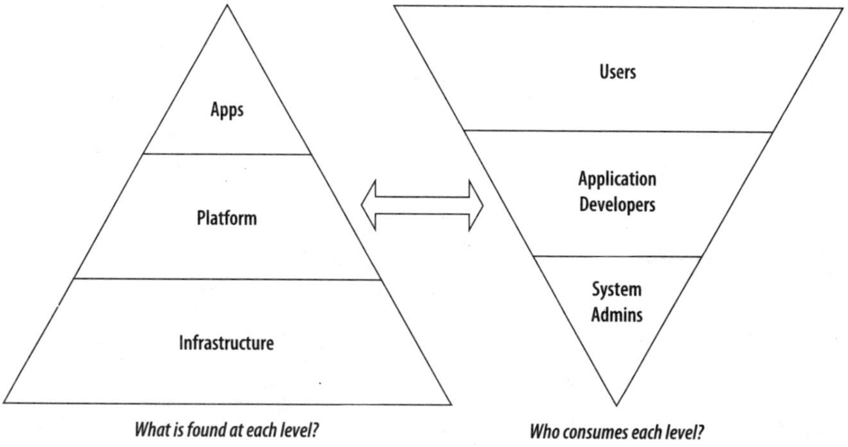

FIGURE 3.2 Cloud service models aligned with their principle consuming populations

Fewer Providers Are Available as More Client Control Is Provided

The rapidly growing number of SaaS options are leveraging the provider's ability to control all details of a service, including the application, platform, and infrastructural elements within their own sphere of control. Fewer providers support client-side application development in PaaS options, where only the platform and infrastructure are managed by the provider.

Only a relatively small group of providers support full client-side development and configuration in IaaS options, where only the infrastructural components themselves (examples include hardware, networking, and storage) are managed by the service provider. The number of cloud computing providers decreases rapidly as the level of client control over customization, configuration, and management of cloud resources increases.

Examining Software as a Service

Software as a Service (SaaS) is often the first example of cloud computing that many users will experience — sometimes without even realizing they are interacting with a cloud at all. Hosted software applications available through a web browser or via a thin client are often indistinguishable to the user, who just wants to run the software application and not worry about application details operating behind the curtain. Figure 3.3 provides some examples of the many SaaS offerings that are available, and this is by no means a complete listing.

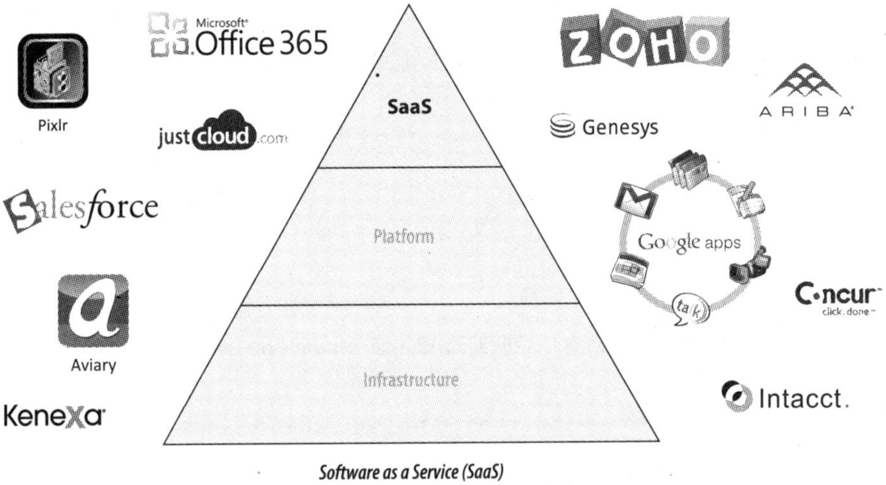

FIGURE 3.3 Some examples of SaaS providers and applications

Like traditional software applications, SaaS offerings provide the end user with some type of application that consumes, produces, or processes electronic information. SaaS products are generally prebuilt and consumed using the provided functionality without significant customization, as in the case of Google Gmail users who simply access the web-based standard email and calendaring application, shown in Figure 3.4.

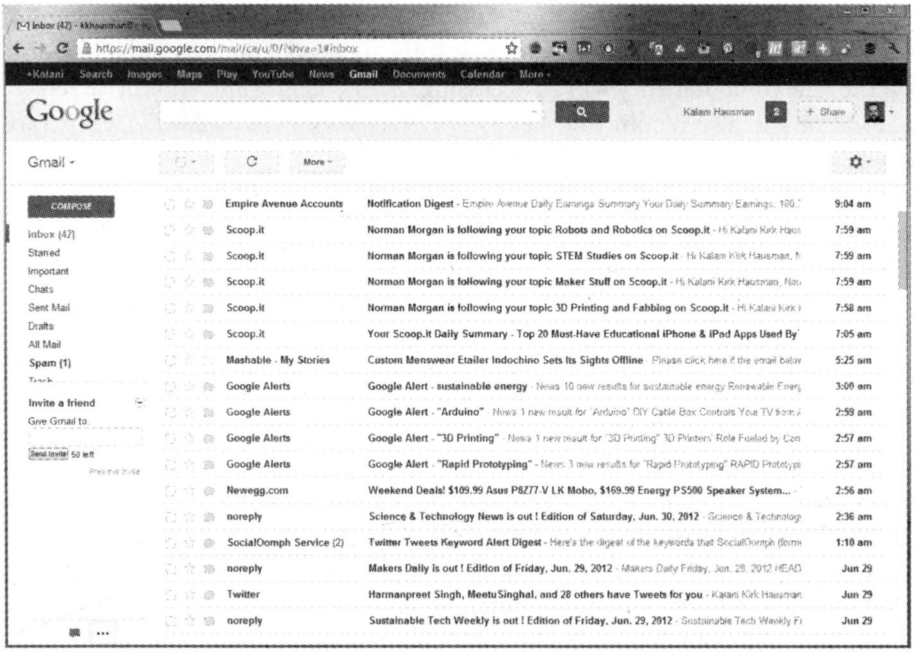

FIGURE 3.4 Example Gmail cloud SaaS client for email, accessed using Google's Chrome web browser

Similar to traditional software products, SaaS alternatives are prebuilt and cannot be changed beyond personalization and configuration settings by the consumer. Cloud SaaS applications offer distinct advantages over traditional locally installed software and are driving the mad rush to bring the cloud into existing enterprise environments.

Traditional software requires a capital expense to purchase and operating expenses to install, update, and maintain. Traditional software application management follows a predictable process:

1. Identify software meeting requirements.
2. Perform capital acquisition for identified software.
3. Install software to client computers.
4. Patch software in maintenance cycle.
5. Perform acquisition fo ftware update.
6. Install software update to client computers.
7. Return to maintenance cycle until next software update.

When a user of traditional software gets a new computer or is moved to an alternate space in the organization, their software applications must be installed on the new computer they will be accessing. Staff changes and enterprise reorganization can also require another round of acquisitions for additional software licensing.

By contrast, SaaS application management requires far fewer steps for the consuming organization:

1. Identify cloud service providers whose software meets organizational requirements.
2. Obtain licensing for identified software service access.

After this, all maintenance, including patches and updates, is handled by the cloud SaaS provider. User mobility and hardware replacements do not affect SaaS application availability so long as a cloud client application such as a web browser is available. Changes to staffing or organizational assignment require purely operational costs for additional access licensing to the cloud service and may simply be retained by the staff member as they change job roles.

The extended availability of SaaS applications also supports additional business processes, such as disaster recovery and business continuity, remote workplace assignment, and collaboration between siloed organizational components or with partners external to the organization's technology envelope.

Many other organizational advantages become possible through SaaS:

- Business agility is enhanced by ensuring that mobile workers retain access to key business applications while visiting new territories or operating through mobile client interaction.
- Displaced employees retain operational capability during widespread natural disasters, and organizational data resources can simply be moved to cloud provider storage outside of the affected area if another Hurricane Sandy–like event should occur.
- Organizations can take advantage of resource sharing between employees working in different time zones or across different geopolitical zones.
- Organizations can implement sustainable "green" initiatives such as remote travel-free employees, who do not require leased space, dedicated equipment, and costly environmental control in expensive central office facilities.

Examining Platform as a Service

Platform as a Service (PaaS) expands an organization's capability to customize application development in the cloud by providing access to cloud program development tools and development environments. Figure 3.5 provides some examples of current PaaS offerings that are available; again, this is not meant as a complete listing.

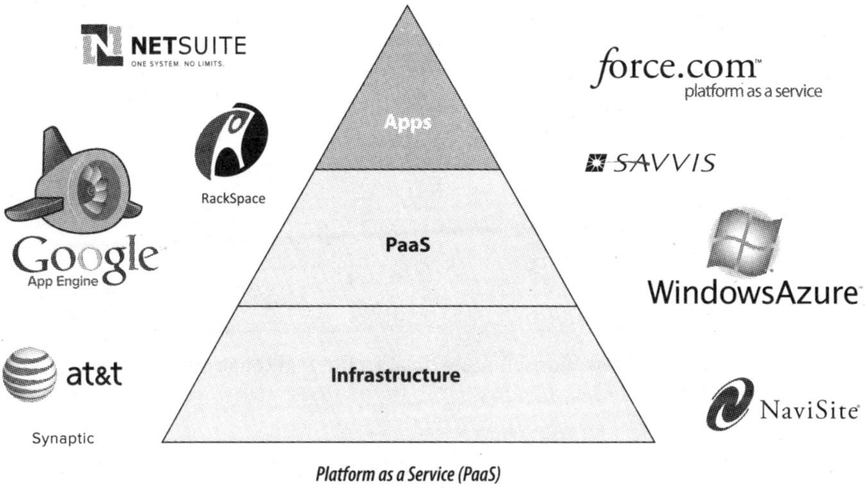

FIGURE 3.5 **Some examples of PaaS providers and applications**

Platform as a Service cloud options are coupled to a particular vendor's technologies, languages, and other features. This is similar to the way that many application development environments are linked to a standard set of tools that their developers will use to create deployable software in traditional enterprise networks. Many PaaS vendors can even link their cloud service platforms to existing development suites to simplify the adoption of new cloud alternatives by existing programming human resources. As an example, Figure 3.6 illustrates the integration between Microsoft's Visual Studio environment and its Azure cloud application service platform. See how the Windows Azure option is listed in the available templates.

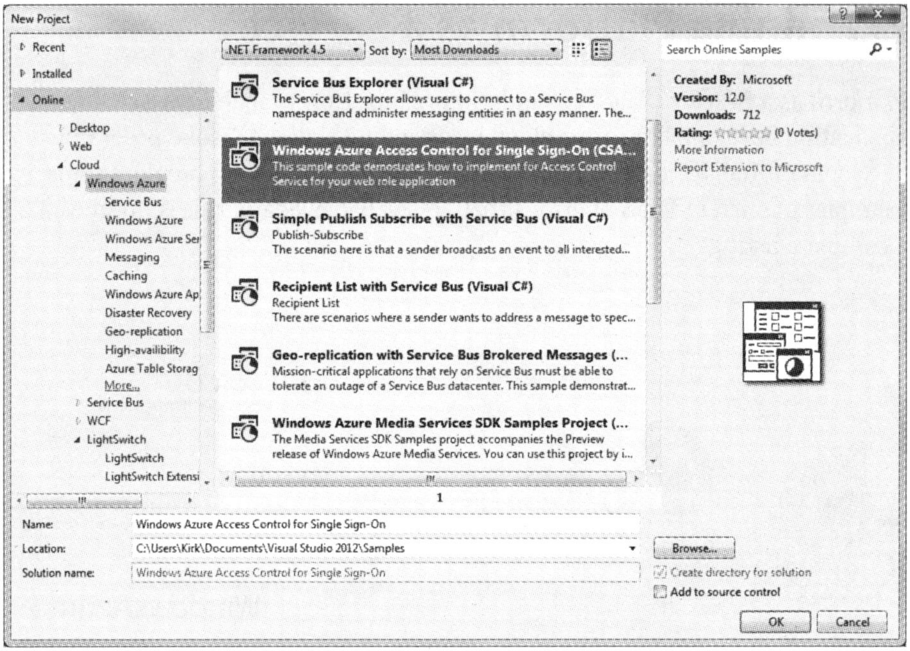

FIGURE 3.6 Creating a new Microsoft Azure cloud service application using Microsoft's Visual Studio development utility

Because the same technologies can be used by application developers for both traditional and PaaS cloud applications, the process of migrating existing software solutions from traditional to cloud hosting is greatly simplified. Even when using private cloud services located in the local data center running atop the same hardware already in place, cloud versions of existing applications can span multiple host servers' resources to allow the same software much greater capacity for expansion and flexibility.

Hosted on hybrid or public cloud services, PaaS applications can scale to meet even a global consumer base. Figure 3.7 provides an example of Google App Engine's PaaS capability used to create one of our favorite fun cloud applications — the Wordle.net service that translates any provided text into a "word cloud" style display image.

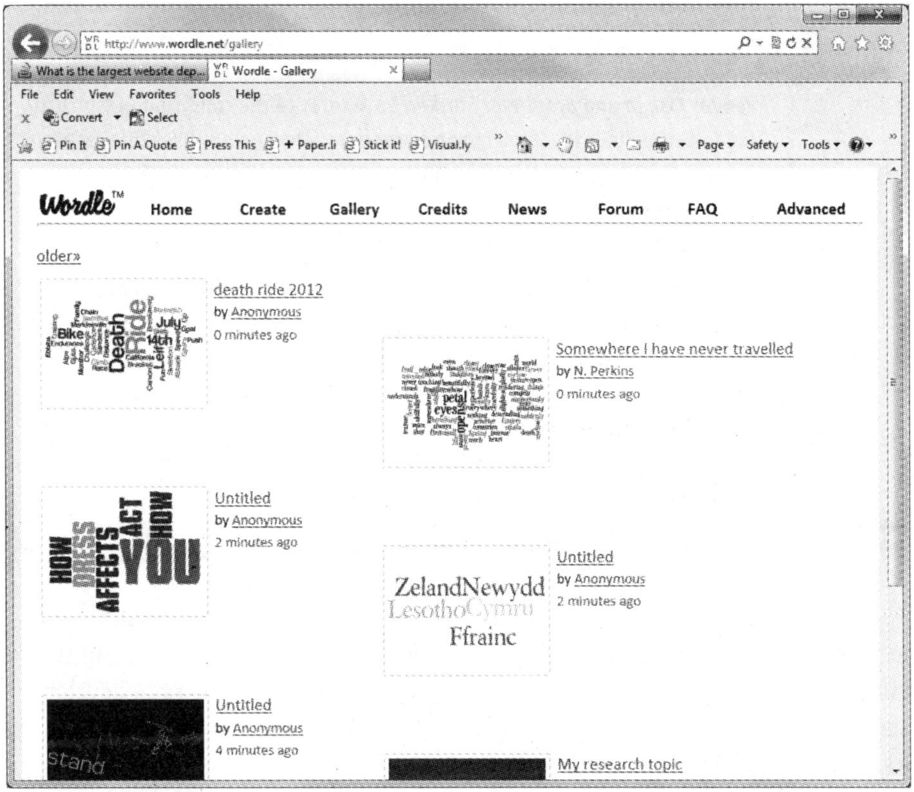

FIGURE 3.7 An example of the Wordle.net application, developed for Google App Engine PaaS cloud application hosting

Because this custom application was developed to run within Google's PaaS application service hosting, its developers were able to rapidly roll out their solution and then expand it as needed to be in the top 11,000 sites worldwide according to the Alexa web statistics service at the time of this writing.

Because individual PaaS vendors provide the infrastructure for their application development cloud services, they get to select which languages will be available for application development on their platform. This leads to concerns of vendor lock-in in a relatively new service environment whose principal hosting agents could change or even shut their doors as cloud hosting options evolve with the market.

What Is Vendor Lock-In?

Vendor lock-in and _proprietary lock-in_ both refer to the condition in which an organization finds itself relying on a proprietary technology base that restricts future migration to alternative solutions without significant costs for transition of supportive technologies. Organizations seeking agility must be careful to manage vendor lock-in constraints in long-range planning.

A good example of vendor lock-in could be sitting on your kitchen counter, in the form of a Keurig coffeemaker, which can make coffee using only its proprietary single-serving packs. This prevents your ability to transition to an exotic version of coffee not already supplied through one of Keurig's licensed vendors. You are locked in to these proprietary packs or must buy a whole new coffeemaker if you wanted to make a cup of Ethiopia Yirgacheffe to hold your focus as you try to concentrate on a difficult task.

Some PaaS vendors have created their own proprietary application development languages, although many try to develop similar analogs to existing languages to diminish the ramp-up time for hiring new programmers to develop applications for their platform. Salesforce.com provides an example of this in its Force.com PaaS proprietary Apex (Java-like) and Visualforce (XML-like) languages. More robust PaaS providers allow programming using standardized and open-source languages to ease adoption and migration of existing organizational applications.

Google App Engine's PaaS application development can be conducted using standardized Java and Python as well as its own Go open-source language. Figure 3.8 shows Microsoft's Azure PaaS's current options, including Microsoft's own .NET suite of languages (including C#, VB .NET, J#), Node.Js, PHP, Java, and Python for software application development of Azure cloud service–hosted applications.

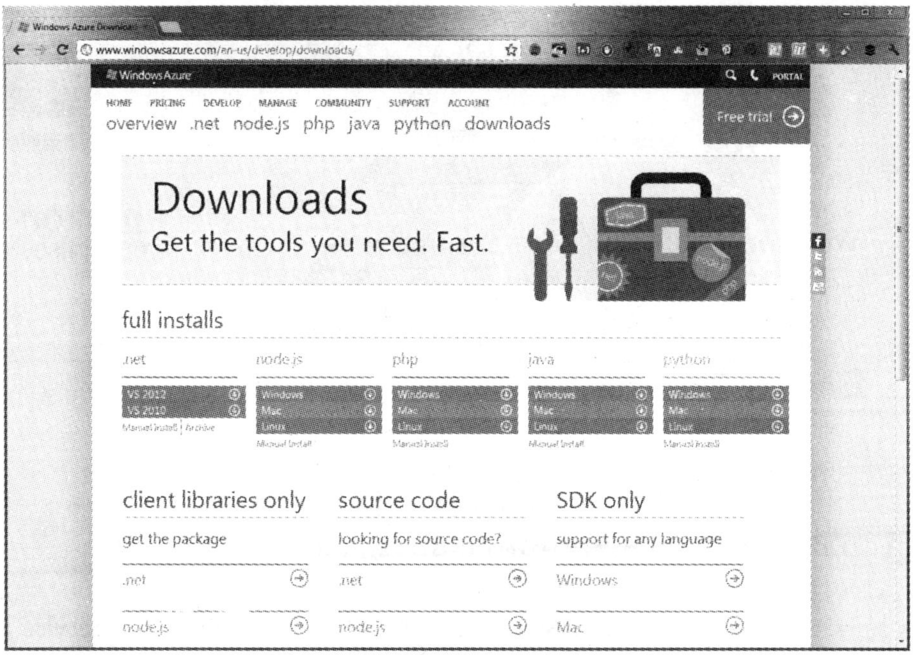

FIGURE 3.8 Microsoft's Windows Azure PaaS development resources illustrating its supported variety of programming languages

Organizations will typically select a PaaS vendor whose suite of languages aligns with existing application development human resources in house to ease adoption of new PaaS software and migration of existing services into the cloud. The close integration of Microsoft's Visual Studio illustrated earlier in this chapter is an excellent example of this convenience, when even the standard programming tools can connect to PaaS deployment targets just as easily as they always have for traditional application deployment servers. Leaders in the PaaS space are trying to future-proof their offerings by providing support for open languages such as Python and Java in order to address concerns regarding vendor lock-in.

Examining Infrastructure as a Service

The third category of cloud services, Infrastructure as a Service (IaaS), allows a client almost complete control over applications, languages, and fundamental resources supporting organizational services such as databases, storage, and networking. Figure 3.9 provides some examples of IaaS providers — a number far less than providers for higher-level service models in the cloud pyramid.

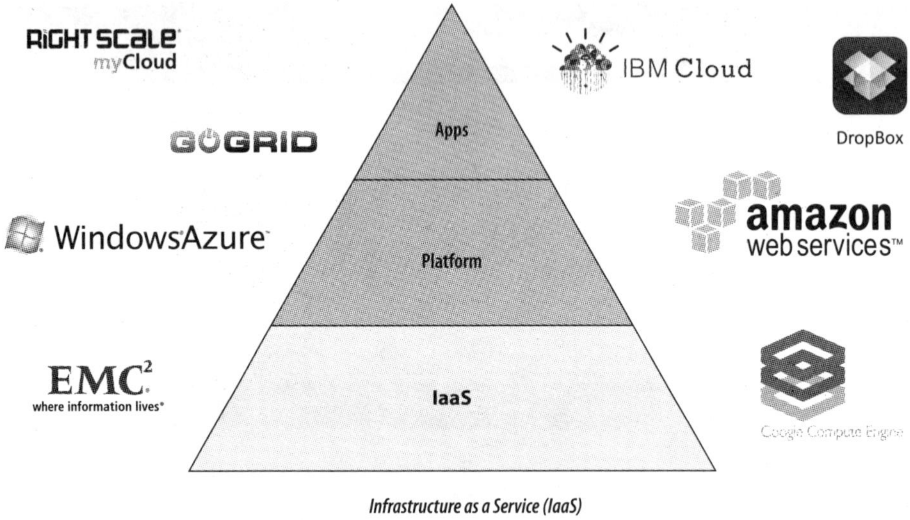

FIGURE 3.9 Some examples of IaaS providers and applications

Infrastructure as a Service is sometimes referred to as Hardware as a Service (HaaS) to reflect its function in providing on-demand hardware-equivalent resources such as storage and network interconnectivity to its clients, who then may provision these resources to meet an organization's particular needs in the form of virtual machines for database services, data file storage, authentication services, and any other functions deemed necessary. This capability means that an organization can contract with an IaaS provider to effectively eliminate local data center server resource requirements while retaining the ability to provision and consume resources through local control and selection.

Figure 3.10 shows the Windows Azure IaaS portal interface, with two virtual machines currently configured as database servers for application development prototyping.

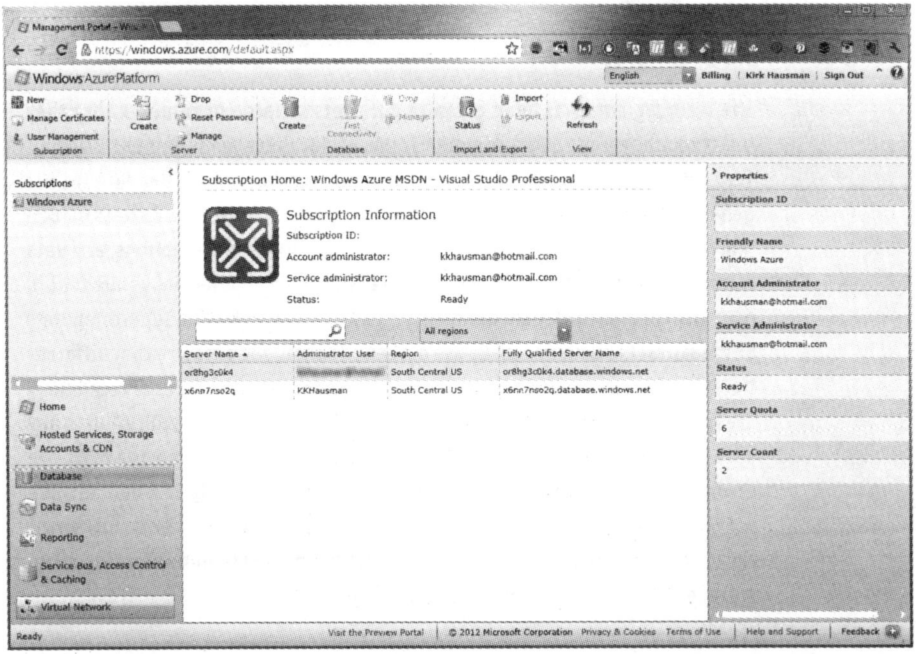

FIGURE 3.10 Windows Azure Platform management console, showing two existing virtual machines configured as database servers for development access using a Visual Studio utility

Controls are present for management of networking, storage and other resources within preestablished limitations allocated to this account. This is an administrative-level tool through which you can provision resources for developers who will then construct applications for end users — affording control of the entire cloud service pyramid from here.

Identifying Emerging Cloud Database Capabilities

We discussed many of the technologies atop which cloud computing evolved — from high-performance computing and virtualization to distributed data resource management — in Chapter 1, "What Is Cloud Computing?" Cloud services have not lost access to their basic functions, and they gain significant advantages leveraging them in the age of "big data" through distributed computing cloud functions and services such as Database as a Service (DBaaS), Data Mining as a Service (DMaaS), Data Warehousing as a Service (DWaaS), and other cloud-specific forms of database management that are being developed.

How Big Is Big Data?

The term *big data* has been given to data sets so large or complex that they resist management using common forms of database management utilities. Traditionally, supercomputers have been necessary to manage big data such as genetic studies, meteorological predictions, and complex physical stress modeling. Modern data analytics for Internet searches, financial predictions, and data warehousing business informatics have expanded the potential venue for big data into common office environments — environments lacking supercomputers or the skill sets needed to make use of them. There is not a set size that differentiates big data from simply large data sets because the capabilities of technology are forever expanding. The term has a general rule-of-thumb application to any data set that cannot be processed in a reasonable amount of time due to its size or complexity. Examples of big data suitable for cloud analysis would include data used for long-term weather forecasting, analysis of economic trends across the entire stock market, and similar tasks whose data sets alone would overrun storage constraints on traditional noncloud hosting.

Sharding

Cloud-based database services can break up a large data set into a number of sub–data sets to be distributed across hosting servers to improve performance and data throughput for very large business applications. MongoDB, for example, is used to manage high-volume transaction databases for SAP's content management service, EA's game download manager, and the *New York Times*'s story submission application. Scaling resources to meet such demands for submission rates in traditional application models would have required specialized and costly high-performance computing solutions for transaction load balancing and high data throughput.

Database Profiling

The potential for unanticipated or undesirable data modification increases with the volume of processed data, requiring database and data analysis to support the integrity aspect of data security. Some DBaaS cloud services such as MondoDB have a built-in database profiling tool that can review big data data sets and data to identify predictable issues that may arise so that application design alternatives can be developed.

Defining Everything as a Service

The lexicon for cloud services aligned with "as a Service" terminology is rapidly expanding and often muddied by media and cloud vendors who redefine "aaS" concepts to best suit marketing for their own unique offerings. The common Dropbox cloud storage presents an example of why attempts to define the specific form of cloud service can be difficult. The web client interface for Dropbox is an example of SaaS, but the Dropbox service is itself a storage component existing as a limited IaaS resource for other application development leveraging its storage capabilities.

Cloud IaaS resources are available for consumption not only by other cloud services but also by traditional constructed applications. Figure 3.11 illustrates this within author Kirk Hausman's WordPress blog, where a standard server-deployed WordPress add-on provides nightly backups to his cloud Dropbox storage allocation. Cloud and traditional resources can be blended to create what is being increasingly referred to simply as Everything as a Service (XaaS). Whatever the future holds, it is clear that cloud computing will enhance flexibility and availability to meet an increasingly mobile global population of consumers.

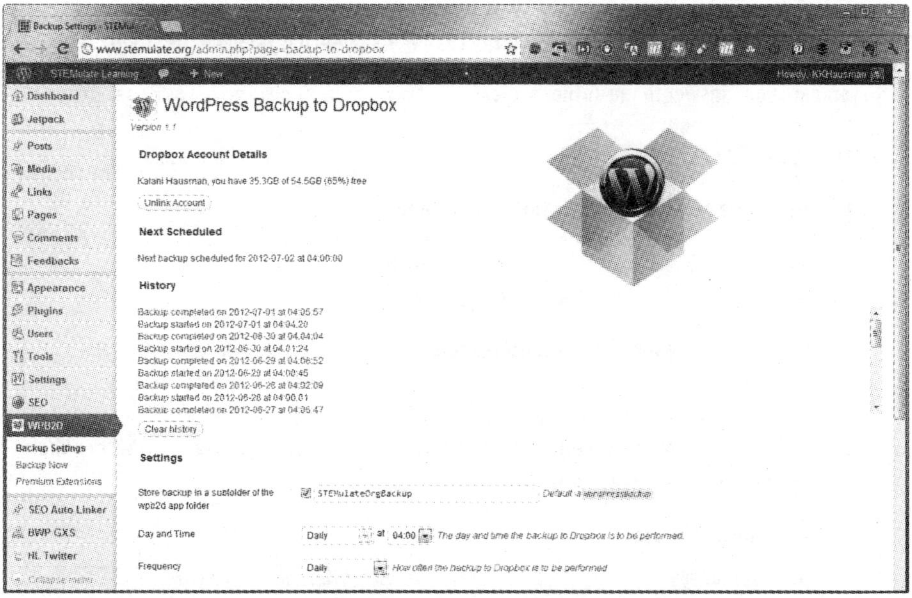

FIGURE 3.11 **A WordPress blog is backed up each night to Dropbox by a third-party application that consumes the IaaS cloud storage aspect of Dropbox.**

We will discuss common examples of current cloud computing services in Chapter 4.

THE ESSENTIALS AND BEYOND

Cloud computing services can be categorized into three main classes of cloud offerings, based on the level of user control and capability for management: Software as a Service, Platform as a Service, and Infrastructure as a Service. The more control a category offers to consumers, the fewer providers there are to meet their needs. The vast majority of current cloud services operate as Internet-accessible applications in the SaaS model, where consumers have little control over application customization or features and simply use the service as it is provided.

As organizations move application development into the cloud using PaaS service hosting or move significant elements of their organizational data center infrastructure into IaaS forms, they can gain advantages of scale and capability over increasingly large data sets provided to a global client base. Building the integration of traditional and cloud services and applications presents one of the greater challenges for enterprise architects as we move toward having Everything as a Service (XaaS) options to meet varying organizational needs.

ADDITIONAL EXERCISES

- Identify cloud service model characteristics using the pyramid model.
- Describe application development options available at each level of abstraction.

To compare your answer to the author's, please visit `www.sybex.com/go/cloudessentials`.

REVIEW QUESTIONS

1. What type of cloud service is the most common?

   A. SaaS
   B. PaaS
   C. IaaS
   D. XaaS

2. True or false? Vendor lock-in concerns relate only to PaaS cloud implementations.

   A. True
   B. False

3. Which level of management is provided by all cloud service providers, whether their products are Saas, PaaS, or IaaS?

   A. Infrastructure
   B. Databases
   C. Applications
   D. Service-oriented architecture

(Continues)

THE ESSENTIALS AND BEYOND *(Continued)*

4. Which category of "as a Service" models is not specifically identified by NIST?
   - A. Software as a Service
   - B. Platform as a Service
   - C. Infrastructure as a Service
   - D. Hardware as a Service
   - E. Everything as a Service
5. Which level of the cloud service model pyramid allows the greatest flexibility for application development?
   - A. Software as a Service
   - B. Platform as a Service
   - C. Infrastructure as a Service
   - D. Hardware as a Service
6. True or false? Application life cycle management in the cloud is slightly more complex than in traditional development models due to the addition of remote resources.
   - A. True
   - B. False
7. What is the term used to reflect the division of a database into smaller data sets for analysis and processing within the cloud?
   - A. Database profiling
   - B. Minimizing
   - C. Sharding
   - D. Subsetting
8. Which NIST "as a Service" model is best suited to full customization for an organization's services?
   - A. Software as a Service
   - B. Platform as a Service
   - C. Infrastructure as a Service
   - D. Everything as a Service
9. At what NIST "as a Service" model level is the current concern of vendor/proprietary lock-in greatest for custom applications developed for the cloud?
   - A. Software as a Service
   - B. Platform as a Service
   - C. Infrastructure as a Service
   - D. Everything as a Service
10. True or false? All cloud services fall into only one of the NIST models: SaaS, PaaS, IaaS.
    - A. True
    - B. False

Current Cloud Technologies

Both CompTIA and EXIN exams expect you to have some familiarity with existing cloud technologies already in use. Although the options will change over time, this chapter will examine representative cloud services in all three primary categories for services in the cloud computing stack: Software as a Service (SaaS), Platform as a Service (PaaS), and Infrastructure as a Service (IaaS). This chapter will also examine the integration of cloud and mobile solutions to empower an increasingly wireless and lightweight spectrum of mobile technology.

- **Comparing traditional technologies and cloud alternatives**
- **Leveraging Software as a Service (SaaS)**
- **Developing within Platform as a Service (PaaS)**
- **Implementing Infrastructure as a Service (IaaS)**
- **Empowering mobile computing**

Comparing Traditional Technologies and Cloud Alternatives

The transformation from a traditional data center and network enterprise toward services hosted in the cloud does not change the expectations or desires of users for capability and familiar interfaces. This chapter provides examples of a number of cloud services that mirror common workstation applications, including cloud-based spreadsheets from several vendors, file storage, and media production services for photographs, music, and even video creation. Table 4.1 lists common cloud equivalents to traditional applications and technologies.

TABLE 4.1 Examples of traditional and cloud equivalents to various application technologies

Technology	Traditional	Cloud Equivalent
User productivity suite	Microsoft Office	Office 365
	OpenOffice	Google Apps
	Lotusphere	Zoho
Audio/video production	Adobe Premiere	Aviary
	Camtasia	NovaCut
	ACID/Sound Forge	WeVideo
Photo manipulation	Adobe Photoshop	Pixlr
Business intelligence	Great Plains	NetSuite
	Quest	SalesForce
	Oracle BI Suite	Workday
File storage	Windows Server	Ubuntu One
	NetApp	SkyDrive
	EMC	Dropbox
Server virtualization	VMware	RackSpace
	Hyper-V	Amazon EC2
	XEN	Windows Azure

Figure 4.1 provides an example of a common traditional desktop application: Microsoft's Excel, a spreadsheet application within the Office suite. Traditional software like this requires installation on the client computer and is available only to consumers accessing the application from the client system, requiring other mechanisms for sharing a spreadsheet document with others consumers.

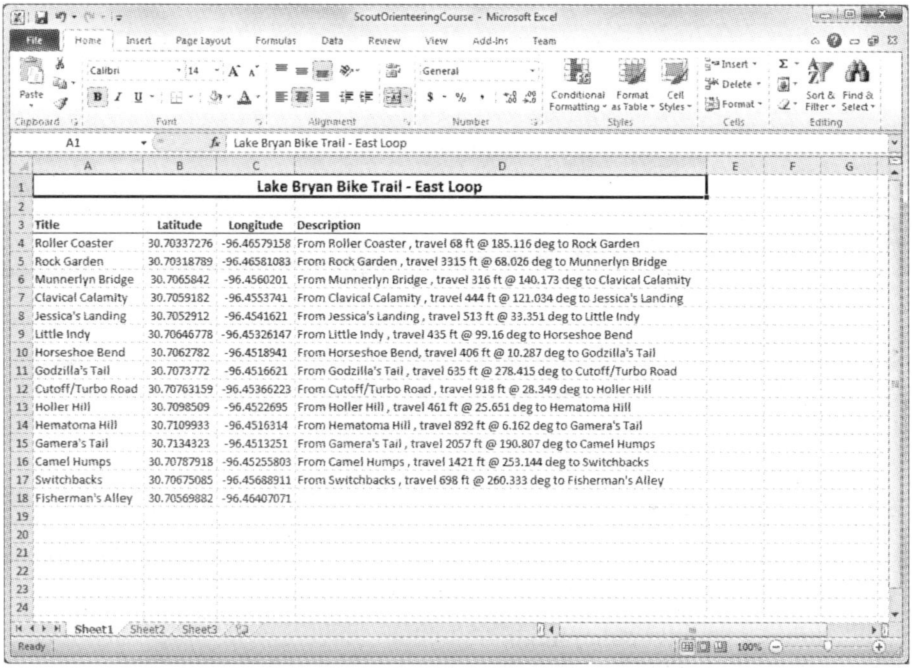

Lake Bryan Bike Trail - East Loop

Title	Latitude	Longitude	Description
Roller Coaster	30.70337276	-96.46579158	From Roller Coaster , travel 68 ft @ 185.116 deg to Rock Garden
Rock Garden	30.70318789	-96.46581083	From Rock Garden , travel 3315 ft @ 68.026 deg to Munnerlyn Bridge
Munnerlyn Bridge	30.7065842	-96.4560201	From Munnerlyn Bridge , travel 316 ft @ 140.173 deg to Clavical Calamity
Clavical Calamity	30.7059182	-96.4553741	From Clavical Calamity , travel 444 ft @ 121.034 deg to Jessica's Landing
Jessica's Landing	30.7052912	-96.4541621	From Jessica's Landing , travel 513 ft @ 33.351 deg to Little Indy
Little Indy	30.70646778	-96.45326147	From Little Indy , travel 435 ft @ 99.16 deg to Horseshoe Bend
Horseshoe Bend	30.7062782	-96.4518941	From Horseshoe Bend, travel 406 ft @ 10.287 deg to Godzilla's Tail
Godzilla's Tail	30.7073772	-96.4516621	From Godzilla's Tail , travel 635 ft @ 278.415 deg to Cutoff/Turbo Road
Cutoff/Turbo Road	30.70763159	-96.45366223	From Cutoff/Turbo Road , travel 918 ft @ 28.349 deg to Holler Hill
Holler Hill	30.7098509	-96.4522695	From Holler Hill , travel 461 ft @ 25.651 deg to Hematoma Hill
Hematoma Hill	30.7109933	-96.4516314	From Hematoma Hill , travel 892 ft @ 6.162 deg to Gamera's Tail
Gamera's Tail	30.7134323	-96.4513251	From Gamera's Tail , travel 2057 ft @ 190.807 deg to Camel Humps
Camel Humps	30.70787918	-96.45255803	From Camel Humps , travel 1421 ft @ 253.144 deg to Switchbacks
Switchbacks	30.70675085	-96.45688911	From Switchbacks , travel 698 ft @ 260.333 deg to Fisherman's Alley
Fisherman's Alley	30.70569882	-96.46407071	

FIGURE 4.1 Microsoft Excel spreadsheet displaying a chart of GPS coordinates from a BSA orienteering bike trek

Figure 4.2 illustrates Microsoft's cloud-based alternative version of Excel within its Office 365 suite. This alternative is reasonably complete in comparison to the traditional desktop application but still lacks certain features regarding macros and other active components because Microsoft's cloud offerings are designed to work in close coordination with their traditional counterparts.

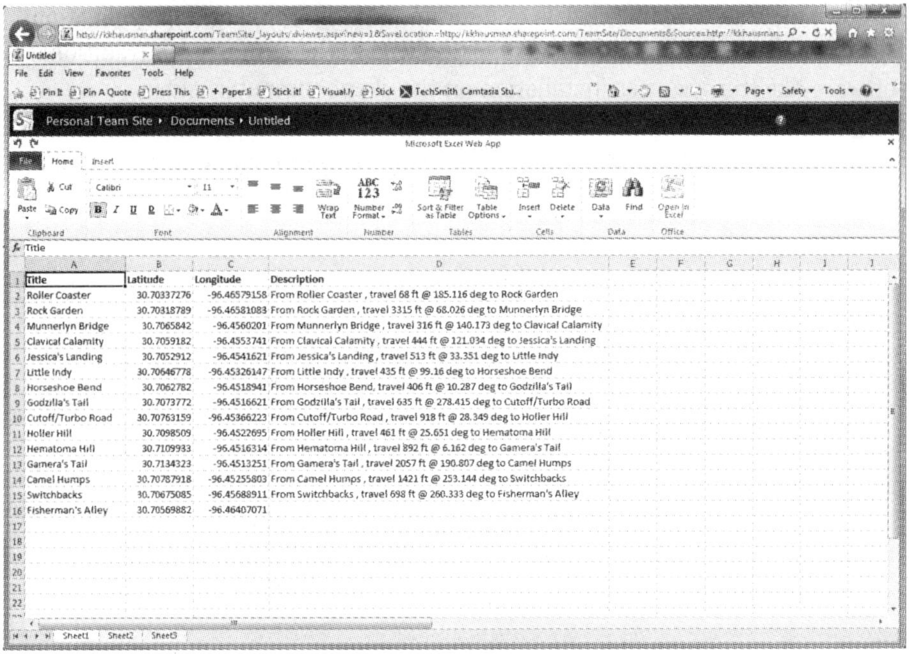

FIGURE 4.2 Microsoft Office 365 cloud version of Excel displaying details of the same trek

One key advantage of cloud-based services is that, being web-based, they are accessible even from machines lacking installed applications like the traditional Microsoft Office suite. Figure 4.3 illustrates a fully in-browser spreadsheet alternative running within the Google Docs suite of applications. Access to this type of application is possible from any browser-enabled computing device—PCs, laptops, hts, and even many data-enabled telephones.

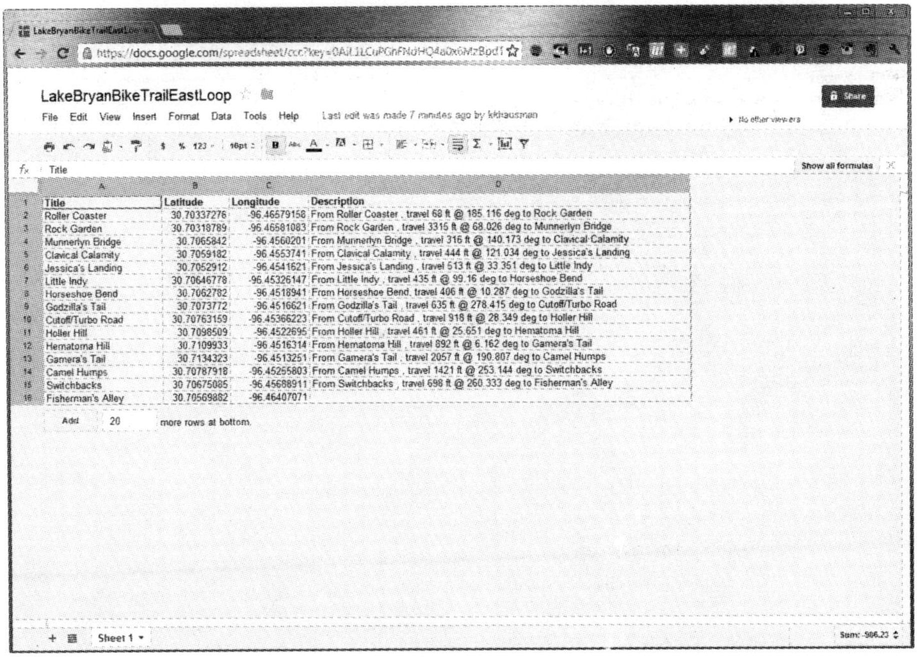

FIGURE 4.3 Google Docs' cloud-based equivalent to Excel, illustrating an entirely in-browser alternative spreadsheet application

Another advantage of cloud-based applications is the relative ease by which documents created by and stored within the cloud can be shared with other consumers. Figure 4.4 illustrates the now-familiar bike trek's GPS data within the Zoho Docs' spreadsheet application, which includes sharing and publishing options directly in the header toolbar. Unlike the Office 365 and Google Docs cloud spreadsheets, Zoho is intended for use as a stand-alone primary user productivity suite and includes functions such as user macros, pivot tables, and other advanced features in its options.

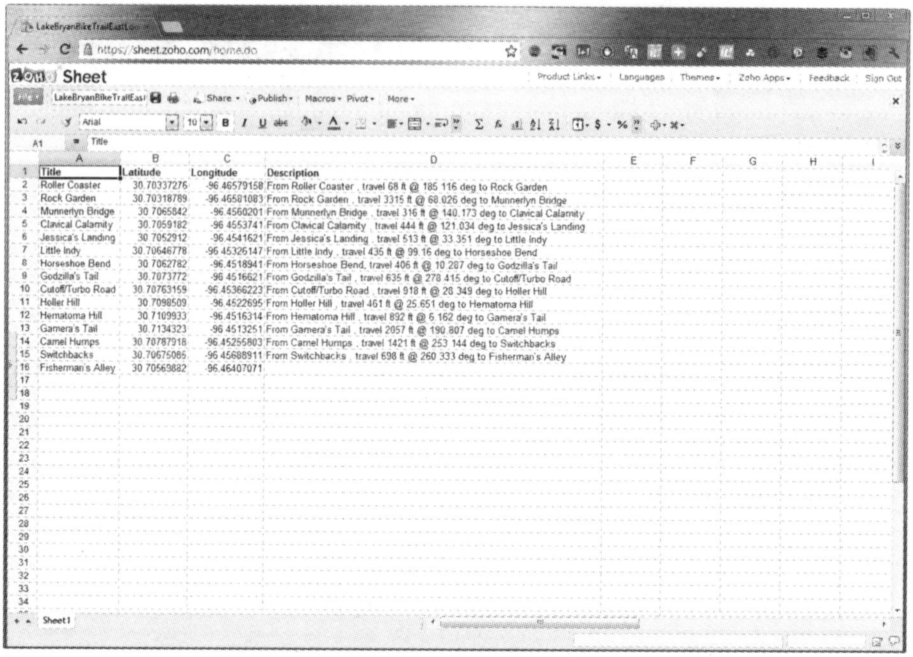

	Title	Latitude	Longitude	Description
2	Roller Coaster	30.70337276	-96.46579158	From Roller Coaster , travel 68 ft @ 185.116 deg to Rock Garden
3	Rock Garden	30.70318789	-96.46581083	From Rock Garden , travel 3315 ft @ 68.026 deg to Munnerlyn Bridge
4	Munnerlyn Bridge	30.7065842	-96.4560201	From Munnerlyn Bridge , travel 316 ft @ 140.173 deg to Clavical Calamity
5	Clavical Calamity	30.7059182	-96.4553741	From Clavical Calamity , travel 444 ft @ 121.034 deg to Jessica's Landing
6	Jessica's Landing	30.7052912	-96.4541621	From Jessica's Landing , travel 513 ft @ 33.351 deg to Little Indy
7	Little Indy	30.70646778	-96.45326147	From Little Indy , travel 435 ft @ 99.16 deg to Horseshoe Bend
8	Horseshoe Bend	30.7062782	-96.4518941	From Horseshoe Bend, travel 406 ft @ 10.287 deg to Godzilla's Tail
9	Godzilla's Tail	30.7073772	-96.4516621	From Godzilla's Tail , travel 635 ft @ 278.415 deg to Cutoff/Turbo Road
10	Cutoff/Turbo Road	30.70763159	-96.45366223	From Cutoff/Turbo Road , travel 918 ft @ 28.349 deg to Holler Hill
11	Holler Hill	30.7098509	-96.4522695	From Holler Hill , travel 461 ft @ 25.651 deg to Hematoma Hill
12	Hematoma Hill	30.7109933	-96.4516314	From Hematoma Hill , travel 892 ft @ 6.162 deg to Gamera's Tail
13	Gamera's Tail	30.7134323	-96.4513251	From Gamera's Tail , travel 2057 ft @ 190.807 deg to Camel Humps
14	Camel Humps	30.70787918	-96.45255803	From Camel Humps , travel 1421 ft @ 253.144 deg to Switchbacks
15	Switchbacks	30.70675085	-96.45688911	From Switchbacks , travel 698 ft @ 260.333 deg to Fisherman's Alley
16	Fisherman's Alley	30.70569882	-96.46407071	

FIGURE 4.4 Zoho Docs' cloud-based equivalent to Excel, illustrating an easily shared version of the orienteering trek

Not only basic user productivity applications can be found in the cloud; full-featured audio and video production suites are available to meet the growing need for multimedia development. Figure 4.5 illustrates a complex production compilation for an animated logo featuring many different layers and video effects. Accessed entirely through a web browser, this suite combines glowing text and rippling multihued backgrounds to produce the striking video display shown in Figure 4.6.

FIGURE 4.5 Aviary cloud-based video production application displaying a complex scripted display of a glowing version of its logo

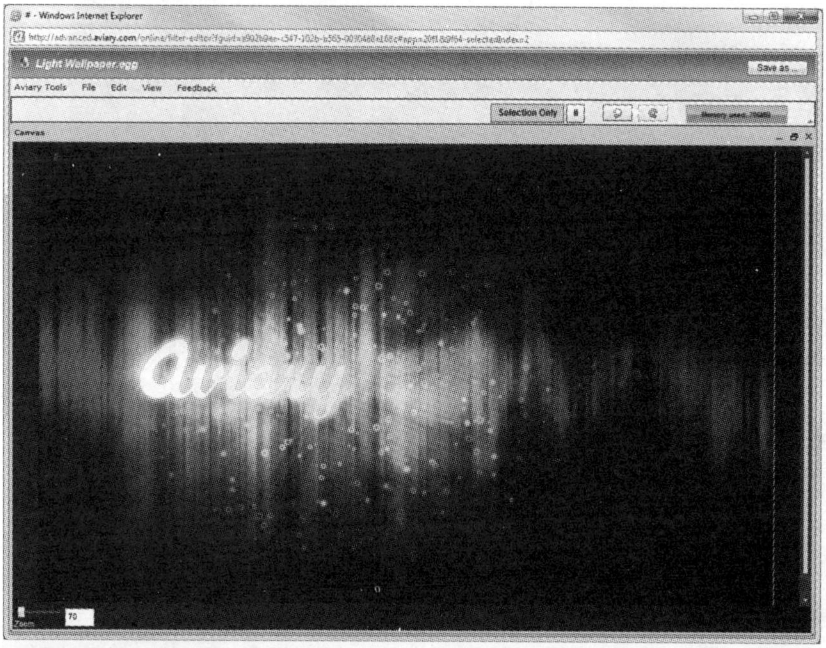

FIGURE 4.6 An animated video presentation of Aviary's logo in its cloud-based video production suite

Aviary's suite bears many of the same functions found in traditional audio/video production suites such as the popular Adobe and Sony products. Cloud-based alternatives to traditional applications are rapidly becoming functional replacements, no longer requiring the technical support necessary for traditional applications installed and maintained in enterprise settings.

Figure 4.7 illustrates the transparent integration of cloud services for email, Twitter, instant messaging, and SkyDrive storage alongside traditional local resources installed directly on the client workstation. A user can access cloud applications through the same interface they use to access traditional applications without even realizing their actions are extending access out into the cloud. Figure 4.8 displays author Kirk Hausman's SkyDrive Infrastructure as a Service (IaaS) storage as it appears when clicked within the Metro interface of Microsoft's Windows 8 operating system.

FIGURE 4.7 Kirk's Windows 8 Metro interface showing both cloud and traditional application components

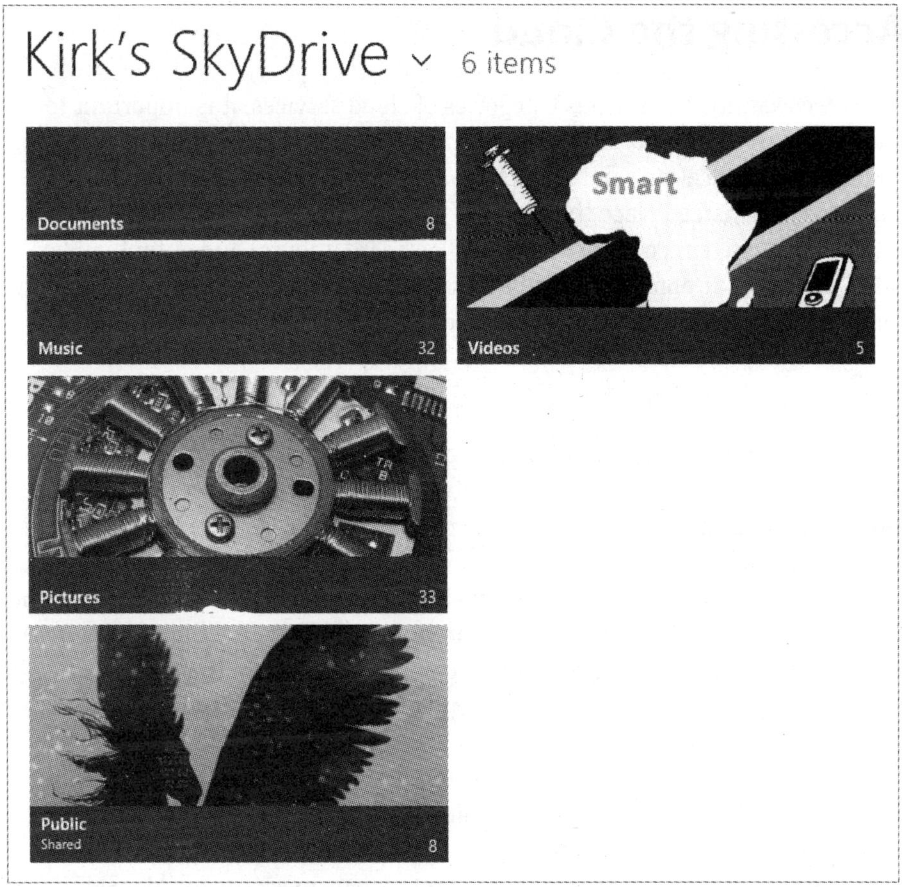

FIGURE 4.8 Kirk's SkyDrive file storage accessed within the Metro interface of Windows 8

Cloud Application Processing

Cloud-based applications gain a significant advantage compared to their traditional counterparts with regard to client systems lacking the necessary resources for their local operation. A thin client or tablet system whose CPU and RAM are insufficient to perform complex tasks like video production can serve as the interface for a suite like Aviary running on its cloud service host machine's resources.

Accessing the Cloud

Before we examine the various categories of cloud services, it is important to understand that in cloud access everything will be conducted over the network. Cloud-based applications and services do not rely on the resources of the accessing device but instead place the power of aggregated servers behind the application. Client systems provide the input (keyboard, mouse) and output (audio, video) between the application and its user but can otherwise be very limited in comparison to traditional workstations in the enterprise network.

Networking in the Cloud

Whether you are accessing local private cloud resources or services from a remote public cloud service provider, networking is the path through which all interaction must travel. Internal private clouds will be configured as a component within the organizational intranet, while public resources are available from service providers via the global Internet. A key element of this access is the TCP/IP standard for network device communication that underlies the Internet, in which each device is assigned a unique numerical address that defines its presence and allows another device to send data and request data from the target destination system.

The various services that allow global TCP/IP interconnectivity to function include functions like the DNS hierarchical naming service that translates a human-readable designation into its numerical address as well as a suite of protocols that facilitate data transport using various mechanisms like SMTP for email, FTP for file transport, and HTTP/HTTPS for web access. These protocols and their functions are grouped into the Open Systems Interconnection (OSI) model, which specifies a seven-layer structure for network communication, as shown in Figure 4.9.

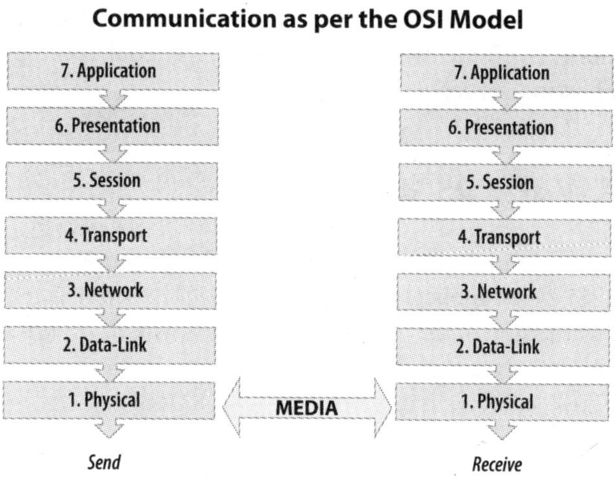

FIGURE 4.9 An example of data communication using the OSI model

Transmitted data is passed down the OSI stack, broken into individual packets with information added at each layer for reconstruction. It is then transmitted over the network media to the receiving system, where the packets are recombined as the data passes back up the OSI model's layers until it is provided to the user or service application at the other end of the connection. This connectivity is used for each communication with the cloud, regardless of type (public, private, or hybrid) or category (SaaS, PaaS, IaaS) of cloud service and is critical to ensuring that client requests for cloud-stored or cloud-provided data and services can occur.

Web Access Architecture

CompTIA refers to the organization of cloud functions against the OSI model of communication as the *Web Access Architecture*. It applies to cloud service access in both private (local network) and public (via the Internet) configurations, whether access is made using a web browser like Internet Explorer, Chrome, Firefox, or Safari on a workstation, tablet, or smartphone or when access is made using a computer without its own local resources, sometimes called a thin client or lean client system. Thin client systems rely on server-based applications and services to take the place of locally stored resources in traditional workstations, often providing only the most basic of input and output functions (keyboard, mouse, audio, video) and a network connection in order to function. A thin client without even a local operating system for connectivity to other services may sometimes be distinguished as an ultra-thin client or a zero client by some vendors. In these systems, the kernel does nothing more than initiate the network connection through which a virtual desktop session can be created on a hosting server.

Leveraging Software as a Service

The majority of applications shown in this chapter so far have been examples of Software as a Service (SaaS) cloud applications. These are packages that consumers just use as they would any other prebuilt application. Any flexibility present is a factor of the application's design, and further development is unnecessary or even impossible by the end user.

Personal Software as a Service Applications

Traditional applications like Microsoft's Excel spreadsheet and Adobe's After Effects video production systems require purchase of the application, installation on client computers, and regular update and patching to maintain the application, with the cycle repeating as upgrades and updates must be purchased and installed in turn. Cloud applications like Zoho's spreadsheet and Aviary's video production require only licensing for a user's account and a browser for access. There are no outright software purchases, no installation requirements, and no patch or update maintenance required by the consuming organization. All such details are handled by the hosting corporation's technical staff and occur automatically from the consuming users' perspective.

Cloud Application Availability

A major advantage of cloud SaaS applications from an enterprise perspective is that users can access their applications from any machine, not only those workstations on which the application has been installed. This eases tech replacement cycles and workforce flexibility because a worker can be moved between organizational locations without losing access to their cloud-based resources.

At their simplest, cloud SaaS applications exist simply as web-accessible components, often wrapped up within other applications like the popular Words With Friends game shown in Figure 4.10. This application allows users to participate in competitive crosswords with friends, whether accessed from a personal computer or a mobile phone or from within other services like Facebook. Connectivity between players across multiple platforms is handled by the cloud service, which also handles calculation of "allowable" words and other functions for calculating scores without consuming additional resources on the client systems.

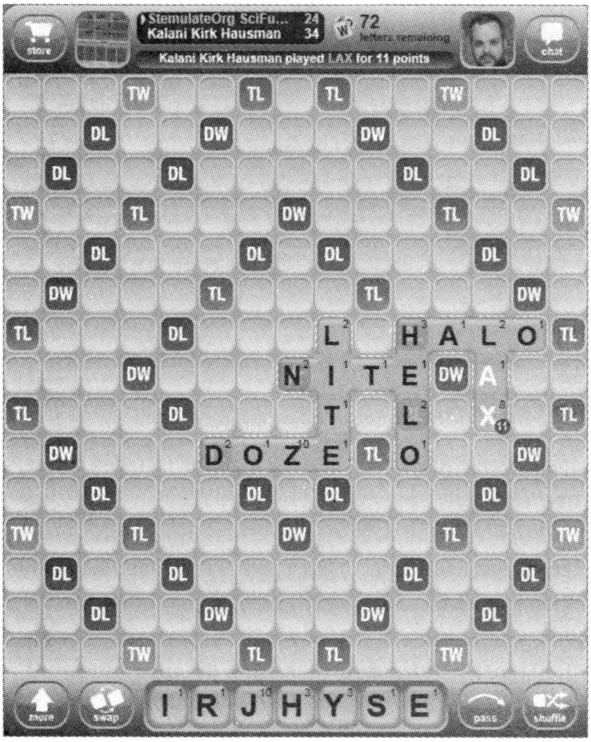

FIGURE 4.10 An example of the popular multiplatform SaaS game Words With Friends

In addition to simple multiplatform apps, cloud SaaS also offers complex fully featured applications accessed within a web browser but running on cloud service host computers' resources. Figure 4.11 illustrates a very capable personal audio editing application as part of the Aviary suite.

FIGURE 4.11 An example of Aviary's audio production application operating within the Internet Explorer browser

Cloud Application Options

Unlike traditional applications, which must be purchased and installed before use, cloud alternatives can easily be tested and replaced simply by accessing a separate website. Flexibility in the cloud-enabled enterprise is maximized, without requiring tech support personnel to learn how to install and maintain a wide variety of different packages. This greatly eases organizational mergers and reorganization, where users can continue to use applications they are already familiar with through nothing more than a new licensing agreement with the cloud service providers.

Instead of requiring all enterprise users to settle on a limited number of application suites installed on particular machines, such as the popular Adobe Photoshop image editing application, users can be allowed to use cloud SaaS offerings from machines at home or work without an additional cost. Figure 4.12 illustrates the Pixlr cloud alternative to Photoshop, with two of Kirk's photographs of local flowers open for editing.

FIGURE 4.12 An example of Pixlr's image editing application with two photos open for edit

Because cloud applications are web-enabled, they also consume other cloud services very well to add information availability beyond that of resources on file servers located in the traditional data center. Figure 4.13 demonstrates Pixlr's access to Kirk's images stored locally as well as in popular social media collections such as Flickr, Picasa, and Facebook. Images produced by Pixlr can also be shared with other consumers within Pixlr's own cloud storage service.

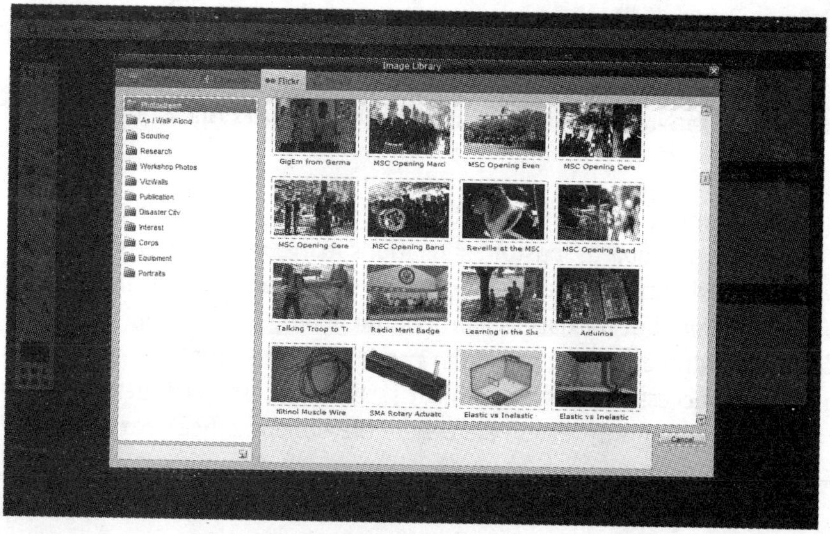

FIGURE 4.13 Pixlr accessing images stored in Kirk's Flickr folders

Enterprise Software as a Service Applications

In addition to personal applications consumed at the individual level, cloud SaaS options for enterprise applications also exist for aggregation of data across multiple individuals, sites, or organizations. Figure 4.14 presents a standard business intelligence (BI) balanced scorecard within the enterprise NetSuite application.

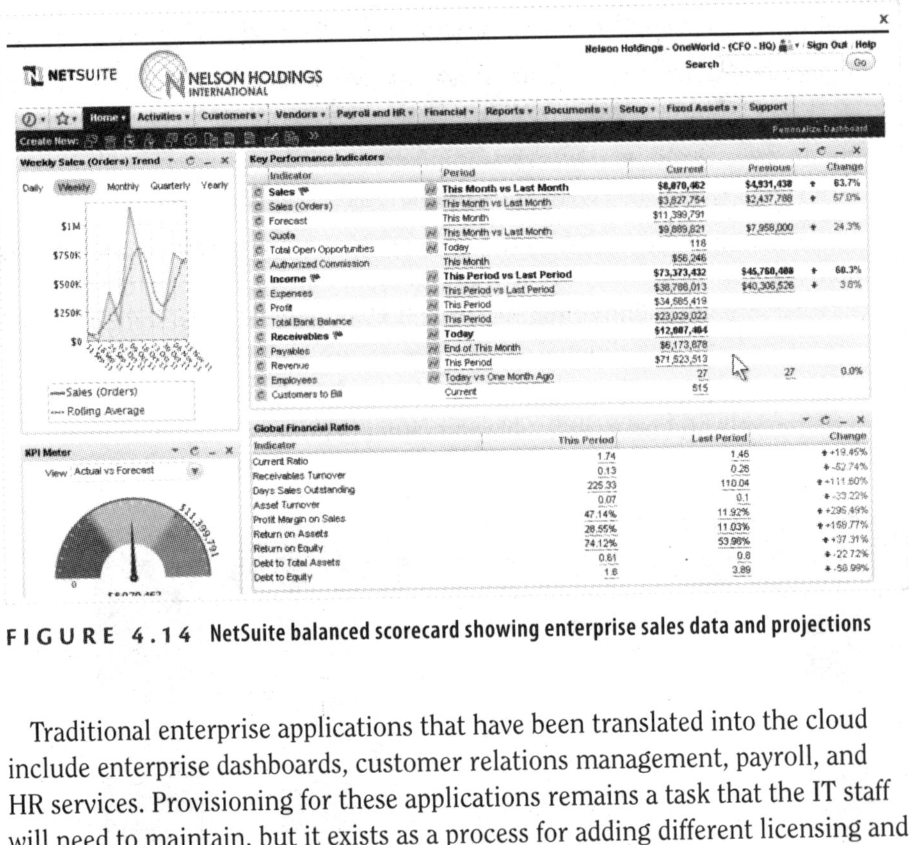

FIGURE 4.14 NetSuite balanced scorecard showing enterprise sales data and projections

Traditional enterprise applications that have been translated into the cloud include enterprise dashboards, customer relations management, payroll, and HR services. Provisioning for these applications remains a task that the IT staff will need to maintain, but it exists as a process for adding different licensing and access control assignments for a particular user's account so that, for example, UserA might have access to sales data while UserB has access to HR details but UserC has only read-only levels of access to the London office's particular details.

Cloud-Specific Software as a Service Applications

Cloud Software as a Service (SaaS) applications go beyond simple apps and replication of traditional desktop applications, extending into entirely new technologies only possible through access to big data resource pools or by performing tasks requiring high-performance computing (HPC). Figure 4.15 demonstrates HPC processing within the Autodesk 123D Catch service using multiple photographic images.

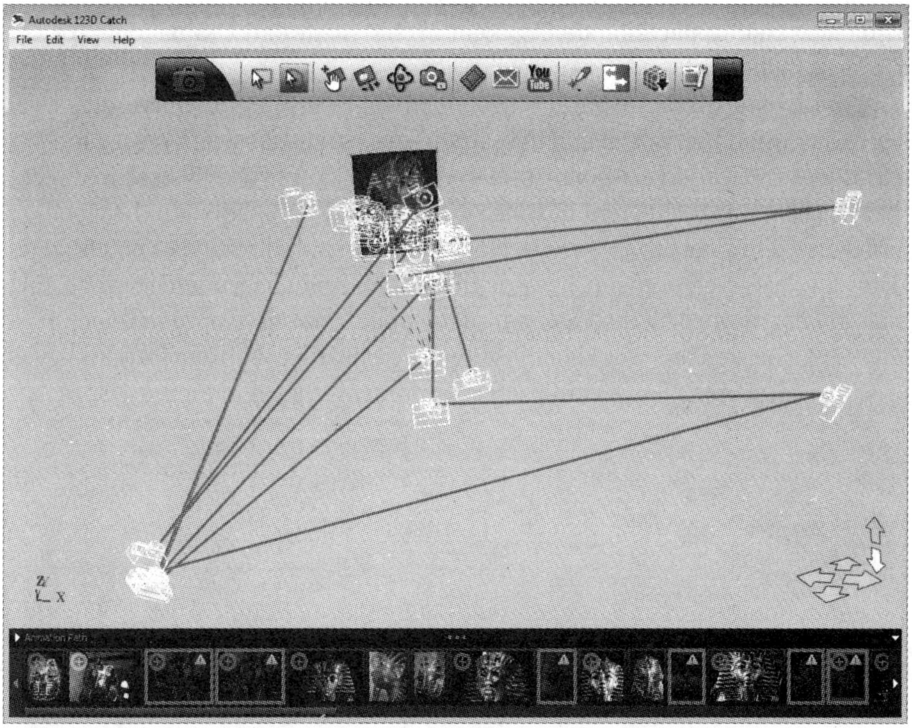

FIGURE 4.15 The 123D Catch cloud application from Autodesk creating a 3D model from images of King Tutankhamen's funerary mask

Cloud-based 123D Catch performs a supercomputing process called *photogrammetry*, where the dimensional shape of an object is calculated by combining multiple photographs and calculating the final shape from changes between images of the object. The final 3D model can be extracted when completed for consumption in animation, CGI, and 3D printing functions. Photogrammetry requires significant CPU power to calculate the object's spatial dimensions, but versions of the application's access interface exist for low-power mobile technologies like Apple's iPad and iPhone for direct input of photographic imagery. The cloud service calculates the photogrammatic shape on its own resources and notifies the user when a final object mesh is available for download.

Developing within Platform as a Service

In addition to preconstructed Software as a Service (SaaS) applications, cloud Platform as a Service (PaaS) providers allow development of customized and personalized applications. Traditional application development is closely aligned with cloud PaaS application development in that many of the same tools are used to develop, test, and deploy applications.

Figure 4.16 illustrates application development for use within Microsoft's Azure PaaS cloud service, using the same Visual Studio application used for traditional application development. Development staff may only need to direct their applications to different hosting sites, easing the transition to the cloud. As discussed in Chapter 3, "Service Models," proprietary lock-in is a potential factor for PaaS environments because the available languages and development tools are determined by the PaaS provider. Applications developed in C# for Microsoft's Azure PaaS would not be directly compatible with applications developed for SalesForce's Force.com PaaS environment, shown in Figure 4.17.

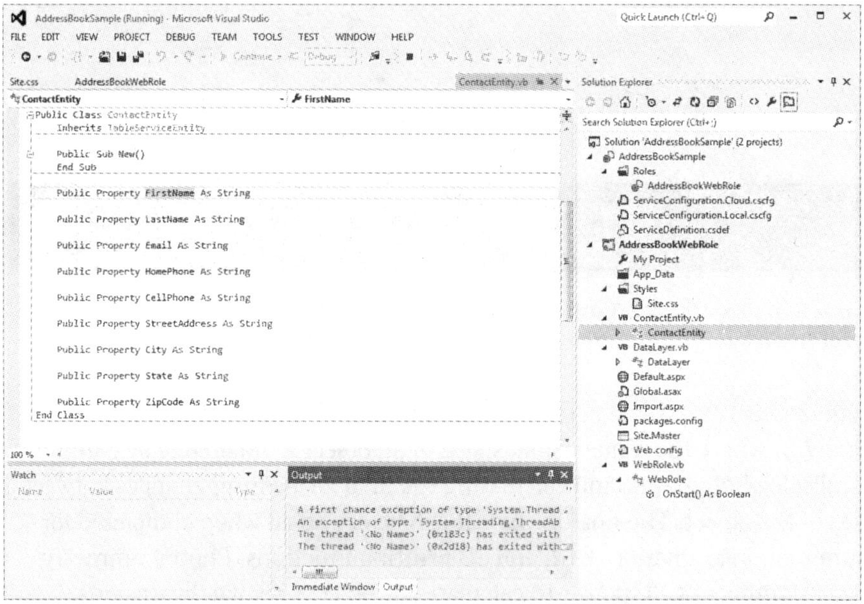

FIGURE 4.16 Cloud application development within the popular Microsoft Visual Studio interface

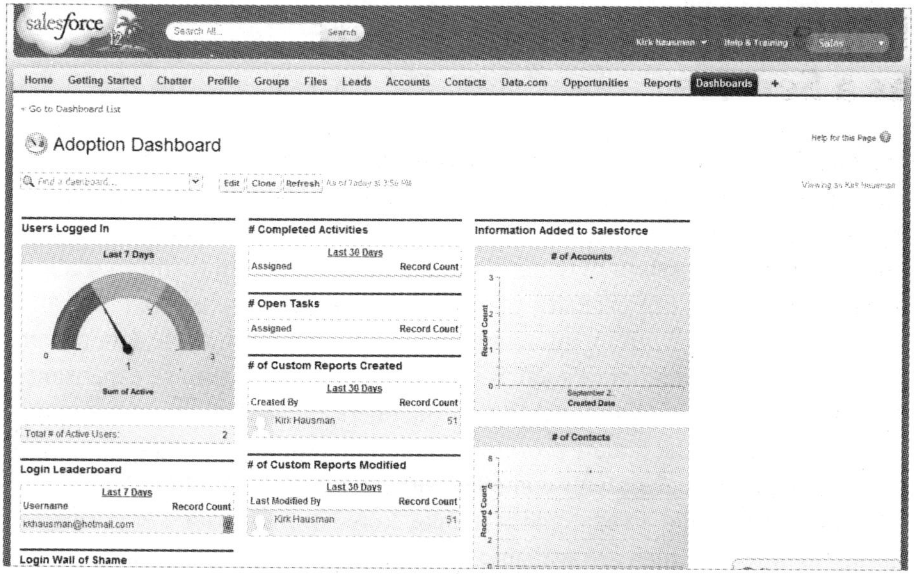

FIGURE 4.17 An example of SalesForce's Force.com PaaS platform

Unlike SaaS software that is updated and maintained entirely by the cloud service provider, PaaS applications are developed, deployed, updated, and otherwise maintained by an organization's own development staff. When staff develops for applications operating in the cloud, resources and services can be accessed by users from within a browser and updates are automatically available when the user refreshes their session.

Sharing in the Cloud

Depending on the PaaS environment's public or private deployment and the network availability to consumers, cloud-based PaaS applications can also serve a global consumer base. For example, a single PaaS application for customer management could be developed for the New York office and then shared by team members in the London and Singapore offices with locational customization, allowing for 24/7 support capabilities using one primary application development effort for all locations.

Implementing Infrastructure as a Service

The final layer of cloud service offerings is Infrastructure as a Service (IaaS), which provides the greatest level of customization and flexibility for a consuming organization by allowing the cloud-level hosting of organizational resources from the operating system to the applications accessed within them. In traditional organizations, infrastructure is managed through purchase of physical servers that must be housed, interconnected, and cooled within the data center itself. Hardware maintenance such as firmware updates and storage expansion is the responsibility of traditional IT staff members and system downtime may be required during the update process. IaaS can involve storage resources, databases, or entire virtual systems complete with their own applications.

Figure 4.18 provides an example of images stored in Kirk's cloud SkyDrive storage allocation, which are available from any web browser along with resources in his Dropbox store and his Google Drive—all cloud IaaS storage services.

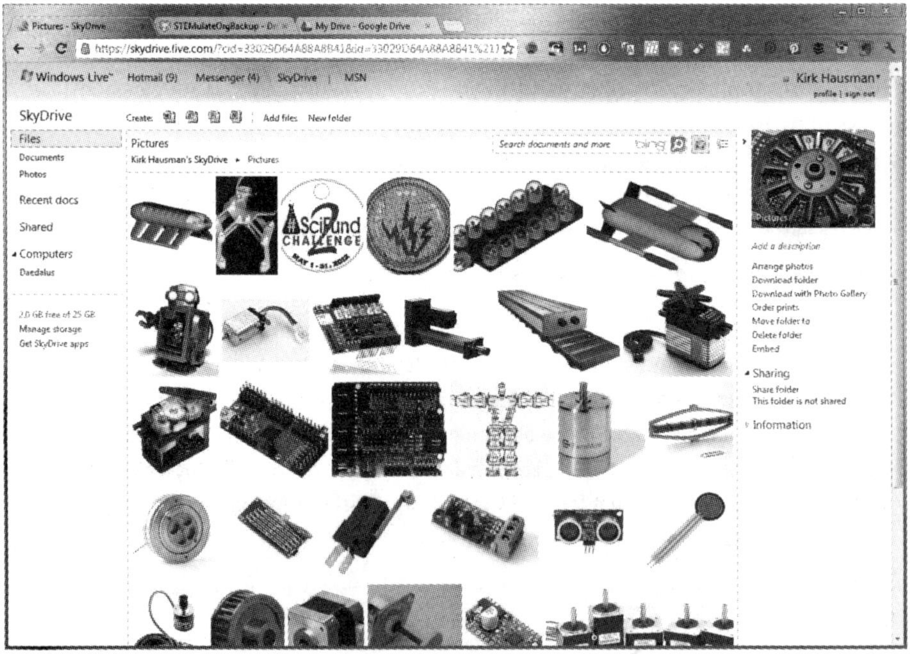

FIGURE 4.18 Images in Kirk's SkyDrive, along with tabs for other cloud IaaS storage services

In public IaaS cloud environments, no hardware purchase is required and hardware management is handled by the cloud service provider. Issues such as power and cooling are handled by the provider using economies of scale and location of cloud data centers in areas with lower costs for energy to provide benefits to organizations in comparison to traditional on-site data centers. Private IaaS cloud environments exist entirely atop resources in the local data center, and all maintenance and management of hardware-level support remain the responsibility of organizational IT staff. In private IaaS deployments, cloud services function as flexible pools of virtualized resources and are effectively simply a further evolution of traditional virtualization.

Many IaaS providers such as Rackspace, Google, GoGrid, and Windows Azure offer the ability to spawn new storage, database, and virtual machine instances as necessary within a pool of resources made available through an organization's resource licensing agreements. Figure 4.19 shows Kirk's resources within the Azure cloud IaaS service, including multiple items in the east, west, and south central areas of the United States as well in Western Europe.

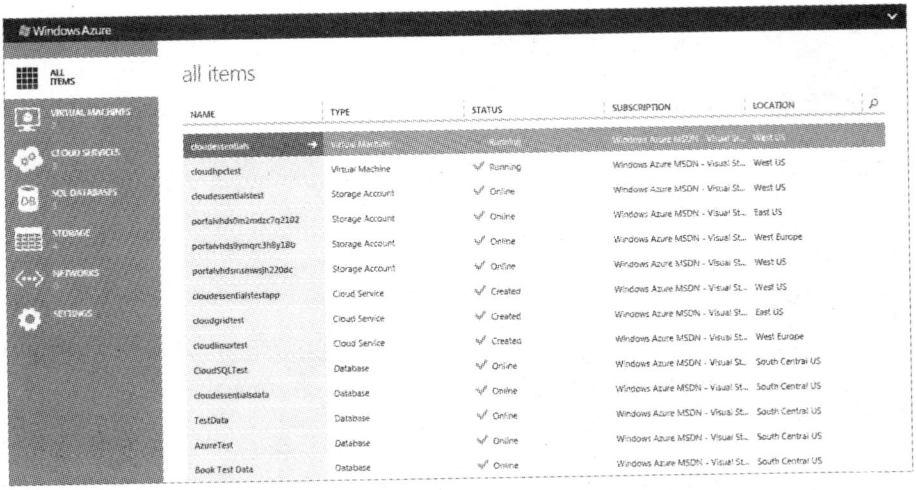

FIGURE 4.19 Windows Azure cloud resources hosted around the world

ACCESSING THE CLOUD

Each resource is available to the others through virtualized networking (local to one another) or over standard WAN connectivity using the public Internet for connectivity. Security considerations for accessing and consuming cloud resources will be covered in Chapter 11, "Security in the Cloud."

Resources in the IaaS scenario are managed and reviewed through dashboards like the one shown in Figure 4.20. Unlike traditional data center resources, additional processing cores, memory, and storage can be added to a cloud server to meet growing need or can be reduced or reallocated to other purposes. Capital expenditures for server hardware can be transformed into operating expenses for resources used in public cloud IaaS offerings.

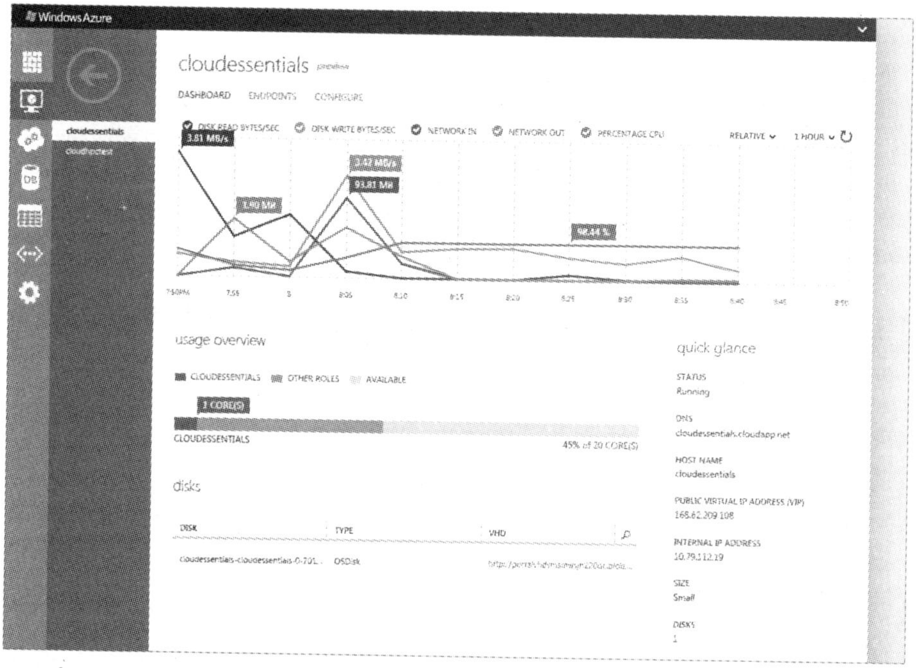

FIGURE 4.20 **Dashboard for Windows Azure showing resource availability and current use for a virtualized server**

New instances can be created by consumers without involving IT staff, selecting resource allocations for each new resource from the available pool as shown in Figure 4.21.

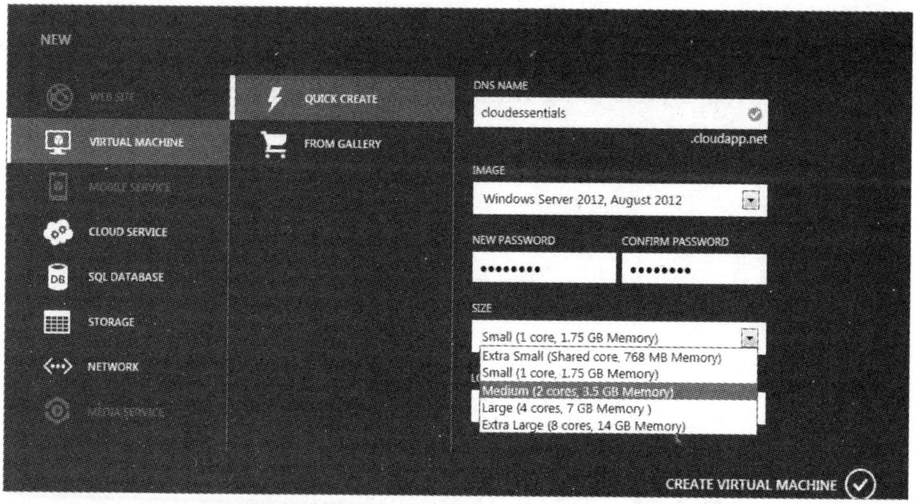

FIGURE 4.21 Creating a new server instance within the Windows Azure management interface

Each new IaaS server can be configured to provide specific services using a simple web-based management interface. Figure 4.22 provides an example of a server being set up for HTTP and WebDAV services.

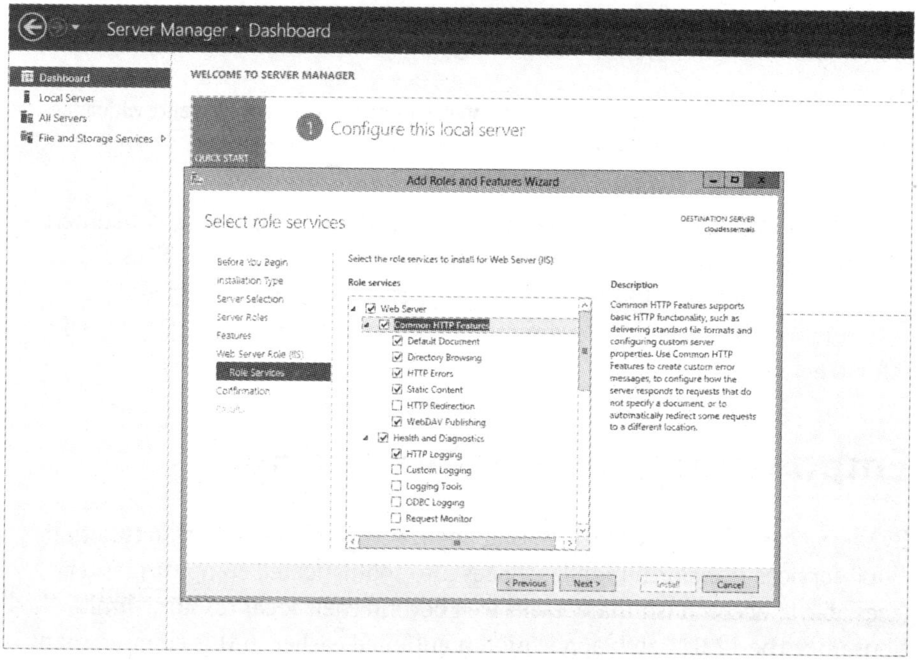

FIGURE 4.22 Configuring a new instance as a web server

Resource configuration, development languages, and even platform can be varied in Infrastructure as a Service (IaaS) cloud offerings as desired, including configuring virtual servers using Windows, Linux, or other operating systems. Figure 4.23 illustrates the current virtual machine images available for rapid instance creation in the Windows Azure service.

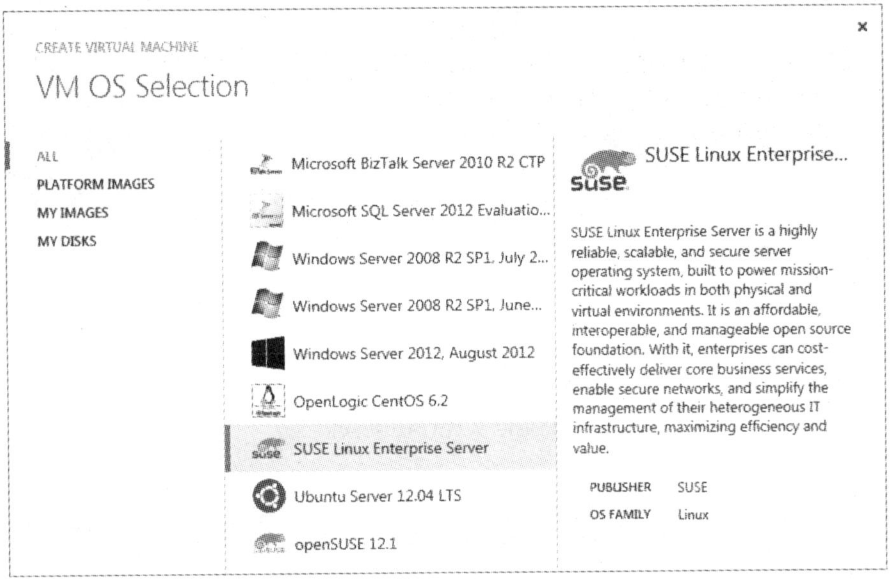

FIGURE 4.23 Selecting an operating system for a new virtual server instance within the Windows Azure cloud IaaS environment

Note that even though Azure is a Microsoft IaaS cloud platform, consumers can create servers using non-Microsoft operating systems such as SUSE Linux, Ubuntu, or CentOS. Unlike with PaaS, proprietary lock-in is lessened in full IaaS solutions because the consumer selects the details for their virtualized infrastructure.

Empowering Mobile Computing

By taking over the "heavy lifting" that applications must perform to function, cloud services transform mobile devices into sophisticated computing interfaces able to accomplish many tasks well beyond their local resource limitations. Like the 123D Catch application mentioned earlier in this chapter, many cloud solutions move CPU-intensive and resource-consuming processing to the service host, while the mobile device serves as a data input and presentation interface alone. This is very similar to the cloud/thin client interaction where cloud services run atop server hardware and only pass input/output data to the consuming device but can also ensure that data transferred to the mobile device occupies the limited bandwidth provided, which is not as troubling for workstations or thin clients with wired network connections.

Figure 4.24 is an example of the Ubuntu One service running on an Android phone, displaying files automatically synchronized between several devices through the cloud service. Music and other forms of data can be played across multiple platforms using this service, while other cloud services provide basic functions that could otherwise overrun available resources on mobile devices, such as antimalware scans that transmit signatures to a remote cloud server for mobile antivirus analysis.

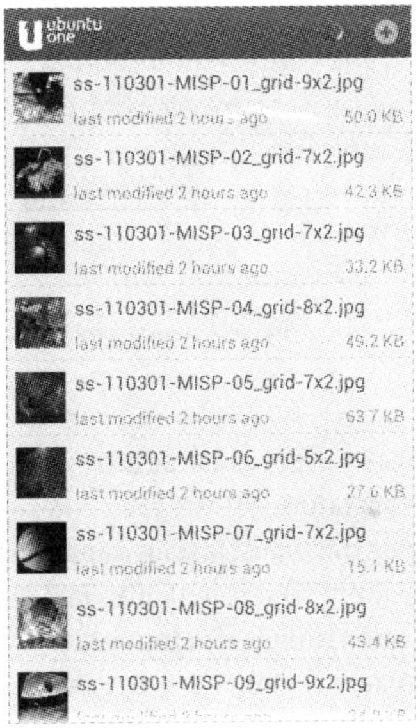

FIGURE 4.24 Mobile access to files stored in the Ubuntu One cloud service

The mobile web is much more interesting when high-speed data networking is available and cloud services integrate with one another. The sequence in Figure 4.25 illustrates this integration as a song that was playing in the background at a local event is investigated. You can see four screen captures from the mobile phone in sequence from left to right, showing the consumption of cloud services that run remotely from the mobile device itself.

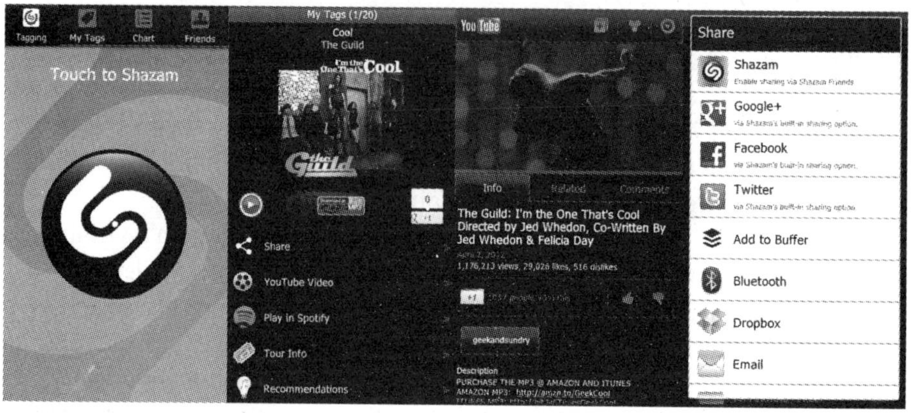

FIGURE 4.25 Four mobile screen captures showing a sequence of operations identifying and sharing music video information

Shazam is a cloud-based analysis service that allows the capture of a segment of ambient audio, called a tag, which it then uses to identify the music that is playing on the background. The tagged music can then be streamed from an integrated service like YouTube or shared to other cloud-based social media and file sharing services.

Flexibility in the Cloud

Cloud SaaS services extend from Gmail to Facebook games and can be accessed transparently to the consuming user. Modern operating systems even integrate cloud PaaS and SaaS applications alongside traditional installed applications without any obvious difference. Virtualized servers within an IaaS cloud environment are accessed using the same technologies for virtualized and physical servers located in the local data center. A move toward the cloud offers an increase in flexibility and a reduction in personnel and capital expenses for the organization, but it can be accomplished without disrupting end users as in the case of traditional enterprise-wide migrations from mainframes to distributed computing or from separate workstations to integrated enterprise resources.

The Essentials and Beyond

Examples of cloud service can be found for all three levels of cloud implementation: Software as a Service (SaaS), Platform as a Service (PaaS), and Infrastructure as a Service (IaaS). SaaS applications are preconfigured and used without customization, while PaaS application development can support customization and personalization of individual applications. IaaS extends customization to include all aspects of the traditional data center while shifting hardware maintenance responsibility to the hosting data center (local for private, remote for public).

Additional Exercises

- Explore cloud alternatives to traditional installed workstation applications.
- Identify cloud applications supporting mobile devices present in the classroom.

To compare your answer to the author's, please visit `www.sybex.com/go/cloudessentials`.

Review Questions

1. What type of cloud service is the most common?

   A. SaaS
   B. PaaS
   C. IaaS
   D. XaaS

2. True or false? Vendor lock-in concerns relate only to Platform as a Service cloud implementations.

   A. True
   B. False

3. Which of the following does not describe the relationship between mobile computing and cloud computing?

   A. Mobile devices serve as data input and presentation interfaces.
   B. Data transmitted occupies the limited bandwidth available to mobile devices.
   C. Cloud services provide functions that could overrun available resources on mobile devices if run locally.
   D. Mobile devices must access cloud services using a mobile web browser.

4. Which category of "as a Service" models is not specifically identified by NIST?

   A. Software as a Service
   B. Platform as a Service
   C. Infrastructure as a Service
   D. Hardware as a Service
   E. Everything as a Service

(Continues)

The Essentials and Beyond *(Continued)*

5. Which level of the cloud service model pyramid allows the greatest flexibility for application development?

   A. IaaS
   B. SaaS
   C. PaaS
   D. XaaS

6. True or false? Application life cycle management in the cloud is slightly more complex than in traditional development models due to the addition of remote resources.

   A. True
   B. False

7. Which type of cloud service model allows the cloud-level hosting of organizational resources from the operating system to the applications accessed within them?

   A. PaaS
   B. IaaS
   C. Public cloud
   D. Hybrid cloud

8. The term *Web Access Architecture* refers to the organization of cloud functions against which model of network communication?

   A. TCP
   B. HTTP
   C. OSI
   D. SMTP

9. What type of client system relies on server-based applications and services to take the place of locally stored resources?

   A. Thick client
   B. Thin client
   C. Desktop
   D. Mobile device

10. All but which one of the following options are advantages of SaaS in the enterprise?

    A. Application deployment and maintenance is performed by the cloud service provider.
    B. Applications do not need to be installed on individual machines.
    C. Data is aggregated across multiple individuals, sites, or organizations.
    D. Customized and personalized applications can be developed.

CHAPTER 5

Cloud Business Value

For most businesses, IT has become a necessity. Hosting IT services in-house can be costly and distract businesses from focusing on their core competencies. As such, IT is becoming less about acquiring the right equipment and more about acquiring the right services. This chapter examines the value of cloud computing from a business perspective.

- **Identifying business drivers for cloud computing**
- **Examining the business impact**

Identifying Business Drivers for Cloud Computing

There are parallels between the changing IT environment today and the changing business telephony environment in the late twentieth century. Many businesses moved away from maintaining their own internal private branch exchange (PBX) systems, which required both equipment and personnel to operate, and toward hosted solutions, letting the local telephone company or another service provider manage their telecommunications.

The business drivers for cloud computing today are the same drivers that brought IT into the business world to begin with: cost, efficiency, and organizational agility.

Reducing Costs and Increasing Efficiency

Generally, the cost reduction stemming from cloud computing can be attributed to economies of scale. This is an economic term that refers to the relationship between per-unit cost and production volume. An increase in production leads to a decrease in per-unit cost by spreading out fixed costs over more units. In cloud computing, economies of scale are achieved through the use of shared resources. A cloud service provider spreads its costs across its entire customer base, allowing each customer access to a greater degree of IT functionality than it would have on its own for the same cost.

With cloud computing, the up-front costs of purchasing new hardware to start an IT project or expand current capabilities are removed, allowing organizations to pay only for the services they use on hardware that the service provider has already purchased. This same variable cost model also allows organizations to scale down services when they are no longer needed or to drop them entirely without having to worry about sunk costs.

Organizations using public cloud services are able shift their IT expenses from capital to operational, which may provide tax benefits. Organizations employing in-house private clouds may be able to reduce their capital expenses due to more efficient use of infrastructure.

Capital vs. Operational Expenses

Capital expenses are those related to fixed assets, including both the original purchase and later improvements. IT-related examples are the costs of computing equipment and software. Operational expenses are those associated with ordinary business operations. IT-related examples include salaries of technical staff, Internet costs, and subscription-based software licenses.

This difference is important in business accounting and tax calculation. The value of a capital expense is spread out (and deducted) over multiple fiscal years, while the value of an operational expense is considered to be used up in the fiscal year in which the expense originated, allowing the full value to be deducted.

Reducing Costs and Increasing Efficiency through Scalability

In networking, a *node* is physical or virtual device attached to a network. This includes, but is not limited to, switches, routers, servers, workstations, and printers.

Scalability, also called *flexibility* or *elasticity*, is a key characteristic of cloud computing. It allows customers to increase or decrease computing resources such as storage, computing power, and network bandwidth dynamically, based on need and the amount the customer is willing to pay. Scaling can be either vertical (scaling up) or horizontal (scaling out). Vertical scaling involves adding resources to a single node, such as memory, processing power, or redundant components. Horizontal scaling involves adding more nodes to a distributed system. This concept is illustrated in Figure 5.1. If both vertical and horizontal scaling are used to address a performance or availability issue, it is referred to as diagonal scaling.

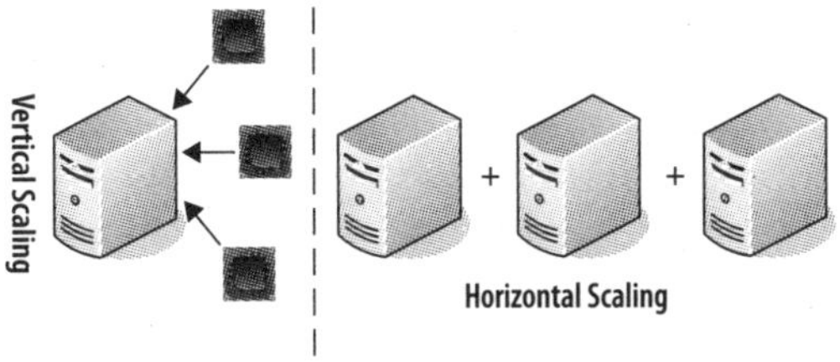

FIGURE 5.1 A high-level example of vertical (adding processors to a server) versus horizontal scaling (adding servers)

This ability can greatly reduce costs for organizations with inconsistent resource needs, such as online retailers that see increased site traffic before holidays or software development companies that need to provision large-scale testing environments periodically.

> Scaling of application services can be handled automatically through the use of a load balancer that monitors traffic and performance attributes and adjusts when necessary.

Improving Security through Economies of Scale

Cloud computing can provide some benefit to security through economies of scale. Cloud service providers may potentially provide a greater level of security than an organization could on its own by spreading the cost across its customer base. The following are some examples of security benefits:

- Increased availability and improved disaster recovery through redundancy and multiple locations
- Security specialists
- 24/7 staffing and monitoring

Not every cloud service provider will have these capabilities, just as not every organization is incapable of having its own highly effective security measures. When evaluating cloud services, as well as individual providers, an organization must take into account the security capabilities of the provider versus its own security capabilities. It must also be aware of any potential data security, privacy, and compliance risks that result from loss of control over data. These topics are discussed in detail in Chapter 11, "Security in the Cloud," and Chapter 12, "Privacy and Compliance."

Reducing IT Administrative Overhead

Cloud computing reduces an organization's IT administrative overhead by transferring routine administrative duties from internal IT staff to the cloud provider. The following list includes some common IT administrative duties:

- Patch management
- Software license management
- Software maintenance and support
- Infrastructure maintenance and support
- Backup and recovery

The time formerly spent on these duties can be reallocated to other work, such as innovation, systems analysis, and IT process improvement. It also allows an organization to reduce its IT staffing levels, thereby reducing HR-related operating expenses.

Increasing Organizational Agility

Organizational agility is the ability to rapidly adapt to changes in the market or industry through identification and realization of opportunities. Cloud computing allows organizations to focus more on their core business activities and less on maintaining an IT environment. It should be noted that this is not a new concept by any means. For years, companies have outsourced IT functions for this very reason.

IT outsourcing, by definition, occurs when an organization enters into a contract with an outside provider to perform IT-related functions instead of performing those functions itself. Those functions may include day-to-day operations, technical support, server hosting, service hosting, and security, to name just a few.

Cloud computing is a form of IT outsourcing that focuses on services, but it does not follow the traditional IT outsourcing model. The primary differences are contract length and scalability. Traditional outsourcing contracts are generally from one to three years. In cloud computing, there is very little commitment required because services are offered on a pay-as-you-go basis. Changes to traditional outsourcing contracts are likely to require a contract addendum or may even need to be postponed until the next renewal cycle. In cloud computing, an organization may scale as needed.

The following are some examples of how organizational agility is facilitated by cloud computing:

Shortened time to market A combination of self-service provisioning of resources and a pay-as-you-go billing model allows organizations to rapidly develop new products (particularly applications or web-based services) without being limited by the cost of computing hardware or being stalled by long procurement time.

Rapid internal development and testing The ability to provision and deprovision development and testing environments on demand provides organizations with greater opportunities to improve their business processes by developing applications internally or testing off-the-shelf software in their environment.

Mobility Global access to organizational enterprise resources is required for organizations with a distributed workforce. Because cloud-based applications are distributed over the Internet and accessed via a web browser, they are easily accessed by various types of mobile devices.

Cloud computing may hinder agility through vendor lock-in. As discussed in Chapter 3, "Service Models," vendor lock-in occurs when an organization finds itself relying on a proprietary technology base, which restricts migration to alternative solutions in the future without significant cost. Vendor lock-in is often caused by the lack of standards in cloud computing, although this is being addressed by groups such as the Cloud Security Alliance, the Distributed Management Task Force, and the Cloud Standards Customer Council.

Examining the Business Impact

It is easy to get caught up in the hype about cloud computing, but not every business will benefit from rapid adoption of cloud services. The decision to move to the cloud, including what to move to what type of cloud, is important, and should be undertaken with care to maintain strategic flexibility.

Strategic flexibility is somewhat related to organizational agility (as discussed in "Identifying Business Drivers for Cloud Computing" earlier in this chapter) but differs in one crucial respect: Organizational agility focuses on reacting and adapting to change, while strategic flexibility focuses on anticipating and preparing for uncertainty.

Moving IT operations to the cloud is risky and full of uncertainty, but this uncertainty can be mitigated by taking the following steps:

1. Evaluate cloud computing costs.
2. Identify the value to your organization now and in the future.
3. Choose an appropriate cloud model.

These steps are discussed in more detail in the following sections.

Evaluating Cloud Computing Costs

The cost benefits of cloud computing may vary by business, particularly with regard to a business's existing IT assets and staffing. Prior to adopting cloud services, it is prudent to calculate the estimated total cost of ownership (TCO) of the cloud services and compare it with the TCO of handling the same services in house.

TCO is the complete cost of an object or service throughout its lifetime, from purchase to disposal, including both direct and indirect costs. The TCO for cloud computing implementation is highly dependent on the deployment model used by an organization. An on-premises private cloud service will have higher capital expenses and other factors affecting direct costs than an external private cloud service managed entirely by the hosting service provider.

The following factors can affect direct costs for cloud computing services:

- Costs directly billed from the provider, such as storage and data transfer
- Hardware and software licensing procurement for private cloud solutions
- Utility costs based on bandwidth and resource consumption for externally hosted forms of cloud computing
- Costs associated with service agreements for guaranteed resource pool availability, virtualized machine count, or other elements of the contractual agreement with a cloud service vendor

The following factors can affect indirect costs for cloud computing services:

- Personnel costs for coordinating cloud and local application development elements
- Costs related to negotiation and management of cloud contractual agreements

- Costs derived from legal or regulatory mandates imposing additional governance criteria into the cloud service provider's operational environment

Direct vs. Indirect Costs

Direct costs are those that can be assigned to a particular process, product, or service. For example, if a company wanted to implement a document imaging system, the cost of scanners would be considered a direct cost. Indirect costs support multiple processes, products, or services. Continuing with the same example, if the imaging system's storage was on the storage area network (SAN), along with files, email, and databases, the cost of the SAN would be indirect.

Identifying Unexpected Costs

Although cloud computing is cost effective, organizations should not allow themselves to be caught off guard by unexpected costs related to the initial migration. Before making the leap to the cloud, ask yourself the following questions:

- How much is it going to cost to transfer my data into the cloud?
- How much is it going to cost for customization?
- How much is it going to cost to integrate cloud-based applications with my locally hosted services?
- How much is it going to cost to test my software to make sure it works in a cloud environment?

Determining Return on Investment

Return on investment (ROI) is a performance measure used to evaluate investment efficiency or compare multiple investments. It is calculated by dividing the benefit of the investment (net gain or loss) by the cost of the investment. The greater the ROI, the better the investment. The formula is as follows:

ROI = (benefit – investment cost) / (investment cost)

Let's look at how ROI factors into an IT scenario. Company XYZ is trying to decide whether it should invest in a new SAN or utilize cloud storage. Factors going into the benefit of cloud storage might include the reduced capital investment, reduction in administrative overhead, and reduced power costs in the in-house data center. The investment cost would include both the up-front costs and the subscription cost for a set period of time. Using this formula, you can determine how long it will take to break even (0 ROI) and to see value (positive ROI). A negative ROI indicates that it will cost the organization money.

Identifying Value Now and in the Future

Businesses may look to cloud computing to solve immediate problems, but they should not stop there. Following are three levels of maturity organizations may reach by leveraging cloud computing:

Utility In the beginning, the business is likely to see some immediate usefulness from cloud computing, such as a reduction in operating costs and increased efficiency. Value is also obtained from increased availability from dynamic allocation of resources as well as resilient and redundant infrastructure.

Process transformation IT exists to support business processes, but all too often business processes are instead determined by the technology being used. Once the dust has settled from the migration, IT staff and business staff can work together to identify opportunities for improvement and implement solutions that leverage cloud computing features.

Business model innovation Whether in the form of new products and services or the business model itself, companies can innovate by maximizing the capabilities of cloud computing.

Choosing the Appropriate Cloud Model

As we discussed in Chapter 2, "Cloud Models," the four types of cloud models are public, private, hybrid, and community. The discussion in this section will be limited to the first three because they are the most appropriate models for businesses. Choosing the appropriate model is a critical decision that will impact planning, cost, and business processes at a minimum.

Public clouds Businesses with the need for variable levels of resources benefit the most from public cloud services, as may small or startup businesses without the ability to invest in infrastructure.

Private clouds Private clouds may be more suitable for businesses that have already heavily invested in computing infrastructure and simply want to use it more efficiently. Private clouds also allow businesses to keep control of their data, which may be required for compliance (see Chapter 12).

Hybrid clouds Hybrid clouds are suitable for businesses that generally would benefit from private cloud services but occasionally have periods of high demand. During these high-demand times, public cloud resources can be used.

Making the Right Decision

Cloud computing is not a one-size-fits-all solution, and not every organization will benefit from it. In addition to the factors already discussed, business model and organization size may determine the level of benefit.

Who Benefits?

The following types of organizations are likely to benefit from cloud computing:

- Startup businesses in particular are likely to benefit from cloud computing, particularly those that have limited staff and financial resources. For this group, entry costs are low because they will not have large amounts of data to transfer.
- Organizations with a workforce that is distributed geographically, is highly mobile, or telecommutes benefit from cloud services.
- Any organization that needs offsite backups can benefit from IaaS offerings such as cloud storage.
- Organizations with internal data centers looking for ways to reduce power costs may be able to reduce the number of physical machines by implementing a private cloud.
- Organizations with e-commerce sites will see benefit from scalability.
- Organizations with IT needs but not enough IT staff will benefit from cloud computing.

Who Might Not Benefit?

The following types of organizations are not likely to benefit from cloud computing:

- Large organizations with significant investment in infrastructure may not benefit from moving that infrastructure to the cloud.

- Organizations with legal or regulatory constraints might not be able to utilize cloud services or may not see their costs reduced due to the need for increased oversight.
- Organizations in geographic areas with poor Internet connectivity may experience reduced availability when using cloud services.

The Essentials and Beyond

This chapter illustrates the blending of information technology and business functions to better align resource consumption and cost with business objectives. Cloud computing will allow technical personnel to develop business sense, while financial management and organizational personnel will develop a greater understanding of technology. This transition represents the maturation of technology from a specialized field of study to a commodity business function supporting the organization's needs.

Additional Exercises

- Identify a common data center job role and critically analyze changes as resources are transitioned to the cloud.
- Identify the business processes in your own organization or educational institution that would be enhanced by the integration of cloud computing resources.

To compare your answer to the author's, please visit `www.sybex.com/go/cloudessentials`.

Review Questions

1. Physical computing hardware is an example of what type of expense?

   A. Operating
   B. Direct
   C. Capital
   D. Indirect

2. Adding additional memory to a server is an example of what type of scalability?

   A. Horizontal
   B. Vertical
   C. Diagonal
   D. Load balancing

3. True or false? An organization should not be concerned with relying on a single vendor or proprietary technology base.

   A. True
   B. False

(Continues)

THE ESSENTIALS AND BEYOND *(Continued)*

4. Which of the following is not a business driver for cloud computing?

   A. Cost reduction
   B. IT staff reduction
   C. Strategic flexibility
   D. Increasing capital expenses

5. Which of the following terms refers to the ability to rapidly adapt to market changes?

   A. Strategic flexibility
   B. Organizational agility
   C. Process transformation
   D. Utility

6. Decreased time to market is facilitated by which of the following cloud computing benefits?

   A. Economies of scale
   B. Pay-as-you-go billing
   C. Mobility
   D. Disaster recovery

7. Which of the following is not an appropriate business reason for choosing a private cloud solution over a public cloud solution?

   A. Management directives to retain full control over hardware
   B. Strict legal requirements for data protection and control
   C. Significant IT investment already made by the organization
   D. Limited Internet connectivity

8. True or false? Organizations with a workforce that is distributed geographically would not benefit from public cloud services.

   A. True
   B. False

9. Which type of cloud would best be used by an organization that wants to leverage its existing IT infrastructure but has occasional periods of high demand?

   A. Public
   B. Private
   C. Hybrid
   D. Community

10. Which of the following tasks cannot be transferred to a cloud computing provider?

    A. Software license management
    B. Backups
    C. Patch management
    D. Ensuring compliance

CHAPTER 6

Cloud Infrastructure Planning

Although their details are hidden from consumers, cloud computing services rely on hardware and network interconnections between hardware elements. Whether you're migrating from a traditional data center to private clouds, implementing a new cloud-centric data center, or planning for remote access of services, understanding the infrastructure underlying the cloud is key to successfully adopting and consuming a cloud service.

- **Understanding cloud networks**
- **Leveraging automation and self-service**
- **Understanding federated cloud services**
- **Achieving interoperability**

Understanding Cloud Networks

Regardless of whether your organization is considering an internal private cloud, an external public cloud, or a hybrid cloud deployment, it is critical to understand at least the basic concepts of networking. Cloud networks are architected to provide the following features:

Scalability Cloud networks must be able to expand to meet variable data consumption requirements required for the utility model of service use.

Resiliency Cloud services rely on network availability, both locally and remote to the hosting data center, and must remain accessible even in the event of loss of power or a network device.

Throughput Cloud networks must support the transfer of large amounts of data, particularly between cloud hosting servers in ways that exceed traditional internal data-center communications.

Simplified management Cloud resources allocation and reallocation must be simple enough that the consuming organization can easily manage configuration and changes without involving traditional IT staff members. This includes data storage, processors, memory, and networking resources all together.

To achieve these goals, the network supporting cloud services must rely upon standards that will suit the capacity, throughput, and resiliency requirements while ensuring that complexity in configuration does not prevent simplified management. Because cloud services are designed for accessibility via the global Internet network, the same fundamental standards for TCP/IP networking are the lingua franca for cloud service interaction and data exchange.

The Open Systems Interconnection Model

The Open Systems Interconnection (OSI) model is used to define and abstract network communications. It comprises seven logical layers based on communication function. Figure 6.1 lists the layers, which are numbered from one to seven beginning at the bottom of the stack (Physical), and indicates which layers are associated with a host and which are associated with media.

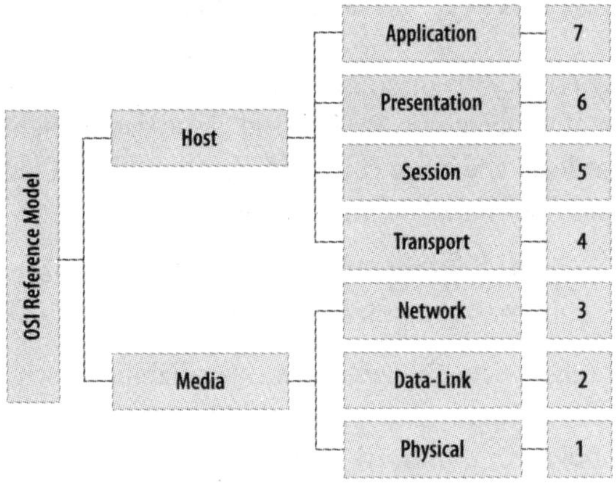

FIGURE 6.1 The OSI reference model

Each logical layer has specific functionality, described in Table 6.1.

TABLE 6.1 OSI model functionality by layer

	Layer	Function
7	Application	Interaction with application software
6	Presentation	Data formatting
5	Session	Host-to-host connection management
4	Transport	Host-to-host data transfer
3	Network	Addressing and routing
2	Data-Link	Local network data transfer
1	Physical	Physical hardware

Private cloud networking is commonly implemented using Layer 2 or Layer 3 technology (or a combination of both), and there is much debate regarding which is the better choice.

Layer 2 Cloud Networks

In a Layer 2 network, elements of the cloud network infrastructure share the same address space (the same network subnet, allowing all addresses to receive broadcasts and service announcements from all others) and interconnect directly through locally switched networking without the need for routers to pass data between participating devices and services. Layer 2 cloud networks can be easier to manage because all IP and MAC addresses share a common network communication partition. Customers will not need to modify their network settings to transition to cloud-hosted service alternatives, but Layer 2 clouds can be overwhelmed if devices are oversubscribed to the point that they begin to compete for network bandwidth until they become congested. Competition is a result of the Carrier Sense Multiple Access with Collision Detection (CSMA/CD) access control mechanism that allows multiple devices to share the same network by transmitting a packet of data and then checking to see if there is another transmission at the same time by another device. If a collision occurs, both devices wait a random amount of time before resending the packet. When a network becomes oversubscribed, it has so many devices that collisions are detected very regularly and delays in data exchange begin to impede data exchange and service availability. Segmenting a network using Layer 3 routers can help to reduce competition by reducing the number of neighbors with which a device will share the same network segment.

Layer 3 Cloud Networks

In a Layer 3 network, cloud resources are interconnected through routers, allowing resources to be located across multiple address ranges and in multiple locations. Layer 3 clouds can bridge resources between locations and require an understanding of subnetwork structure to properly separate groups of devices into manageable "neighborhoods" to reduce competition and data collisions between devices. In return for this added complexity of management, Layer 3 cloud resource counts can be expanded to include a virtually unlimited number of devices due to the network segmentation provided by routed subnetting. Routed subnetting functionally breaks up the network into many subnetworks, similar to neighborhoods of homes broken up by separate feeder roads so that all traffic does not have to share the same access route. Layer 3 networking also allows widely separated network subnets to exchange data, routing packets across public or private network connections more like telephone calls, which can establish connections between devices in different area codes to connect offices in different locations.

Combined Layer 2/3 Cloud Networks

To bridge separated network address ranges using Layer 3 routing while also taking advantage of the simplicity of Layer 2 device interconnection and discovery, it is possible to implement combination networks that use Layer 3 routing to create virtual Layer 2 network connections. These combination networks essentially create network bridges that can transparently route data between different subnets while allowing Layer 2 device broadcasts and services announcements to be detected by all devices across all linked subnets. This may sound complicated, but it works in the same way that professional conference call systems do, creating a bridge between speaker phones at separate offices so that anyone speaking can be heard by all other participants in the linked offices.

Internet Protocol Version

The OSI model is a simplified organization of the basic layers of networking that form the Internet and other TCP/IP networks, both publicly routed (Internet) and private (used only inside an organization). These networks depend on unique device addressing using the Internet Protocol standard, which identifies the address of a device just as a physical address defines where your mail is delivered. For example, a post card addressed 1313 Mockingbird Lane, Sunnyvale, California, tells the postal service to route your mail to California and then to Sunnyvale, where it is sorted by street to the stack for delivery on Mockingbird Lane, where the postman drops it into the box at 1313 to get the mail to its intended address.

The Internet Protocol defines network and device identification that accomplish this in much the same process used by the postal service — although with faster delivery of data that does not require hand delivery. At the time of publication, the world is in transition from Internet Protocol version 4 (IPv4) to Internet Protocol version 6 (IPv6), and so are cloud service providers due to the inherent scalability of IPv6.

IPv4 addresses are 32 bits long (4 bytes), which means there are a maximum number of 2^{32} addresses (> 4.2 billion). This may sound like a large number, but when you consider the proliferation of Internet-capable mobile devices and consumer electronics, it's not very many at all. IPv6 addresses, on the other hand, are 128 bits long, which means there are a maximum number of 2^{128} addresses (> 340 undecillion).

1 undecillion = 1,000,000,000,000,000,000,000,000,000,000,000,000

In addition to increased address availability, IPv6 has the following improvements over IPv4:

- Removal of broadcasting, which reduces network congestion
- Improved routing speed
- Automatically generated host identifier that eliminates the possibility of IP address conflict

Organizations considering moving to the cloud may want to also have a plan for transitioning to IPv6, or at least running both IPv4 and IPv6 until they are able to make the full transition. Because IPv6 has been an approved standard for over a decade, most computing equipment (including mobile devices) should be IPv6 enabled. Organizations considering a private cloud may even be able to use IPv6 alone from the beginning. Not all cloud service providers support IPv6, so this should be part of vendor selection criteria.

Network Challenges

In addition to changes in IP address systems, networks face additional challenges as their use continues to expand to meet new services and technologies. The biggest challenge for cloud networks is latency, which can result from several different factors. Network latency is the amount of time it takes for data to get from one network node to another. The following factors contribute to network latency:

Network node count Using an inadequate number of network devices such as switches and routers can cause latency. It benefits cloud networks, private or public, to use network devices designed specifically for cloud computing and to fashion a network of sufficient numbers of devices to meet need.

Number of hops The more nodes data packets traverse, the greater the delay as each gateway node in turn inspects and updates packet headers. A cloud network should include multiple paths between endpoints and a mechanism to leverage connectivity across as few devices as possible within reasonable costs.

Transport protocol latency High-throughput networks between cloud devices may require alternative transport protocols, such as Fibre Channel or InifiniBand, which have bandwidth capabilities exceeding those of more common switched Ethernet network interconnects. Cloud networks often bear much in common with networks used in high-performance computing environments due to the higher level of resource utilization than found in traditional data center environments.

Network congestion Both the number of network devices and the bandwidth available to each device influence network congestion. While dedicated point-to-point connections can simply transmit on one medium and receive on another, modern internetworking protocols operate using a Carrier Sense Multiple Access (CSMA) mechanism to share the same network medium. Internetworking protocols with collision detection (CSMA/CD) or collision avoidance (CSMA/CA) improve performance by detecting when multiple devices are trying to communicate at the same time, applying a random delay to each before attempting a retransmission. When too many devices are connected to the same network segment, collisions become more numerous and lead to congestion between devices.

Infrastructural Changes

In traditional data centers, shown in Figure 6.2, the bulk of network communication passes from local access interconnects up through aggregation devices to core high-bandwidth network paths, many of which may implement wide area network (WAN) protocols in favor of local area network (LAN) alternatives to gain greater overall throughput between network segments. When connectivity between resources over the public Internet is required, data communication passes through a gateway bridging the core network and the Internet service provider's connection.

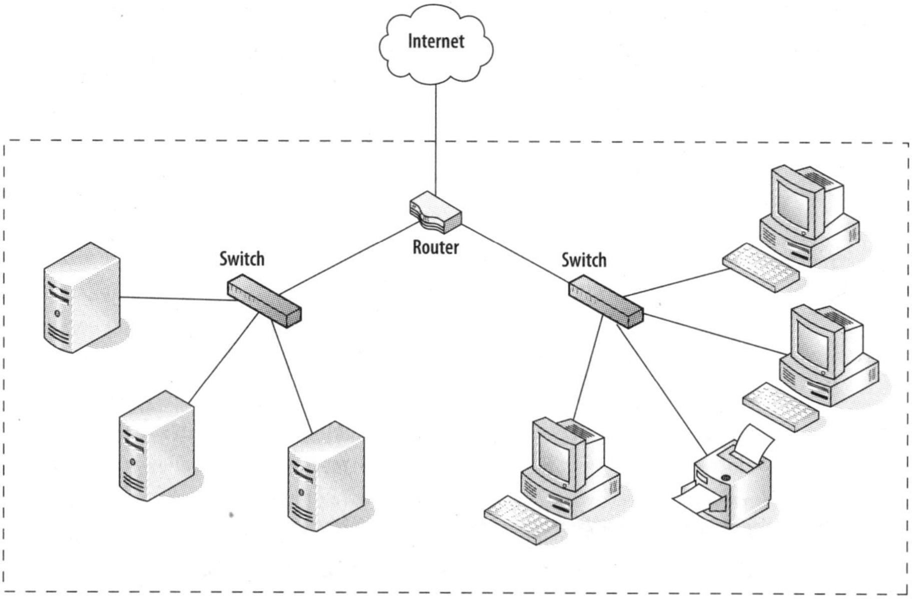

FIGURE 6.2 Traditional data center connectivity

Traditional data center internetworking connections generally do not consume the full bandwidth available because resource pools are isolated within each hosting device. Cloud resource pools are shared and interoperate across many host servers, requiring a much higher degree of continuous and sustained communication at the same networking level.

In networks developed for cloud service interconnections, the layering of network devices is reduced and protocol separation is simplified. This is done by connecting a limited number of devices to high-speed "leaf layer" devices that can handle direct switching between local devices and data pass-through to even higher bandwidth spine connections, which might involve newer 40 GB or even 100 GB connections at the time of this writing.

When the aggregation process is eliminated, and the hop count of device layering, network latency is reduced and data is more rapid in direct exchange between cloud data center devices. Network broadcast isolation at the leaf layer reduces congestion and enhances device-to-device throughput, transferring the bulk of data exchange from a vertical transition across the traditional data center network to a horizontal transfer between cloud service host devices. Because each leaf handles only a few racks worth of servers, device oversubscription is eliminated and total device count capacity is greatly expanded across the entire cloud network. Reduction of device count between any two points also reduces network latency, improving individual communication efficiency between endpoints.

Virtual Extensible Local Area Networking

Vendors such as Intel, VMware, Arista, and Broadcom have developed a technology that creates Layer 2 tunnels, the Virtual Extensible Local Area Network (VXLAN). VXLAN is an example of software-defined cloud networking (SDCN). Fundamentally, VXLAN provides Layer 2 tunneling connections between cloud services separated by Layer 3 network segmentation.

VXLAN endpoints (Virtual Tunnel End Points, or VTEPs) provide gateway connections between virtual network segments and standard TCP/IP routed networks so that these virtual networks can transparently interoperate within the traditional data center. VXLAN segments have one limitation compared to traditional networks: A MAC address must be completely unique within a virtual network, so clustered host servers must leverage failover mechanisms that allow for different network interface card (NIC) MAC addresses. To properly handle internetworking connections, VXLAN headers identify endpoints using a unique combination of the virtual network identifier (VNI) and the endpoint's MAC address.

The additional network packet data that facilitates tunneled internetworking communication over VXLAN connections marginally reduces data throughput in comparison to true Layer 2 networking but allows an organization to manage and consume its cloud services without concern as to their location or host network address space. VXLAN can be integrated within existing networks without need for retrofitting and is a standard implemented by multiple vendors' products, protecting against proprietary lock-in constraints.

Leveraging Automation and Self-Service

One of the essential characteristics (as well as a key selling point) of cloud services is self-service provisioning. Virtual servers, applications, storage, and other services can be provisioned by the organization on demand.
Figure 6.3 shows an example of self-service provisioning using Microsoft Azure, configuring a new Windows Server 2012 virtual machine with two CPU cores and 3.5 GB of allocated RAM. Other options presented at the left of the same interface allow the provisioning of cloud services, SQL databases, data storage pools, and virtual networks within the Azure pool of resources.

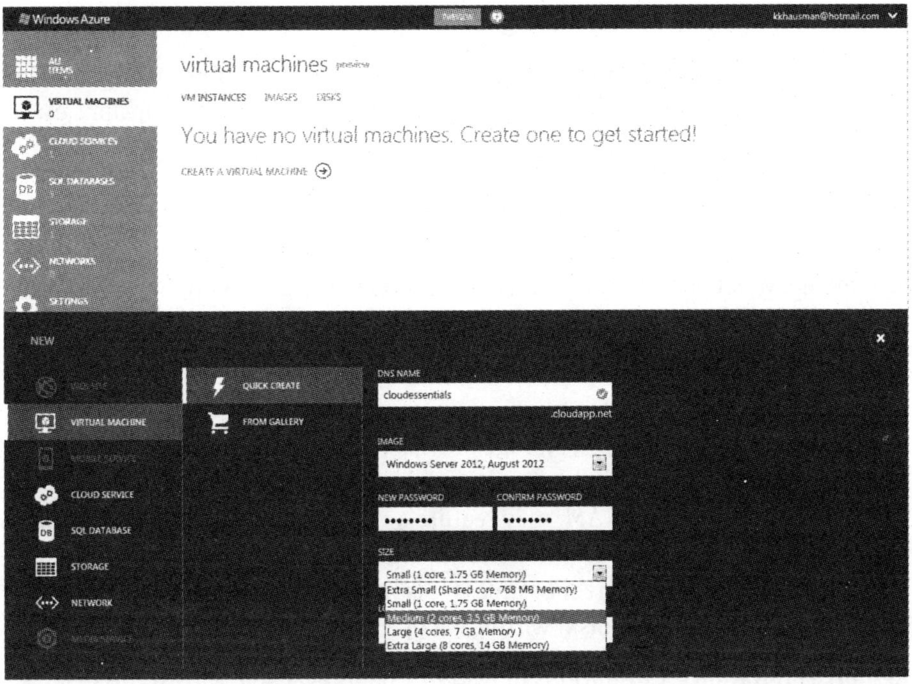

FIGURE 6.3 Self-service provisioning of a new virtual machine within the Azure IaaS administration console

In Chapter 5, "Cloud Business Value," we discussed some of the benefits of self-service provisioning, such as increased organizational agility, but it is important to note the risks involved. Generally, management consoles are designed to allow both IT staff and business staff to provision resources. Without some manner of oversight or governance, or at least effective communication between business staff and IT staff, this could lead to increased costs, duplication of resources, or security risks. As such, internal processes should be in place prior to allowing business staff to provision resources.

Virtual server sprawl is very easy, so the tendency to stand up a new server without releasing the resources allocated to an existing system can rapidly expand an organization's costs. Just like playing poker in Vegas using an account card rather than real money, designating cloud resources within a web interface lacks the "reality" of designating a particular machine in the data center for a new project, and cleanup seems unnecessary unless organizational policies include regular review and deprovisioning of virtual servers that are no longer needed.

Automation in Provisioning

On-demand self-service provisioning is not possible without automation, and to be effective, automated cloud services must include the following capabilities:

Data recovery Data backup and recovery can be automated to increase data availability in the event of a system failure or network outage.

Resource pooling This capability allows computing resources such as storage, memory, network bandwidth, virtual servers, and processing power to be assigned dynamically or upon request.

Provisioning policies Provisioning policies are used by cloud service providers to define provisioning attributes (parameters used to identify resources) related to various services. For example, storage provisioning policies may be used to automatically increase storage capacity when needed. Certain forms of resource provisioning, such as adding RAM, may require a reboot to effect the change unless migration between virtualized instances is available. Similarly, added data storage capacity may require a reboot unless it is handled as a separate partition (as if it were another separate disk) within the operating system.

Resource limitation Limitations of resource pools available within the self-service interface must be clearly evident to prevent costly overruns when electing to stand up a new server, database, or storage pool. Figure 6.4 illustrates this within the Microsoft Azure administration interface, showing the resources allocated to a VM from the account's available capacity.

FIGURE 6.4 **Windows Azure administration console displaying one server taking up 8 cores out of 20 allocated to this account**

In addition to direct limitations in terms of total required pools, limitations need to be managed for automated provisioning of cloud resources in terms of type of resource and administrative functions such as data protection that can be configured. Users might be able to provision a new database but not a new virtual network, and they might be able to configure the data backup type and frequency for the database but not for a file server based on automation settings in the new resource provisioning self-service interface.

Benefits of Automation

Cloud service automation has a number of advantages over the traditional data center resource allocation process:

Hidden complexity Automation takes care of resource availability without requiring operators to understand the location and type of individual host server equipment.

Availability Automated cloud self-service makes it possible to manage resource allocation and provisioning even during off-hours, weekends, and holidays when the IT staff is otherwise engaged.

Standardization Limitations configured within the self-service interface ensure that new allocated resource pools conform to established standards for quality management and ease of support.

Resource utilization Power consumption and resource management can be configured to improve an organization's data center carbon impact.

Understanding Federated Cloud Services

With regard to cloud services, *federation* refers to the collection of multiple cloud resource pools into a single manageable whole. The VXLAN technology mentioned earlier in this chapter can be used to bridge multiple different clouds located in various Layer 3 network segments, forming a single Layer 2 cloud network environment through virtualized networking.

Federated cloud services expand this integration to allow an organization to grow beyond local data center resources, as in the case of cloud bursting, when a service demands resources beyond local limits and can integrate externally provided hosted services to meet expanded requirements. Federated cloud services like CloudSwitch, shown in Figure 6.5, make it possible to migrate services such as cloud-hosted virtual machines between private and public cloud hosting through the same type of web client as the one used to originally provision each resource.

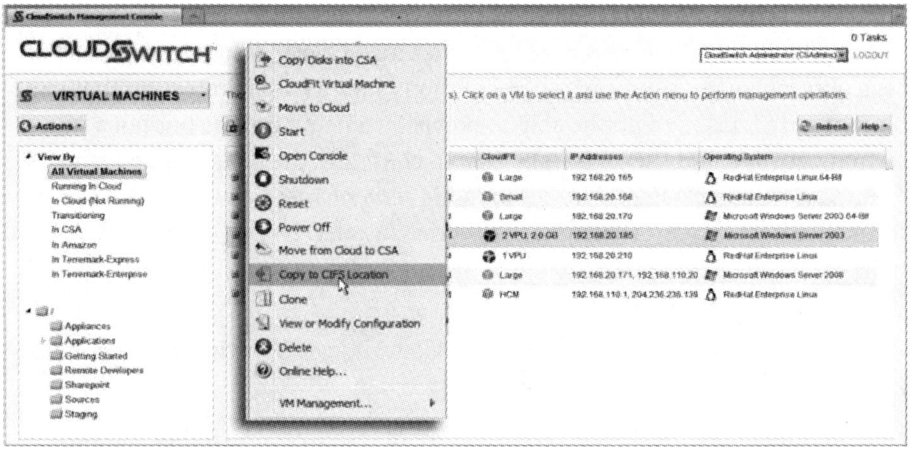

FIGURE 6.5 **Demonstration of the CloudSwitch administrative interface, being used to copy a virtual server to the public cloud**

Federated cloud services can provide interconnections between clouds functioning in private/private, private/public, and public/public configurations, allowing multiple clouds to be managed as a single cloud resource pool.

Encryption and Storage Gateways

Federated cloud resources are protected through encryption and standards for passwords and digital certificates. Organizations employing federated cloud services should consider setting up a cloud storage gateway, which is a local server that ensures data protection by handling encryption and data compression when accessing, modifying, backing up, or recovering data from cloud-based file storage. The storage gateway also functions as a standard pass-through for cloud storage, allowing an organization the ability to consume resources from multiple vendors without concern for the storage vendor. This acts to protect against proprietary lock-in for cloud storage resources and allows use of multiple storage providers' services at the same time.

Storage gateways can provide multiple functions:

Backup The cloud storage gateway integrates with data recovery suites to handle backups and data recovery options.

Caching The storage gateway can store regularly accessed data to improve response time in comparison to repeated access against the original storage server.

Compression Gateways can provide data compression services to reduce network bandwidth requirements for storing and retrieving file data.

Encryption Cloud storage gateways ensure that all data is properly encrypted before transport or storage, protecting cloud-hosted data against unauthorized access or modification.

Achieving Interoperability

One of the greatest challenges to cloud adoption is interoperability, which can be defined in the following ways:

- The ability to move resources, such as applications, between service providers
- The ability for services running in different clouds to access a common set of data or share information
- The ability to use a common set of management tools with services from multiple providers

In general, current cloud providers' services rely on proprietary storage formats, so, for example, an Azure instance cannot be directly ported to EC2 hosting. One way to improve interoperability is through an orchestration layer. In a noncomputing environment, orchestration is the arrangement or organization of elements toward a desired goal or effect. In cloud computing, an orchestration layer is a mechanism to arrange, organize, integrate, and manage multiple cloud services. There are a number of vendors offering cloud orchestration tools. Most are aligned with a particular spectrum of technologies; for example, Cisco's products are intended to orchestrate interconnections between Cisco-compatible products and may not work on some other forms of cloud access or hosting technologies. The following vendors are among those offering cloud orchestration tools:

- Cisco Intelligent Automation for Cloud
- Citrix CloudPlatform
- Flexiant Cloud Orchestrator
- IBM SmartCloud Continuous Delivery
- NephoScale Cloud Orchestration Suite
- RightScale Cloud Management

Even with the proper tools, some organizations may find managing multiple cloud services difficult and instead turn to a cloud broker to handle it for them. A cloud service broker is an entity that acts as a middleman between cloud service providers and consumers. In addition to aggregating and integrating multiple services into a single service, cloud brokers may add value to the aggregated services, such as identity management or performance reporting.

Cloud Computing Standards

To achieve coordination and interconnection between cloud services and service providers, an organization must select standards for its cloud technologies. Like the OSI model and TCP/IP protocol suites mentioned earlier in this chapter, standards are, by definition, a set of established rules, principles, and requirements — an approved model. Cloud service providers that follow the same standards are much more likely to be interoperable than those that follow their own proprietary model. Part of the selection process of cloud service providers should always involve identifying the standards they have adopted to reduce the risk of vendor lock-in.

There are several standards bodies involved in cloud computing, including the following:

Cloud Security Alliance (CSA) This group focuses on audit and security standards for cloud computing.

Cloud Standards Customer Council (CSCC) One of this organization's goals is to influence standards development based on cloud user requirements.

Distributed Management Task Force (DMTF) DMTF has several working groups involved with developing standards for management interfaces, audit data, interoperability, software license management, and virtualization.

IEEE Standards Association (IEEE-SA) IEEE-SA has several active projects for development of cloud computing standards, covering topics such as portability, interoperability, and federation.

National Institute of Standards and Technology (NIST) NIST addresses cloud computing standards in its Special Publications 500 series, in particular SP 500-291, *NIST Cloud Computing Standards Roadmap*. Security standards can be found in the Special Publication 800 series and are discussed in Chapter 11.

Organization for the Advancement of Structured Information Standards (OASIS) OASIS is developing standards for identity management, data sharing, privacy, and portability, among others.

Storage Networking Industries Association (SNIA) SNIA's Cloud Storage Initiative developed the Cloud Data Management Interface (CDMI) standard. This standard describes the processes for assigning metadata that defines required services, such as backup or encryption.

Standards for Private Clouds

Private clouds can be configured to meet standards such as NIST and ISO standards, regulatory mandates related to credit card information and protected health care information, or other functional guidelines as currently employed in the traditional data center.

Standards for Public Clouds

Public cloud providers adopt standards for audit and security management, such as ISO 27001 and 27002. Additional provisions for organizational regulatory mandates such as SOX, PCI, and HIPPA must be negotiated by an organization as part of its public/hybrid cloud service-level agreement (SLA).

The Essentials and Beyond

Cloud deployment scenarios take advantage of new techniques for network interconnections between services and resource pools. New technologies for virtual networking, self-service automation, and federated cloud service management tools like the storage gateway enhance utilization and flexibility for organizations moving into the cloud. Care must be taken to apply suitable standards for interoperability and security controls when moving away from the traditional data center, but many options already exist for both private and public cloud service hosting.

Additional Exercises

- Identify regulatory mandates that would have to be included in a public cloud migration of their organizational infrastructure and that are familiar to class participants.
- Walk through a comparison between Layer 2, Layer 3, and VXLAN tunneled Layer 2 cloud networks.

To compare your answer to the author's, please visit `www.sybex.com/go/cloudessentials`.

Review Questions

1. When networks are architected for cloud services, which quality addresses the ability to expand to meet variable data requirements?

   A. Resiliency
   B. Simplified management
   C. Scalability
   D. Throughput

(Continues)

THE ESSENTIALS AND BEYOND *(Continued)*

2. VXLAN provides virtual ________ layer connections across _________ layer networks?

   A. Data-Link, Network
   B. Physical, Data-Link
   C. Transport, Physical
   D. Network, Transport

3. Which factor contributes to network latency primarily because of oversubscription?

   A. Congestion
   B. Number of hops
   C. Node count
   D. Protocol latency

4. Which capability of cloud service automation allows memory and processing power to be dynamically assigned?

   A. Provisioning policies
   B. Data recovery
   C. Resource limitation
   D. Resource pooling

5. __________ cloud services can provide interconnections between cloud functioning, allowing multiple clouds to be managed as a single cloud resource pool.

   A. Hybrid
   B. Federated
   C. Layer 2
   D. Layer 3

6. Congestion occurs when devices begin to interfere with one another as they compete for available network capacity and can be addressed by expanding the available bandwidth or _____________.

   A. Selecting transport protocols with higher latency
   B. Selecting transport protocols with lower latency
   C. Reducing the number of hops between devices
   D. Segmenting subnetworks to limit collisions

7. Which benefit of cloud automation eases Christmas data center support in particular, compared to traditional data centers?

   A. Hidden complexity
   B. Standardization
   C. Availability
   D. Resource utilization

8. Which function of cloud storage gateways is intended to improve response time to data requests?

   A. Backup
   B. Caching
   C. Compression
   D. Encryption

(Continues)

THE ESSENTIALS AND BEYOND *(Continued)*

9. Which of the following is *not* a definition for cloud interoperability?

   A. The ability to move resources, such as applications, between service providers

   B. The ability for services running in different clouds to access a common set of data or share information

   C. The ability to arrange, organize, integrate, and manage multiple cloud services

   D. The ability to use a common set of management tools with services from multiple providers

10. Which cloud standards body is focused on audit and security standards for cloud computing?

    A. Cloud Security Alliance (CSA)

    B. IEEE Standards Association (IEEE-SA)

    C. National Institute of Standards and Technology (NIST)

    D. Organization for the Advancement of Structured Information Standards (OASIS)

CHAPTER 7

Strategies for Cloud Adoption

Whether adopting individual cloud services or migrating fully into the cloud, organizational change and planning are key elements required for potential success. Before transitioning toward a new technology base, the organization's cultural state and business goals must be identified and solutions found to address emergent business requirements, whether they include cost efficiencies, resource scalability measures, or global accessibility needs.

- **Aligning cloud deployments with organizational goals**
- **Identifying the impact of cloud adoption to business processes**
- **Understanding the importance of service-level agreements**

Aligning Cloud Deployments with Organizational Goals

Any organization that is considering adoption of cloud services must start by identifying the type of cloud service components it intends to take advantage of before starting plans for integration with an existing enterprise network. In a general sense, cloud "as a Service" options can be aligned with the OSI reference model, as illustrated in Figure 7.1. The Open Systems Interconnection (OSI) model is used to characterize network communication functions and was discussed in Chapter 6, "Cloud Infrastructure Planning."

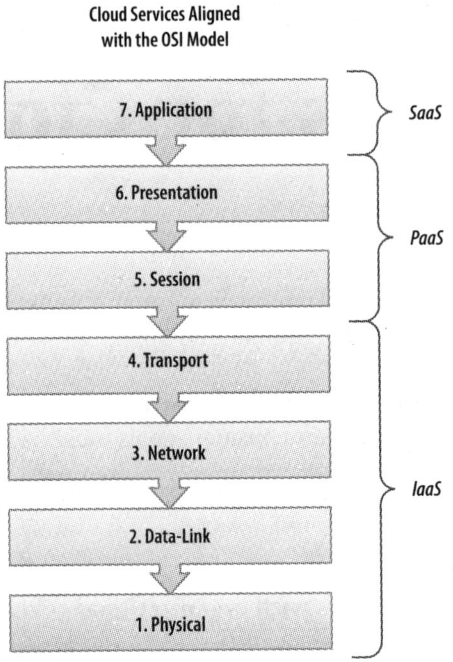

FIGURE 7.1 Cloud services aligned with the OSI reference model

Organizations need to understand the type of cloud services they will be consuming. Email is a common enterprise application to migrate into the cloud, so a Software as a Service (SaaS) application like Gmail might only include Application layer elements of the OSI model being provided by the cloud service provider.

All other elements of the network infrastructure — such as networking interconnections and client systems like workstations, tablets, smartphones, thin clients, and terminals — must be provided by the local enterprise when used for accessing cloud resources. The cloud service provider will of course have its own internal network resources to support its internal operations, but these will not be exposed to the consuming organizational users who require only network access and a compatible browser for consumption of the web-accessible service. Consumers for Google's Gmail service are familiar with this because they can make use of the cloud-based email system through any browser equally well whether from their desktop or a mobile device.

An organization that wants to leverage Platform as a Service (PaaS) development for custom applications might need cloud services covering only

Presentation or possibly Session layer elements to expose the custom application programming interface (API) for consumption by the organization. However, if an organization wants to include cloud Infrastructure as a Service (IaaS) hosting of entire virtual desktop environments to meet its business objectives, then the cloud service provider may handle components extending from the Network layer up (for Layer 3 networks) or even the Data-Link layer (for Layer 2 networks) requiring only Physical layer networking to be provided by the organization itself.

For a new startup, organizational goals are more readily defined without legacy technology considerations. In startup environments, cloud service offerings can support all elements of their business data requirements, from file storage and database (IaaS) solutions up through custom application development (PaaS) and even user productivity suite (SaaS) components, without concern for their integration with existing resources, which would create complexity for existing organizations with extensive existing enterprise technology resources. For an existing enterprise network, compatibility will be a major factor in planning the migration to cloud service alternatives. A single service provider like Amazon might be able to support all of these components from a clustered virtual network providing highly redundant resources with redundant mirrors on multiple continents, including database and service elements combining to create a custom Microsoft SharePoint/Exchange collaboration portal accessible by organizational personnel located anywhere in the world.

Alternately, an established organization that needs only a smaller set of resources like enterprise resource planning (ERP) support from a vendor such as NetSuite or customer relationship management (CRM) services from a different cloud provider like Salesforce may leverage cloud gateway services to bridge disparate alternatives. Cloud federation and service gateways were discussed in Chapter 6.

Cloud Service Provider Business Requirements

As we discuss business requirements for cloud service providers, you should be aware that CompTIA's criteria for the Cloud Essentials exam includes the expectation that cloud service providers should maintain a framework based on open Java-based SaaS standards as a preference to those with proprietary languages or APIs. EXIN only notes that service selection may be affected by compatibility but does not offer a particular technology such as Java as being preferential in selection.

Selection of cloud service providers involves many factors, including an assessment of how long the vendor has been providing cloud services and what its uptime has been like during this period, whether the cloud vendor's technologies are compatible with the organization's existing enterprise, and if the vendor's offerings meet the detailed requirements identified during planning for migration into the cloud. Additional criteria might be included in selection, such as the portability of cloud technologies to an alternate vendor, typically based on the application toolset options available for PaaS development. Other considerations include security requirements and legal or compliance mandates that must be met by the service-level agreement (SLA) with the vendor. We will discuss SLAs in greater detail later in this chapter.

Identification of cloud service vendors will also include an assessment of liabilities such as limitations on total cost of operations, data security options available for disaster recovery, and planned maintenance cycles and service downtime scheduling. These details should be included in the assessment of cloud service providers to meet an organization's needs. For this assessment to be successful, the organization should consider the following questions:

- Is the service model appropriate for an organization's business needs? If a business requires only a new email service, then a simple SaaS solution might take care of its needs. If it needs a fully virtualized network and integrated servers and services, then IaaS service providers might need to be brought into the pilot.
- Does the vendor's deployment model (private, public, hybrid) meet the organization's needs and regulatory mandates? A simple privately owned commercial operation might have few regulatory mandates, while publicly traded businesses might have constraints on information protection and reporting from various legislative and regulatory directives such as the Sarbanes-Oxley Act of 2002.
- Does the change in security auditability from organizational data center to cloud data center hosting impact legal or regulatory mandates? Many industries, such as the health care industry, have requirements for auditing any access to protected information, which may require additional details in the contract with a cloud vendor hosting file and data storage of health information.
- Does the vendor have an established track record in providing the identified service with uptime that meets the organization's uptime constraints, including planned maintenance and unplanned historical downtimes? A new entrant into the cloud service arena might

not have sufficient redundancy and scalability to meet expanding needs, while an existing provider with an established cloud hosting data center structure will already be adept at adapting to transient changes in consumption.

- Can the cloud service provider scale to meet all known and planned organizational expansions? When an organization is selecting a vendor, it is obvious that the vendor's services must meet the immediate needs being addressed by the current project, such as email, but the selection of a particular vendor may complicate other later projects involving other cloud services such as a full CRM suite that must integrate with the email service. It is best to make vendor selections based on all known current and planned projects to ensure that a selection made early in the process does not preclude opportunities later when second order projects are undertaken.
- Will the vendor negotiate an SLA meeting the organization's requirements and mandates? Some cloud service vendors may be able to tailor the SLA and other contract terms to meet an organization's specific requirements and mandatory constraints, such as a governmental organization that may not want its backup data transferred to a data center outside of the government's geopolitical borders to retain "control" over legal findings and public information requests for data stored by the service provider. If the cloud service vendor's operations involve transferring services to data centers in northern areas to take advantage of cooler climates during the summer, this could preclude their adoption by a client organization with mandates for data control.
- Do the vendor's facility redundancy provisions (for example, power, network, and air handling) and disaster recovery provisions meet the organization's recovery point objectives? Because cloud service providers may have multiple client organizations, it is critical to address disaster recovery and business continuity recovery objectives in the contract to ensure that the organization's resources will be recovered within an acceptable window of time after an incident.
- Can the performance measures of the cloud vendor's services be monitored and verified by the organization? Cloud resources will generally be located remotely from the client organization in public and community cloud environments, requiring agreements with the hosting service to allow monitoring and validation of performance

measurements that could otherwise be identified as an attack profile by the host vendor's intrusion detection systems.

- Will the vendor's cloud servers be engaged in multitenancy with other clients likely to experience extended attacks (for example, online gambling sites)? Because a cloud service vendor can engage many different client organizations, contracts specifying conditions of multitenancy will protect against an organization's services sharing the same host data center equipment as vulnerable targets of opportunity for hackers or online activists.
- Will the cloud vendor's services be affordable during both peak and baseline operations? Contract negotiations with the service provider should include the pilot's level of operation or even a planned baseline for consumer access. It's also important that it include details specifying capability to address sudden peaks in access together with controls and limits restricting cost in the case of extended periods of excessive use like those accompanying distributed denial of service attacks.
- Are the cloud service vendor's systems protected in an auditable manner against logical, physical, and environmental hazards? As with contractual agreements for performance monitoring, cloud service contracts should include provisions for audit and review of all levels of security. This is particularly important when organizational data falls into a protected category with regulatory mandates that must be met.

Identifying the Impact of Cloud Adoption to Business Processes

Prior to adopting cloud computing services, an organization must fully understand the impact they will have on existing business processes. It is important to keep in mind that both technical and business staff must work together to determine the impact on their particular department. This necessarily begins with identifying and understanding organizational business processes and their dependencies.

Culture and Business Changes

The change in computing resources from capital expense (CAPEX) to operating expense (OPEX) as discussed in Chapter 5, "Cloud Business Value," and self-service provisioning may change an organization's financial processes, particularly with regard to how budget, return on investment, and profitability are calculated. Additional success factors when planning adoption of cloud services include a range of management and cultural changes necessary to prepare for migration. These will not predetermine success, but an organization cannot move toward a new technology base without including fundamental changes in expectations that accompany the new technologies' own peculiarities.

A common complaint is the idea that "if you cannot touch your data, you do not own your data," leveraging the idea that locally hosted resources are inherently better protected, more readily available, or more rapidly brought back online during interruptions due to maintenance, power outages, or network attacks. These complaints derive from overconfidence that local personnel provide expertise in all of these areas to a greater degree than those at a cloud provider's data center. Aside from the ability for management to personally contact and yell at the technicians tasked with correcting an issue affecting downtime, this is unlikely to be true for all possible technologies when compared to cloud service providers like Amazon, Google, and Microsoft who can call on an effective army of technical professionals with deep skill sets in the event of an outage.

In addition to changing the cultural expectations regarding data access, protections against external exposure should be included in SLAs and hosting contracts to ensure that the same legal and regulatory protections are provided by the hosting company as when data resources are stored in local data centers. This adds legal constraints and transfers penalty costs for noncompliance to the vendor associated with violations to ensure that security and protective measures are maintained. This can be handled as part of the organization's risk management process by considering business, technical, and legal risks associated with cloud service adoption and the development of practices or service requirements to mitigate each risk to an acceptable level.

Business risks such as proprietary lock-in can be addressed by selection of standards available from multiple vendors, while technical risks like resource exhaustion can be addressed by establishing limits and expansion of service provisions in the cloud service contracts, and even legal risks such as data disclosure due to hacking can be addressed by mandating encryption standards to be used during storage and transport of data. Risk in the cloud is addressed much like risk anywhere else in an enterprise network because any system that is publicly accessible can become the source of a risk, and planning must include mechanisms to mitigate (reduce), eliminate, transfer, or accept each.

Audits of vendor services and facilities and monitoring will need to be included in contracts and SLAs, particularly when multitenancy might include nonorganizational services and data supported by the same hosting hardware. Other security provisions such as penetration testing and production system vulnerability scanning should be conducted with prior notice to the vendor just as when performing these tests on non-cloud-hosted data resources to ensure that an organization's tests do not impose hardships on other hosted resources sharing the same pool of cloud resources.

Management Changes

In addition to changes in risk management mandated by the remote locale of cloud data resources, an organization must include changes to infrastructure, service, financial, and vendor/partner management practices as well.

Changes to infrastructural management might include tech refresh cycle realignment with network access instead of desktop workstations, requiring efforts to ensure that updated and continued expenditures remain visible to executive sponsors and key stakeholders. A new workstation is highly visible, while an update to the network or gateway might have no obvious value to those determining organizational infrastructural budgets and expenditures.

Service management may need to be adjusted, depending on whether help desk functions are retained by the local data center group or if they will be aligned with the cloud vendor's own help desk services. If escalations include a cost per use, contracts should include details on cost limits and pre-negotiated incident costs based on responsibility and type of service desk request. Service-level agreements will require significant attention when cloud-hosted services are adopted, and the organization's legal staff should be included in any agreements negotiated between the organization and the service provider.

Financial management will need to change to address the shift from capital expense data center costs to operational service-use-related costs but also should address considerations for the expansion or transfer of software licensing and related service expenses that may be folded in the cloud vendor's offerings or might need to be purchased in addition to existing agreements. Client access license (CAL) models, for example, might be in place for the existing technologies used in local data centers but may need to be updated for consumption of cloud-hosted versions available from the vendor.

Testing for Readiness

As we mentioned at the start of this chapter, any cloud service adoption must start with the identification of cloud services that would benefit an organization's business operations, which will in turn determine the type of service provider (SaaS, PaaS, IaaS) that will be needed. After identifying desirable cloud alternatives to existing data center services, an organization can test its own readiness for the migration through a series of actions within its own operational sphere of control.

1. The first step to test an organization's readiness for cloud migration is to test against internal or limited-scope cloud services in a pilot program. This will allow discovery of operational pain points and development of interoperability intermediaries — such as service-oriented architecture (SOA) wrappers — where necessary to support legacy services not yet ready for cloud migration.
2. Cloud service opportunities within the organization should be identified based on business needs such as resource expansion and cost control and then communicated with other business units to ensure that the road map is understood and that processes are developed and tested for service integration.
3. Results from the pilot program should be reviewed by a cross-functional team representing all business elements of the organization. This team will monitor the new services and identify areas that might create issues.
4. Technical and financial provisions should be negotiated to address any issues identified by the cross-functional team to determine if the road map needs to be changed to meet the organization's business needs. The results from any changes will be transmitted back to the cross-functional team for success validation.

Change and Project Management

To ensure that proper change controls are present throughout the transformation from traditional data center to cloud services, the transformation should be integrated into the organizational continuous improvement process. By iteratively reviewing business needs and available cloud alternatives, an organization can ensure that its technologies continue to evolve and better align with business requirements over time. Adoption of a standard process for project, program, and portfolio management will ensure that communications for and between members of the change control board and cross-functional review team are preserved and will support notification and involvement for key stakeholders and executive sponsors.

Understanding the Importance of Service-Level Agreements

A service-level agreement (SLA) outlines the expected level of service a customer can expect to receive from a service provider, the metrics used to measure said service, and the roles and responsibilities of both the service provider and the customer. It is a critical part of any service-oriented vendor contract. If multiple services are being received from a service provider, they may all be covered in a single SLA or each service may have its own SLA.

An SLA serves as an intermediary between the cloud service provider and a client organization, as illustrated in Figure 7.2. A typical service provider SLA includes the following components:

- A breakdown of services provided and excluded
- Costs for services
- Duration of the agreement
- Responsibilities of the customer and the service provider
- Availability and performance requirements
- Service monitoring and reporting
- Remediation and liability (or lack thereof) for service disruption
- Dispute resolution procedures
- A mechanism for reviewing and updating the SLA, including a change control process

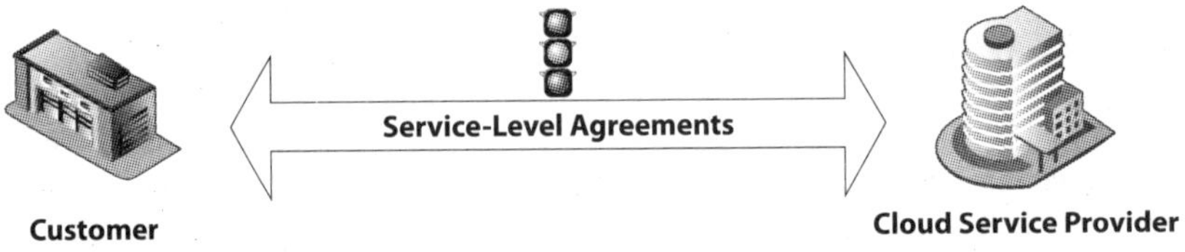

FIGURE 7.2 Service-level agreements control client expectations and service provider responsibilities.

Service-level objectives (SLOs), also called service-level targets, are quality-of-service measurements used to measure service provider performance.

Typically, service providers have a standard SLA they offer that is generally favorable to the service provider. Some service providers will engage in negotiations with a customer and include a customized SLA into the contract, while others will not. A noncustomizable SLA may also be referred to simply as terms of service. Organizations with critical or confidential information, or those subject to regulatory compliance, should review the SLA carefully, preferably with assistance of legal counsel, to ensure that it meets security, privacy, and compliance needs. (See Chapter 11, "Security in the Cloud," and Chapter 12, "Privacy and Compliance," for more information.) If it does not meet required needs, appropriate provisions should be added.

Cloud Service-Level Agreements (SLAs)

Due to the nature of cloud computing, certain elements need to be present in cloud SLAs that may not necessarily apply to traditional computing SLAs. The following list includes a few of the cloud-specific considerations:

- Data location
- Service multitenancy
- Transparency (data breach notification)
- Disaster process recovery notification
- Legal data release notification
- Data ownership

When Standard Terms of Service Just Won't Do

In January 2012, the United States Government amended the Family Educational Rights and Privacy Act (FERPA) to require that vendors having access to confidential student data be formally designated as authorized representatives by institutions of higher education. This effectively prohibited institutions of higher education from storing or processing confidential information such as email or student data on systems managed by cloud service providers that offered only standard terms of service. This example applies to education; however, there may be other applicable regulations that apply to your industry. See Chapter 12, for more information on regulatory compliance.

The Essentials and Beyond

Cloud deployment scenarios take advantage of new techniques for network interconnections between services and resource pools. New technologies for virtual networking, self-service automation, and federated cloud service management tools like the storage gateway enhance utilization and flexibility for organizations moving into the cloud. Care must be taken to apply suitable standards for interoperability and security controls when moving away from the traditional data center, but many options already exist for both private and public cloud service hosting.

(Continues)

THE ESSENTIALS AND BEYOND *(Continued)*

ADDITIONAL EXERCISES

- Identify regulatory mandates familiar to class participants that would have to be included in a public cloud migration of their organizational infrastructure.
- Walk through a comparison between Layer 2, Layer 3, and VXLAN tunneled Layer 2 cloud networks.

To compare your answer to the author's, please visit `www.sybex.com/go/cloudessentials`.

REVIEW QUESTIONS

1. Adopting cloud services will impact an organization's financial management due to which of the following changes?

   A. Cost of technical support escalations

   B. Changes in software licensing

   C. Shifting technology from a capital to an operational expenditure

   D. Both B and C

2. Which of the following is not an indicator of the organization's ability to successfully adopt cloud services?

   A. A successful pilot

   B. A fully staffed help desk

   C. Identification of regulatory requirements

   D. Executive management support

3. What instrument identifies the roles and responsibilities of both the customer and the cloud service provider?

   A. Service-level objective

   B. Web hosting agreement

   C. Service-level agreement

   D. Software license agreement

4. What is the role of a cross-functional team representing all business elements of an organization in determining readiness for cloud services?

   A. To participate in the pilot program and identify areas of concern

   B. To negotiate costs for services

   C. To ensure that the SLA benefits the organization more than the provider

   D. To manage the cultural change that will occur during and immediately after the transition

(Continues)

THE ESSENTIALS AND BEYOND *(Continued)*

5. Which of the following is not a critical success factor in selecting a cloud service provider?

   A. The provider is able to provide the appropriate level of security for the organization's data.

   B. The provider's offerings meet identified organizational requirements.

   C. The provider uses open, Java-based standards.

   D. The provider's uptime meets the organization's availability needs.

6. Of the following activities involved in cloud services adoption, which should be performed first?

   A. Implement a pilot program.

   B. Identify business processes and their dependencies.

   C. Identify and compare vendors.

   D. Identify the appropriate services and deployment models.

7. With regard to an organization's readiness to adopt cloud services, which of the following is not one of the goals of a pilot program?

   A. Identification of the type of service provider needed

   B. Identification of problems with interoperability

   C. To provide data to a cross-functional team for analysis

   D. To test the implementation plan in a controlled environment

8. Which of the following SLA elements should be of high concern to an organization considering putting mission-critical data or services in the cloud?

   A. Services provided and excluded

   B. Dispute resolution

   C. Availability and performance requirements

   D. Costs for services

9. Prior to cloud services adoption, technical and business staff must work together to perform what action?

   A. Identify business processes and their dependencies.

   B. Determine changes to the organization's infrastructure.

   C. Determine the impact to business processes.

   D. Both A and C.

10. Cloud service opportunities should be identified based on what criteria?

    A. Business needs

    B. Regulatory requirements

    C. Cost control

    D. Security requirements

CHAPTER 8

Applications in the Cloud

Throughout this book, we use commonly known applications to illustrate the use and architecture of a cloud application. Most of the applications mentioned, such as Dropbox and Salesforce.com, are Software as a Service (SaaS) applications. SaaS applications may use a backend based on the Platform as a Service (PaaS) or Infrastructure as a Service (IaaS) architecture.

This chapter describes how cloud applications are built based on the different prerequisites tied to a PaaS or IaaS provider for public clouds, technologies used in a private cloud, and interoperability in a hybrid cloud environment.

- **Understanding the role of standard applications**
- **Developing cloud-ready applications**
- **Migrating applications to the cloud**
- **Preparing for technical challenges**
- **Identifying and mitigating risks**

Understanding the Role of Standard Applications

For lack of a better term, we will use *standard application* for any application that is not a *cloud application*. As described in Chapter 1, all standard applications, even those that are designed for single users running on a stand-alone computer, can be broken down into three basic logical tiers: presentation, application (or logic), and data. To better understand these layers, see Figure 8.1.

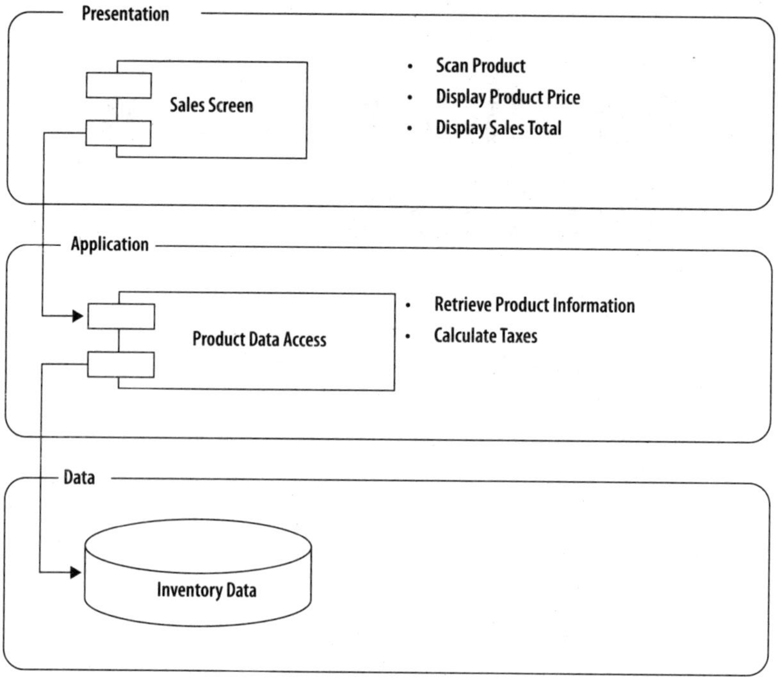

FIGURE 8.1 An example of the logical tiers in a point-of-sales application

If you examine the checkout use case for a basic point-of-sale application, you will be able to identify the different functions that make up the presentation, application, and data tiers. Figure 8.2 shows a sample detailed use case for a checkout service. The use case is broken down into three simple operations: scan item, calculate total and tax, and payment. The very first operation, *scan item*, can be described as follows:

1. The clerk is presented with the option to type the item code or scan it.
2. The system retrieves description, unit price, and tax information for the item.
3. The system updates current list of items in sale and calculates current total.
4. The system displays current item information and current total.

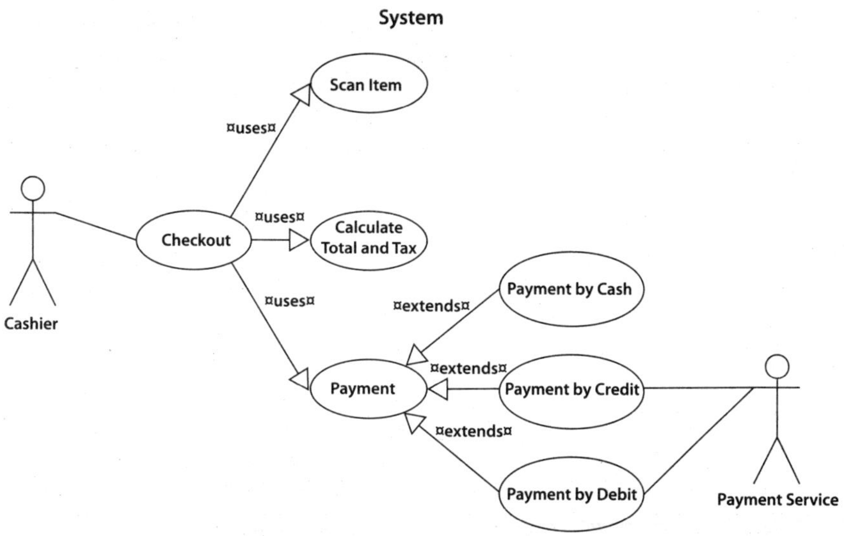

FIGURE 8.2 Checkout use case

WHAT ARE USE CASES?

Use cases in software development are ways of communicating intent among all team members in a software development project. They are something that end users, developers, project managers, and stake holders can all understand and relate to.

A single use case cannot be used to describe all the necessary details of any application. But taken this single case study, you can construct an application using the logical division of layers, as shown in Figure 8.3.

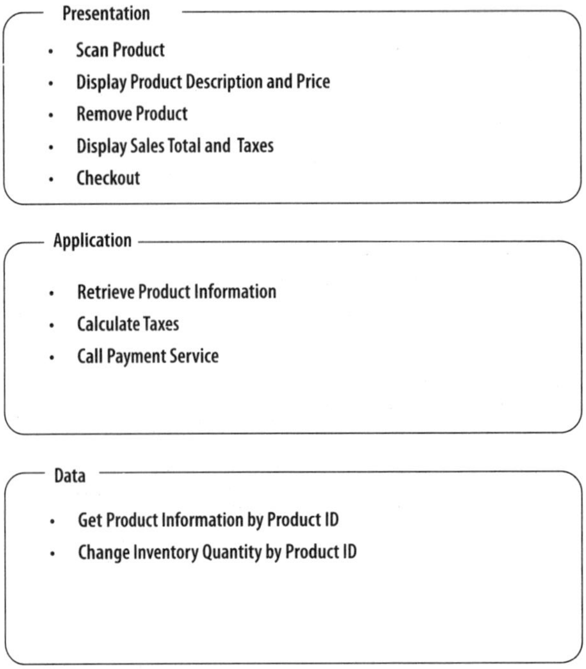

FIGURE 8.3 Checkout use case functions broken into layers

There is a lack of context on this simple point-of-sale application. Is it used by a single user in a small shop, a local supermarket, a popular chain, or even an online store? Without the context, there is no way of deciding the actual physical structure of the application. Each one of these different contexts will drive the application design to a different physical structure, such as desktop, distributed, web based, or cloud.

Desktop Applications

A desktop application has the advantage of being able to use all the application programming interfaces (APIs) made available by an operating system to ensure that its look and feel are familiar to users who work with that same operating system every single day. And the fact that the data consumed is not shared with other users or applications allows developers to create a desktop application a lot faster than, for instance, the type of application that might require concurrent access to data, sharing of information, and communication across a network.

An example of a desktop application would be a simple word processing application that stores everything you type in a file on your local hard drive. You do not need access to the Internet or any other network, interaction with another user, or access to any other service over the network.

Desktop applications will not end because of cloud computing. They will still be needed in several situations where access to external data or services is not needed or possible. In the early 1990s, one of the authors of this book traveled across the Amazon carrying electronic voting machines to distant villages where electricity was not present. These voting machines were powered by batteries and tallied votes locally. At a later time, they would produce data to be sent over dial-up connections to another computer for general tallying.

A word processing application and this type of vote-casting application are only two examples of desktop applications that will resist the trend of web-based and cloud applications. Some applications are better off left in a desktop environment for ease of use and maintenance and sometimes simply because of technology limitations.

In the case of the hypothetical POS application described previously, if the application is to be used in a small shop, with a single point of sale, all three logical layers could run on the same, and only, point-of-sale computer. A single application could provide the user interface with regular elements of a common operating system and the logic within the same process. This single application could also contain code that accesses data stored in the computer hard drive in any format the application is able to read and write to. For an example of this type of application, see Figure 8.4.

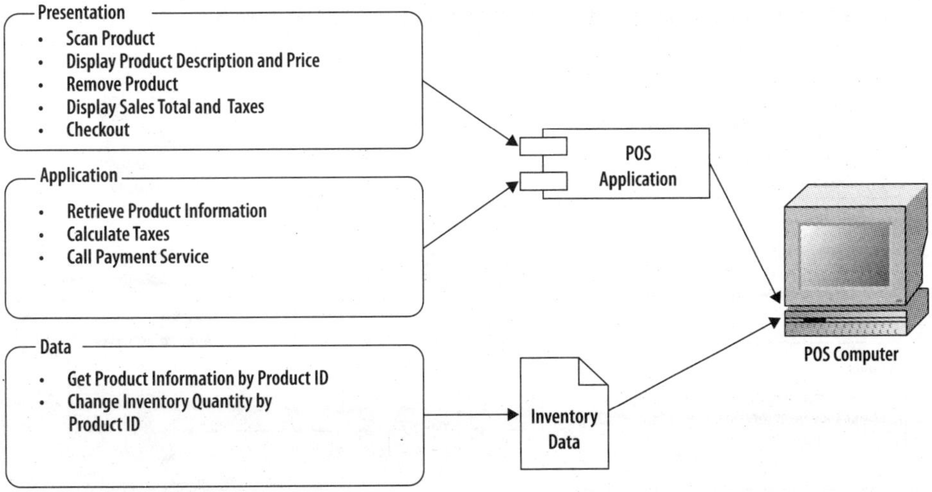

FIGURE 8.4 Representation of the POS application as a desktop application

The data layer would contain a list of all products sold in the store along with their unit price and available quantity in stock. When a product is sold, the application retrieves its information and, once the sale is complete, decreases the inventory.

Distributed Applications

Chapter 1 included a discussion of distributed application design. In reality, true cloud applications must be designed as distributed applications. This is covered in more depth in the section "Developing Cloud-Ready Applications" later in this chapter. For now, take our small shop with a single cashier, and imagine sales are going well. The shop is growing. Lines are forming at the single point of sale. Something must be done to decrease this line or customers will shop elsewhere. A new point of sale is needed. But what if sales keep growing and more customers come in? Maybe two points of sale are not enough. More might be needed.

The application design must now change to allow for the use of multiple points of sale and possible future growth. Currently the data is stored in a single file, in the one and only computer available. All the inventory data is listed there. Any point of sale that's added will need access to this data. There is now a real need to physically separate the data from the rest of the logical tiers.

Because the new points of sale will still be in the store, the store can decide what type of operating system to use and maintain the one currently in use, preserving the user interface. The data must be now placed on a separate physical computer, accessible to all points of sale. And the logic can run on the computer storing the data, on the computers used as points of sale, or on a separate computer dedicated to the application tier, depending on processing and scalability needs. For an example of this type of application, see Figure 8.5.

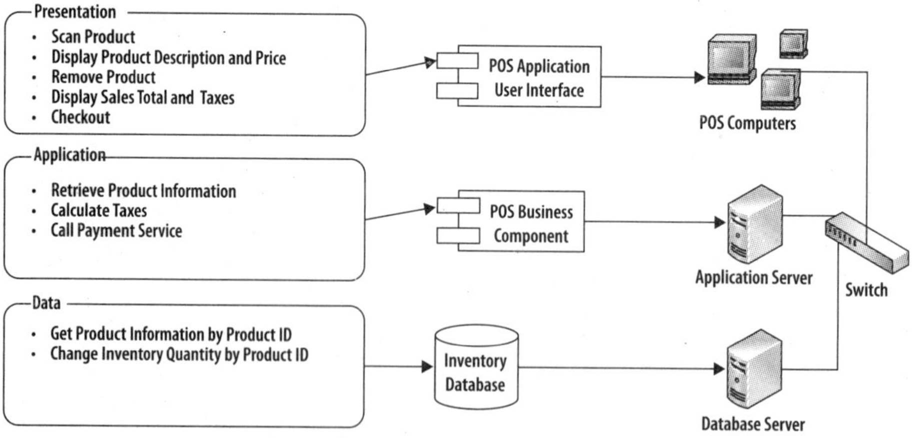

FIGURE 8.5 Representation of the POS application as a distributed application

When designing distributed applications, software architects have to take into account the needs for availability and scalability of the solution as a whole. Single points of failure must be avoided at all costs. For instance, what happens if the one computer holding the inventory data for the store were to break? None of the points of sale would be able to access the data and make a sale.

Several techniques can be used to handle availability. Each point of sale could have a cached copy of the data. In this case, if the server hosting the data is not available, a point of sale can still be used to make a sale as long as the data it contains cached is trusted. All sales would be stored locally until the data server is back online. At this point, data from all points of sale can be copied to the data server and synchronized. Of course, this requires changes to the application design and code. Another solution would be to use failover clustering to provide high availability. Failover clustering would not require changing any of the code for the application but comes at a higher hardware cost. For an example of a highly available multitiered application, see Figure 8.6.

Failover Clustering

Failover clusters provide high availability and scalability to certain server workloads. Two or more servers share access to the same data being handled by the application and are exposed to the network as a single virtual computer (not to be confused with virtualization). This virtual computer has its own name and IP address. When a computer requests access to the service by using the name or IP address of the cluster, one of the servers that is part of the cluster, referred to as the *active node*, responds. If the active node fails, one of the remaining nodes assumes control of the resources managed by the cluster.

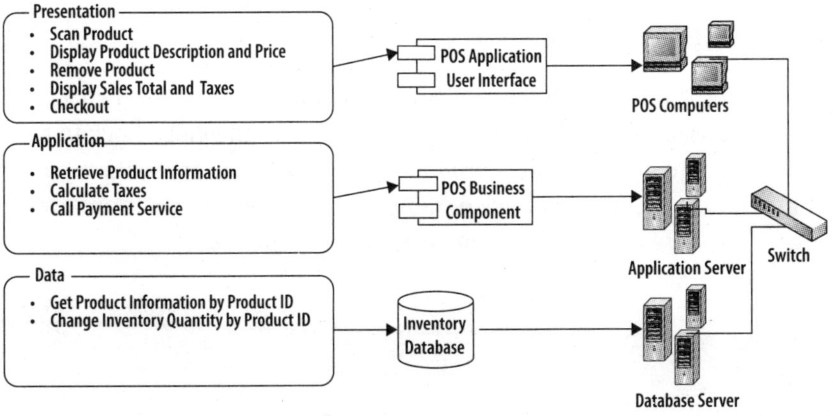

FIGURE 8.6 Representation of the POS application as a highly available distributed application

Web-Based Applications

Standard distributed applications can be used to solve most high availability and scalability needs of an organization. Most applications found on the premises of different organizations today are standard distributed applications. Just as with desktop applications, there will always be a place for standard distributed applications in an organization.

However, standard distributed applications require control of the entire enterprise architecture. If devices with different operating systems are needed in the presentation layer, a different user interface for each must be designed and developed. The APIs used to communicate between the physical layers may also require configuration of firewalls to allow the communication to flow.

Going back to the example POS application, imagine that sales are booming. All of a sudden customers are calling in from other states asking about products, wanting to purchase them. The existing inventory is not enough to handle these new orders. Deals are struck with suppliers to allow accessing their existing inventory when selling products that are not available in the store. And to help serve out-of-town customers, a web storefront must be created.

Once more, the entire physical structure must change. The point of sale needs to be available over the Internet for the customer. There is no way of limiting what type of computer or operating system that customer is using. And there is no way to train these new customers on the existing point-of-sale application. An interface that's common to all must be used, something that is available to anyone who has access to the Internet. The presentation layer must change. Scalability is now more important than ever.

This is where web applications come in. There is a fine line between cloud applications and web applications that will be covered in the next section, "Cloud Applications." For now, consider the new design in Figure 8.7.

Cloud Applications

Years go by, and the once-small shop with a single point of sales now generates thousands of transactions a day. Customers from all over the globe flock to the company's website to order its latest products. The web-based application holds up well but requires the maintenance of hundreds of servers. IT costs are over the roof, and response times for scaling up are not acceptable.

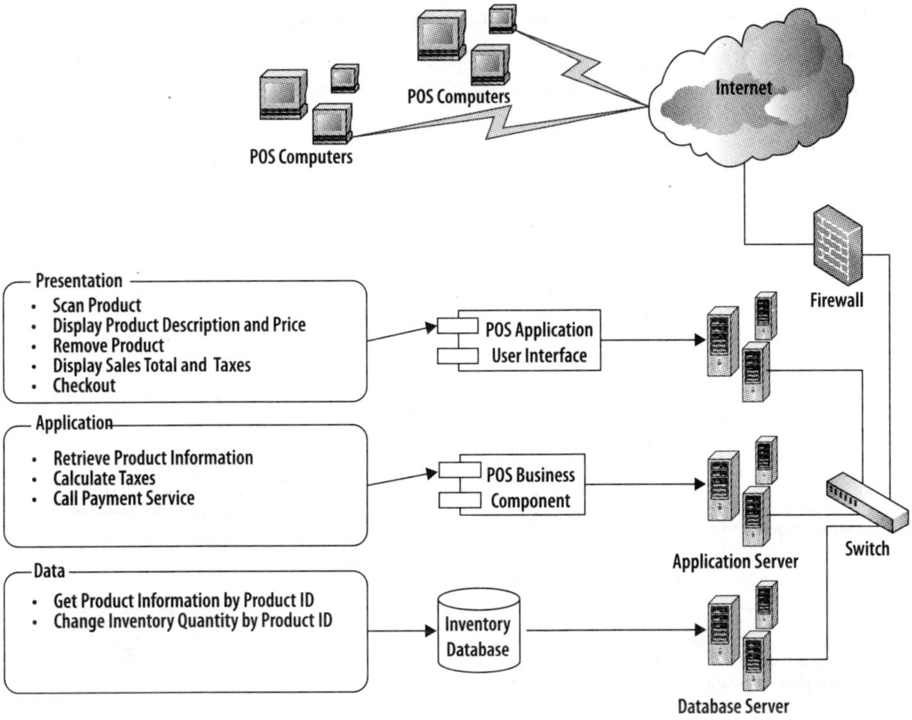

FIGURE 8.7 Representation of the POS application as a web application

On top of the existing infrastructure problems, the company decides to invest in a multimillion-dollar marketing campaign on TV during the upcoming Super Bowl. It is hard to estimate the number of users who will access the website during and after the massive TV campaign, but the site must stay online and accommodate for the increasing number of users.

Super Bowl

The Super Bowl, the annual championship game of the National Football League (NFL) in the United States, has been the most watched American television broadcast of the year. In 2013, the Super Bowl drew an audience of more than 111.3 million viewers.

This is the ultimate cloud application scenario. Reduce the number of servers on premises, and use automated scalability. Once again, the physical design of the once-simple POS application must change. For an example of this type of application, see Figure 8.8.

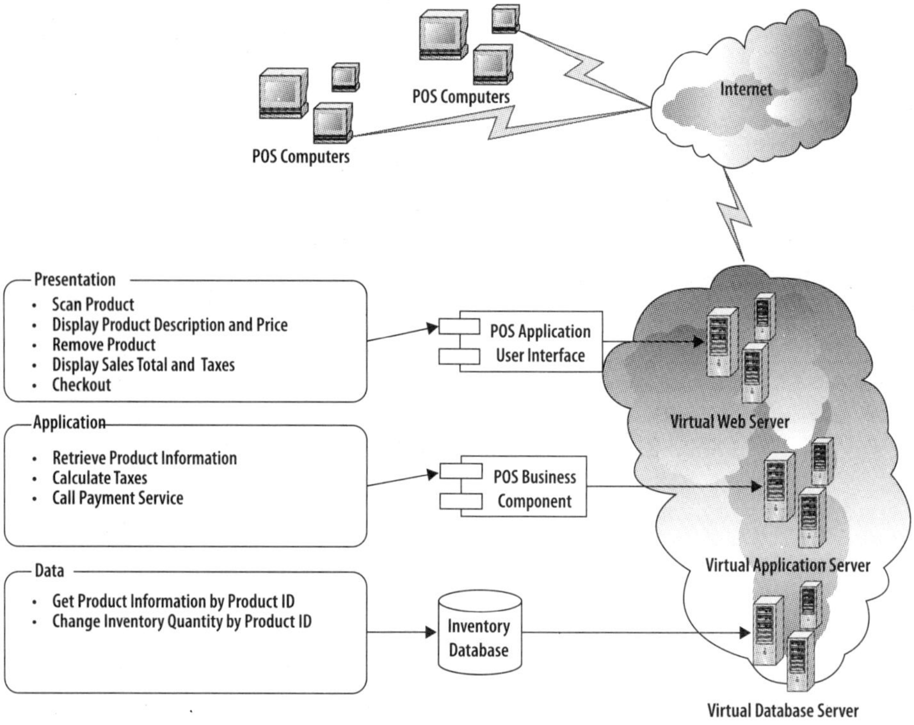

FIGURE 8.8 Representation of the POS application as a cloud application

Developing Cloud-Ready Applications

Not every application should be migrated to the cloud. It is important to identify which types of application will benefit from cloud computing and then ensure that those applications are designed to be cloud-ready.

Cloud-Ready Application Patterns

The main technical characteristic of a cloud-ready application is the need for elasticity. You should automatically scale out when usage is high to accommodate the required compute needs and scale down when compute needs decrease, cutting costs.

Based on elasticity, four main patterns can be easily recognized for cloud-ready applications, covered next.

Start Small, Grow Fast

This is the typical scenario for startup companies. Scalability is vital if the product goes viral, yet investment should be minimized at all costs. Relying on the popularity of an application is a gamble, and if no one adopts it, there is no need to spend thousands of dollars to keep servers running at all times. However, if it becomes the next Facebook and usage spreads exponentially, the infrastructure must be able to respond and scale up quickly. Figure 8.9 shows the relationship of resource consumption and time in a start small, grow fast design pattern.

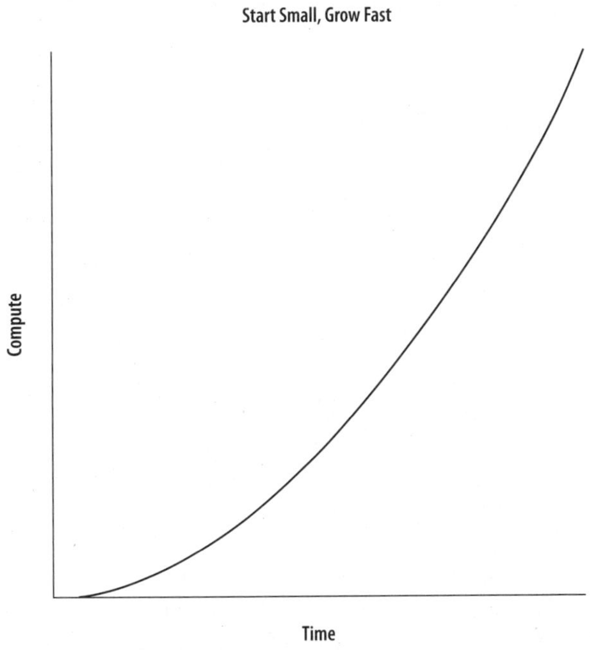

FIGURE 8.9 Start small, grow fast

Predictable Burst

Predictable bursts are well known to e-commerce applications. A new release of a product (think iPhone) or marketing campaign (Super Bowl) can cause an e-commerce application to suffer a burst that is both welcome and predictable.

This type of burst is often linked to a single event, and it is very possible that cloud computing may be used for just this one-time event. Figure 8.10 shows the relationship of resource consumption and time in a predictable burst design pattern.

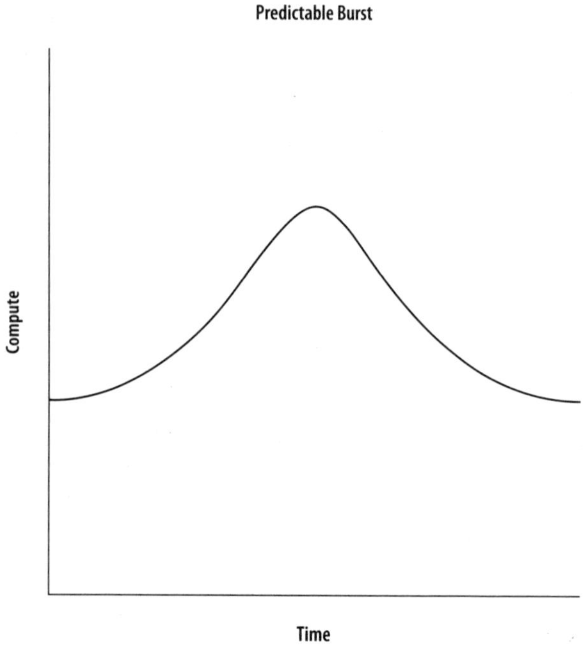

FIGURE 8.10 Predictable burst

Unpredictable Burst

This pattern is very similar to the predictable burst, but here there is no association of the burst to an event — or maybe not to an event that can be predicted, such as the September 11, 2001, terrorist attacks. After the attacks, news websites could not handle the amount of traffic being generated by user access. Some websites, such as CNN.com and MSNBC.com, removed their video, audio, and even photo feeds from their sites to ensure that their main pages could be loaded. Figure 8.11 shows the relationship of resource consumption and time in an unpredictable burst design pattern.

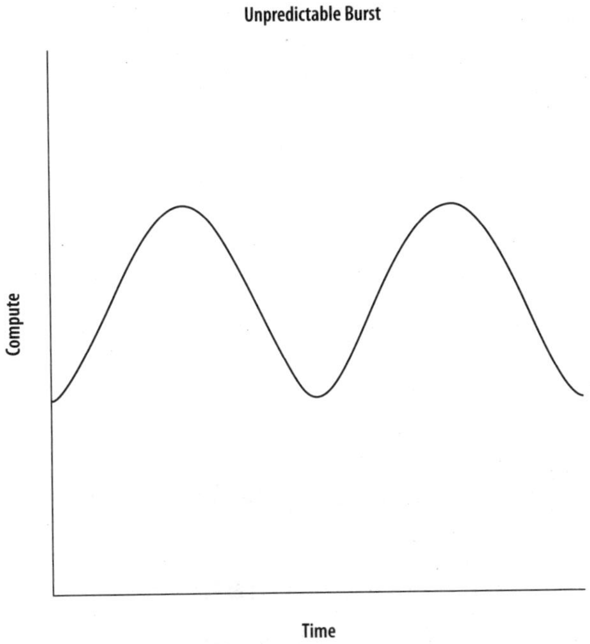

FIGURE 8.11 Unpredictable burst

Periodic Processing

Almost every single enterprise has one application that is heavily used during a specific period of time and then forgotten completely. They are a lot easier to spot at the government level, with applications such as tax processing and election voting, but also happen in private organizations for payroll processing and annual review, for example. The amount of compute time required for such applications in such a short period of time does not justify the investment on an infrastructure that will be left without use for long periods of time. Figure 8.12 shows the relationship of resource consumption and time in a periodic processing design pattern.

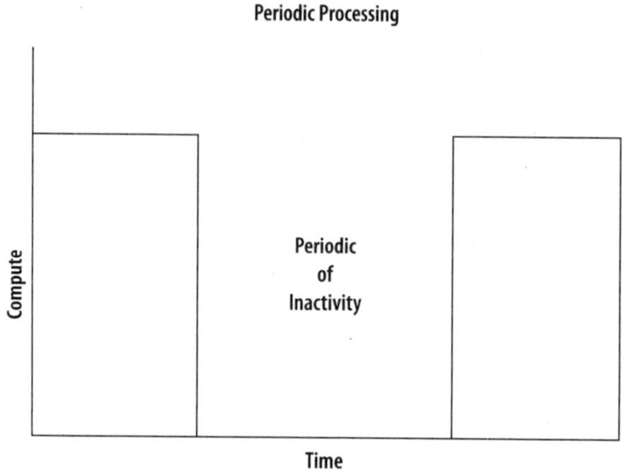

FIGURE 8.12 Periodic processing

Cloud-Ready Application Development

Cloud-ready applications can exist on a standard distributed environment but also take advantage of the benefits of cloud computing. When designing a cloud-ready application, developers must take into account two main factors:

Stateful vs. stateless applications Stateful applications require information about objects to be maintained between calls to a server. Because in a distributed environment, especially in a cloud environment, there is no guarantee that the same server will answer subsequent requests from a client, stateful objects should be avoided at all costs.

IaaS vs. PaaS There are no standards for PaaS-based applications. Each provider uses different APIs based on its platform. Choosing a specific provider might force a lock-in with a technology that cannot be migrated later to a different provider. Use IaaS unless you are comfortable with the technology used by a PaaS provider and you do not foresee a change in the technology used.

When deciding on an IaaS provider to use, it is important to evaluate their offerings based on the following factors:

Pricing plan Providers offer pay-as-you-go plans, monthly plans, yearly plans, or any combination of these. Try to estimate what your usage will be to identify the best pricing. Thoran Rodrigues published an article on TechReplubic early in 2012 showing that the monthly price for a 1 CPU, 2 GB RAM cloud server at that time varied anywhere from US$40 to US$270 for 720 hours (24 hours for 30 days in a month). His full study can be found at the following location:

www.techrepublic.com/blog/datacenter/11-cloud-iaas-providers-compared/5285

Service-level agreement (SLA) Providers guarantee an SLA of anywhere from 99.9 percent to 100 percent. Be aware of 100 percent SLAs and ensure that financial guarantees are in place if the provider is not able to deliver the SLA specified by contract.

Number of data centers The more the merrier. Smaller providers like ReliaCloud, GoGrid, and Bit Refinery have one or two data centers, while providers like Rackspace, Amazon, Terremark, and Go Daddy have more than five data centers spread all over the world. These numbers were accurate at the time this book went to press and may change with time.

Certifications Ensure that the provider has any certifications required for your application, such as Payment Card Industry Data Security Standard (PCI DSS) or Statement on Standards for Attestation Engagements No. 16 (SSAE 16) and Statement on Auditing Standards No. 70 (SAS 70).

Support Some providers have extensive support over the phone, while others only handle support tickets online and maybe be slow to respond. Make sure your enterprise's needs are met by the support offered by the chosen provider.

Monitoring Once again, the level of monitoring varies a lot by provider. Some providers do not have any built-in monitoring, requiring the installation of third-party tools and extra services, while others have integrated monitoring tools available at no extra cost.

Instance types Most providers have a set number of servers that can be used, with a specific number of CPUs, amount of memory, and operating system. Others have fully customizable instances.

Data transfer cost Most providers charge for outbound data transfer; some also charge for inbound data transfer.

Migrating Applications to the Cloud

Most candidates for cloud-based applications are already being used in the enterprise. Looking back at the cloud-based application patterns discussed earlier in this chapter and reflecting on the existing applications in the enterprise architecture of any organization will result in a list of several applications that are good candidates for cloud computing.

Once these applications are identified, it is necessary to decide how they can be migrated to the cloud. Some applications can be completely replaced by existing SaaS applications, others can be easily migrated to an IaaS provider, and a few can take advantage of existing PaaS offers. It is important to identify the type of service to use because it will affect how the application might need to change and associated costs for maintaining it once it's migrated. Table 8.1 describes the migration choices and their differences.

TABLE 8.1 Migration choices

Migration to	Pros	Cons
SaaS	Least cost Replaces current application with existing SaaS offering	Less flexibility for customization
PaaS	Lower cost than IaaS using comparable operating system and support No operating system maintenance	Provider technology lock-in Changes to existing application
IaaS	Minimal code change to application Use of familiar development technology	Operating system maintenance

Different IaaS and PaaS vendors provide guidance on migrating existing applications to their environment. Here are some of these guides:

- Windows Azure:

`www.microsoft.com/en-us/download/details.aspx?id=29252`

- Amazon EC2:

`aws.amazon.com/documentation/ec2/`

- Rackspace:

`rackspace.com/knowledge_center/article/rackspace-open-cloud-migration-considerations`

Preparing for Technical Challenges

As mentioned, not every application is fit to be a cloud application. Distributed applications that require automated scalability and high availability and are more CPU bound than I/O are the applications that can easily benefit from cloud computing. The basic rule of thumb is very simple: Applications that process large amounts of data and are I/O bound should remain on premises; those that require processing small amounts of data and are CPU bound can benefit from cloud computing.

The reason for the CPU-bound versus I/O-bound decision lies in one of the main technical challenges found with cloud-based applications: moving data over the Internet. Bandwidth can become very expensive when large amounts of data need to be transferred in and out of a cloud-based application. For example, Amazon charges US$0.12 per GB of data transferred out of its data centers. An application that generates 10 TB of data a day will cost US$1,200.00 a day just on data transfer. Not only is that a financial challenge, it is also a technical challenge to transfer that amount of data over the Internet in places where connectivity to the Internet may still rely on analog dial-up lines. The following list summarizes some of the challenges cloud-based applications face today:

Big data Big data applications are applications that generate several terabytes of data a day. For example, eBay generates over 150 TB of logging data every day. Moving this data out of a public cloud can cost hundreds of thousands of dollars a month.

Unstructured data Flat files tend to require a lot of processing for parsing data into a more manageable format and therefore consume compute resources that are costly. Structured tabular data should be used whenever possible.

Security Personally identifiable datasets and trade secrets require protection. A lot of organizations believe that data is more secure in their facilities than on the cloud. The reality is far from that. Sensitive data can be stored in the cloud if the necessary measures are taken. And it can be more secure than storing it locally. This is covered in more detail in Chapter 11, "Security in the Cloud."

Compliance Certain countries do not allow for personally identifiable data (PID) to cross geographical boundaries. This is a common issue in the European Union. Cloud providers duplicate data across their data centers, causing compliance issues for PID.

Learning curve Software architects and developers need to be trained in the development of cloud-based applications and may be required to learn proprietary APIs to create new applications in a PaaS environment.

Identifying and Mitigating Risks

Risk is defined in Information Technology Infrastructure Library (ITIL) 2011 as the possibility that an event will occur and affect the ability to achieve an objective. Every enterprise should follow a risk management process that includes at least the following steps:

Risk identification Anyone in the enterprise should be able to present a basic risk statement in the form of a simple sentence stating that IF a certain event occurs THEN a specific objective will not be met.

Risk classification The risk management team is responsible for looking at identified risks and classifying them by analyzing their root cause, possible outcome, and type of risk (availability, integrity, performance, security, etc.).

Risk prioritization Different risk management processes prioritize risks differently. The simplest way to prioritize risks is to attribute a value to the probability of the risk happening and the impact of the risk to the organization. Assigning numeric values to these factors will allow the multiplication of one by the other to come up with a risk factor. The higher the risk factor, the more dangerous the risk.

Risk planning Once risks have been prioritized, it is necessary to decide what to do about them. Some risks can be avoided by changing how the associated task is performed. Some can be mitigated by changing the scope of the task, and some might simply be accepted and a contingency plan created in case they occur.

Risk monitoring The top risks in the risk management list for the enterprise should be monitored closely, and triggers must be defined to allow the enterprise to identify when they happen and roll out its contingency plan if necessary. Once a risk becomes reality and is dealt with, it goes back into the classification step because its probability of happening again, and it impact, may change.

These are some of risks associated with cloud computing:

Vendor lock-in Many cloud service providers offer development tools that are proprietary and work exclusively within their cloud environment. The more applications an organization develops with these tools, the more the organization is locked in with the provider, making it harder to move providers if needed.

Security and compliance Some organizations are required to comply with regulations and laws such as the Sarbanes-Oxley Act of 2002, the USA Patriot Act, the Health Insurance Portability and Accountability Act of 1996 (HIPPA), and the EU Data Protection Directive, among others. Depending on the services offered by the cloud service provider, the organization might not be able to obtain the necessary security incidents logs required by these regulations.

IT organizational changes If cloud computing is highly adopted and in consequence the IT personnel is drastically reduced, morale among the remaining members of the IT staff could be at risk.

Cloud service provider maturity Most cloud service providers are young companies or represent a new line of business for well-established companies. The longevity and profitability of cloud offerings are yet unknown. At the time this book was published, several cloud service providers were restructuring their offerings because they were not profitable.

Reliability and performance issues Cloud service providers offer SLAs for the service they sell. However, they might be unable to meet these requirements if multiple tenants require scaling out at the same time.

High-profile targets Well-known cloud service providers are high-profile targets for cyber attacks. The more high-profile customers they have, the more likely it is for hackers to try to break into their systems.

Over-scalability due to DDOS Distributed denial of service (DDOS) attacks are hard to identify and can be seen as legitimate attempts to access an application. If there is no limit in the number of instances an application can bring online to allow for scaling out, a well-designed DDOS attack might inflict a costly penalty on the scalability of an application by spawning several virtual machines and increasing compute time.

For more information about cloud risks and security, please see Chapter 11.

The Essentials and Beyond

This chapter illustrates the different types of application that might benefit from a cloud computing environment and describes the process of developing cloud-ready applications. It also describes the technical and organizational challenges faced by companies that are "getting in the cloud" today.

Additional Exercises

- Identify a list of commonly used applications that are good candidates for becoming a cloud-based application.
- Identify who the customers for these applications would be, whether they are from within the organization or actual company customers.

To compare your answer to the author's, please visit `www.sybex.com/go/cloudessentials`.

Review Questions

1. What are the three basic logical tiers of a distributed application? (Choose three.)

   A. Presentation
   B. Application
   C. Network
   D. Data
   E. Internet

2. What is the main limitation of a desktop application?

   A. Lack of manageability
   B. Lack of reliability
   C. Lack of security
   D. Lack of scalability

3. True or false? All distributed applications are web applications.

   A. True
   B. False

4. What are the main advantages of using a web-based distributed application? (Choose two.)

   A. Availability
   B. Scalability
   C. Security
   D. Reliability

(Continues)

The Essentials and Beyond (Continued)

5. Which of the following is a design pattern of cloud-based applications?

   A. Predictable volume
   B. Constant processing
   C. Unpredictable burst
   D. Big data

6. What type of application design is preferable for a cloud-based application?

   A. A design that uses stateful objects
   B. A design that uses stateless objects
   C. A design that uses in-memory state management
   D. A design that uses client-based state management

7. Which of the following is an advantage of migrating an application to an IaaS provider?

   A. No operating system maintenance
   B. Lower cost than PaaS
   C. Minimal code change
   D. Lower cost than SaaS

8. Which of the following is not a risk associated with cloud-based applications?

   A. Vendor lock-in
   B. Reliability
   C. Security
   D. Lack of development tools

9. True or false? Big data applications are perfect candidates for cloud-based applications.

   A. True
   B. False

10. Which of the following risks leads to an increased cost for running a cloud-based application?

    A. Security compliance
    B. IT organizational changes
    C. DDOS attacks
    D. Cloud service maturity

CHAPTER 9

Cloud Service Rollout

Once the decision to go to the cloud has been made, it is time to roll out the solution. Cloud service rollout plans will vary depending on the type of cloud service used (SaaS, PaaS, or IaaS) and the vendor being used.

In this chapter, we will cover cloud service rollout and break it down into the following topics.

- **Identifying vendor roles and responsibilities**
- **Identifying organizational skill requirements**
- **Transitioning to live environments**
- **Preparing for incident management**

Identifying Vendor Roles and Responsibilities

Cloud service vendors have extended the commonly used terms of agreement generally seen in software licenses to the cloud environment. When buying a cloud service online, customers click through a predefined list of licensing options that defines the user agreement and can finish the purchase only if all terms are accepted. This trend is slowly losing power, especially when it comes to larger organizations. One of the key aspects of moving to the cloud is to provide access to data anytime, from anywhere, on any device, and to be able to dynamically scale. Larger organizations understand that terms must be present in the service agreement to guarantee the delivery of those services and define what happens when the terms are not met.

One of the most important factors when deciding which vendor to use as a cloud service vendor is the ability to negotiate the legal terms of the service agreement. The service agreement must include a list of roles and responsibilities for both the customer and the cloud service vendor. When negotiating these terms, the following topics must be covered:

Contract renewals Most vendors have an automatic contract renewal clause. Larger organizations tend to stay away from such contracts.

Contractual protection All cloud service vendors work with a service-level agreement (SLA) that describes the availability of their services and any penalties that might be accrued in case the SLA is not met. Beyond the SLA, organizations should also look for protection and assurance on data access and privacy controls, documented policies on data protection, security certifications, and application of rules and regulations.

Insurance Even with the SLA and other assurances in place, it is recommended to have insurance coverage in case there is an interruption to the organization's business due to the inability of the vendor to maintain the necessary service terms. Some vendors will have insurance in place; others will not.

Data loss Data loss can be caused by either the vendor or the customer, depending on where and how data is stored. Larger organizations tend to share the responsibility of data storage more often than smaller organizations. The ability to have an in-house copy of the data must be discussed and added to the service terms.

Data location Most vendors copy the data stored across data centers in different cities—and sometimes even countries. Different countries and unions have laws that govern where data can be stored for services provided within their geographical span. Organizations and vendors must be aware of the regional laws to which they must abide and ensure that they are dealt with in the terms of service.

Data ownership The data stored with the vendor should be the property of the customer, not the vendor. Depending on the type of data being stored, it is necessary to protect it from being shared across other organizations and used by the cloud service vendor themselves. Another important item to include in the terms of service is the process of handing the data over to another vendor, in case the customer decides to change vendors in the future. Of course, this is harder in SaaS scenarios because the vendor hosts the applications and their data format might not be the same as a different vendor for the same service.

The Cloud Industry Forum (CIF) developed a white paper in 2011 called "Cloud: Contracting Cloud Services, a Guide to Best Practice" that discusses the best practices for negotiating cloud services contracts; it is available at `cloudindustryforum.org`.

The Cloud Industry Forum

The Cloud Industry Forum was established in 2009 to provide transparency through certification to a Code of Practice for credible online vendors and to assist end users in determining core information necessary to enable them to adopt these services. As listed on `cloudindustryforum.org`, their goals are as follows:

- **To sustain a credible and certifiable Code of Practice for the cloud industry.**
- **To continually encourage the widespread adoption of the Code of Practice by industry players.**
- **To champion the widespread adoption and use of cloud services based upon the trust and assurance that can be achieved through the Code of Practice.**
- **To leverage the Code of Practice through international affiliations and partnerships.**
- **To support other appropriate cloud-based initiatives that complement the purpose of the Code of Practice (such as standards bodies seeking to provide common standards for security, privacy, and interoperability).**

The following are best practices for negotiating a cloud service contract:

Choice of law Organizations looking for a cheap or standard cloud service should contract under the vendor's standard terms, including the choice of law. Other organizations should raise the issue of contract negotiation with the vendor and choose the law based on their territory coverage.

Data control Vendors should disclose the list of data centers used to store the data, including backups. The SLA between the vendor and the organization must also specify how backups are handled.

Service availability Vendors should have documented management systems, processes, and resources. Organizations should be able to access the average available time provided by the vendors in the different layers of services offered. And consequences for not meeting the SLA must be clearly identified.

Liabilities and indemnities Organizations should specify the purpose of contracting with the vendor so that it is clear that, unless the service adequately addresses this purpose, it is pointless to enter into the contract. This purpose could be addressed in the SLA. A vendor may offer an introductory period to enable the customer to evaluate the service before a full-term contract comes into effect.

Deletion of Data Vendors should maintain a copy of the data being hosted even if the customer is not paying and not able to access the data. Before data is deleted, the customer must be notified with enough time to resolve any existing disputes.

It is also important to understand that the vendor responsibilities vary depending on the type of cloud service being offered. SaaS vendors will have more responsibility over the service provided than PaaS vendors, and PaaS vendors will have more responsibility than IaaS vendors. Figure 9.1 shows the vendor responsibility by type of cloud service.

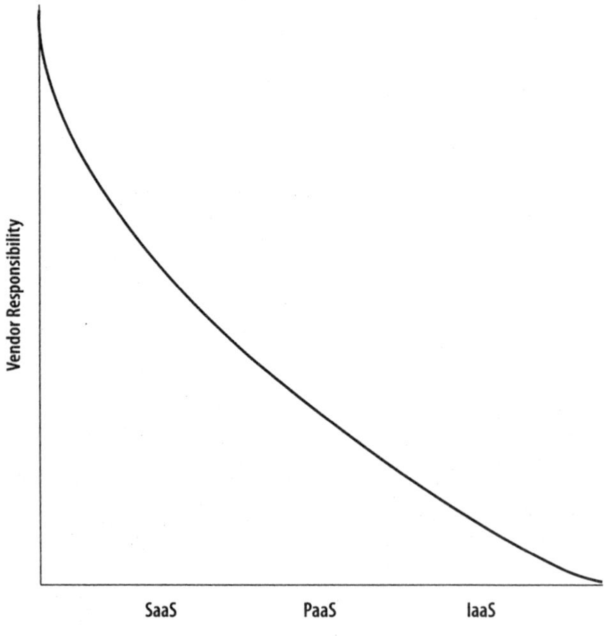

FIGURE 9.1 Vendor responsibility by type of service

Identifying Organizational Skill Requirements

Moving an application to the cloud usually means transferring technical responsibilities of all or part of the application to a vendor. Although technical skills are basically transferred to the vendor, they are still required at different levels depending on the type of cloud service acquired. The customer may not be required to maintain expertise on the technology used to create and maintain SaaS applications, but they must understand how the applications work and their limitations. Figure 9.2 shows the relationship between technical skills required by cloud service.

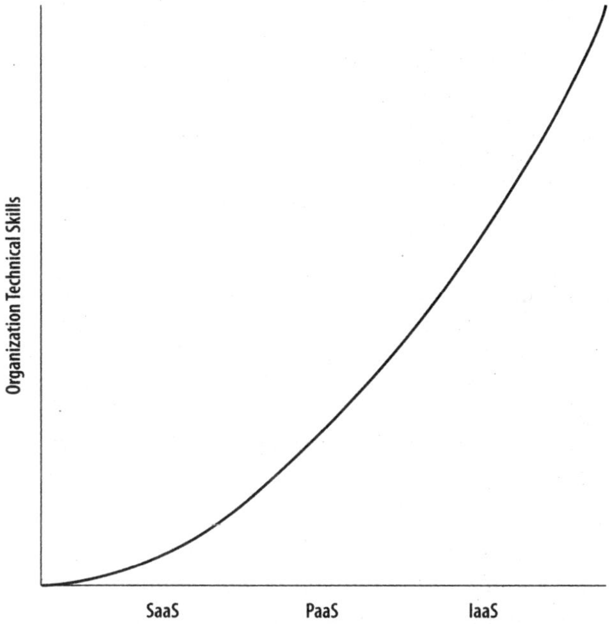

FIGURE 9.2 Technical skills vs. cloud service

Whether an organization is hosting their own cloud; contracting SaaS, PaaS, or IaaS from a vendor; or using a hybrid cloud implementation, more than just technical skills are required to ensure that cloud computing is being used in the best possible way to support the organization's needs:

Software as a Service (SaaS)

Looking back at the definition of Software as a Service, vendors provide access to a full application online to their customers. As an organization looking at contracting an SaaS vendor, the skills required to ensure the SaaS solution meets the needs of the organization are listed below.

Technical skills Since the vendor will maintain the application, technical skills acquired by the organization to maintain a SaaS solution are minimum. Depending on the scale of the project, organizations might have their service desk operators trained on basic usage of the SaaS solution. Yet, some SaaS providers will also provide help desk services, which should be integrated with the service desk maintained by the organization. This integration can be as simple as having service desk operators redirect calls to the vendor's support website or call center.

Even though most SaaS vendor provide monitoring tools and reports that show the overall availability of the service to their customers, it is important to monitor the SaaS solution from the organization's perspectives. This can be done by using synthetic transactions, as you will see in Chapter 10.

You must also consider whether the new SaaS solution is replacing an existing service. In this scenario, you might need to migrate the existing data from the existing solution to the SaaS solution.

In summary, the technical skills required by the organization to maintain a SaaS solution contracted from an outside vendor are:

- Basic skills on using the solution for service desk and training purposes.
- Monitoring skills to ensure the SaaS solution is accessible to end users.
- Migrate data from existing solutions to the SaaS solution.

Project management skills SaaS solutions are developed and maintained by a vendor. As an organization, when acquiring a SaaS solution, you must be able to manage the implementation of the solution within your organization. Users must be trained on the new solution, and if the solution replaces an existing system, data may have to be imported from the existing system into the new SaaS solution. From a project management perspective, you have to:

- Create and implement a training and adoption plan.
- Create and implement a data migration plan when required.
- Create and implement a pilot program.

Vendor management skills As discussed previously in this chapter, service terms and SLAs must be negotiated with cloud vendors carefully. Going to the cloud means trusting a vendor to keep applications running. Dealing with these vendors becomes a daily activity, and vendor management skills are one of the most important skills needed when dealing with cloud computing for SaaS, PaaS or IaaS solutions.

With SaaS solutions specifically, you must be able to negotiate the right SLA terms and ensure that the requirements for the solution are met by the vendor's service. Once the service is in production, you must be able to communicate efficiently with the vendor on SLA monitoring metrics, problem management, and change requests. In summary, these are the actions required for vendor management when acquiring a SaaS solution:

- Negotiate the SLA
- Communicate on SLA metrics
- Manage expectations for changes in the system

Data integration and analysis skills Data storage in a SaaS solution is done by the service provider. Due to that, if you are migrating an existing application to a SaaS application, you need to work with the vendor to plan how data will be migrated from the current on-premises solution to the new SaaS solution.

Business and financial skills The organization must be able to make a case for cloud computing and show the return on investment (ROI). It is necessary to have metrics in place that can be used to tell if the business performance being met by an application matches the cost of keeping it in the cloud.

Security and compliance management skills Organizations are regulated differently based on their type, type of data handled, and location. An overarching understanding of these many regulations, such as Sarbanes-Oxley (SOX) and Health Insurance Portability and Accountability Act (HIPAA), becomes extremely important when hosting data in the cloud.

Platform as a Service (PaaS)

Looking back at the definition of Platform as a Service, vendors provide access to a set of Application Programming Interfaces (APIs) and the necessary infrastructure to host virtual machines that run a set of pre-defined operating systems. As an organization looking at contracting a PaaS vendor, the skills required to ensure the PaaS solution meets the needs of the organization are listed below.

Technical skills Since the vendor will maintain the operating system for the virtual machines, technical skills acquired by the organization to maintain a PaaS solution are directly related to the application being developed. By building on top of the skills required to maintain a SaaS solution, when migrating to a PaaS solution organizations need to ensure their developers are well trained on the APIs being offered by the PaaS vendor.

In summary, the technical skills required by organization to maintain a PaaS solution contracted from an outside vendor are:

- Basic skills on using the solution for service desk and training purposes.
- Monitoring skills to ensure the PaaS solution is accessible to end users.
- Migrate data from existing solutions to the PaaS solution.
- Development skills on the APIs provided by the PaaS vendor.

Project management skills PaaS solutions are developed and maintained by the organization, with the exception of the operating system running on the virtual machines, which is maintained by the vendor. As an organization, when acquiring a PaaS solution, you must be able to manage the implementation of the solution within your organization. Users must be trained on the new solution, and if the solution replaces an existing system, data may have to be imported from the existing system into the new PaaS solution. From a project management perspective, you have to:

- Create and implement a training and adoption plan
- Create and implement a development plan
- Create and implement a data migration plan when required
- Create and implement a pilot program

Infrastructure as a Service (IaaS)

Looking back at the definition of Infrastructure as a Service, vendors provide the hardware and connectivity necessary to maintain applications hosted on virtual machines. As an organization looking at contracting an IaaS vendor, the skills required to ensure the IaaS solution meets the needs of the organization are listed below.

Technical skills Since the vendor will only maintain infrastructure necessary to host the virtual machines in an IaaS solution, technical skills acquired by the organization to maintain an IaaS solution includes all the skills previously discussed in the PaaS section, along with the skills necessary for operating system deployment, and maintenance.

In summary, the technical skills required by organization to maintain an IaaS solution contracted from an outside vendor are:

- Basic skills on using the solution for service desk and training purposes.
- Monitoring skills to ensure the IaaS solution is accessible to end users.
- Data migration from existing solutions to the IaaS solution.
- Development skills on the APIs chosen by the organization.
- Deployment skills on the operating system, or systems, chosen by the organization.
- Patch management skills on the operating system, or systems, chosen by the organization.

Project management skills IaaS solutions are developed and maintained by the organization. As an organization, when acquiring a IaaS solution, you must be able to manage the implementation of the solution within your organization. Users must be trained on the new solution, and if the solution replaces an existing system, data may have to be imported from the existing system into the new IaaS solution. From a project management perspective, you have to:

- Create and implement a training and adoption plan
- Create and implement a virtual machine deployment plan
- Create and implement an operating system patching plan
- Create and implement a development plan
- Create and implement a data migration plan when required
- Create and implement a pilot program

Transitioning to Live Environments

The transitioning of a cloud-based application from a test environment to a live environment varies depending on the type of cloud service being used. SaaS applications often are the easiest ones to deal with because they are mostly owned by the vendor and the switch from test to live does not require any changes by the customer.

PaaS vendors like Microsoft and Salesforce.com provide a test environment in which virtual machines can be executed to run a cloud-based solution before moving into full production. These vendors often provide the capability needed to copy the test environment settings, including virtual machines, virtual switches, and applications to a live environment.

IaaS vendors and PaaS vendors work in a similar way. However, IaaS vendors might not provide any tools for migration, leaving it up to the customer to create a new live environment based on an existing test environment. It is necessary to check with the vendor to understand what kind of migration support is offered by its specific platforms.

Hybrid scenarios, where the organization has a private cloud and a public cloud, deal with migration to a live environment in different ways. Once again, the choice of technology will dictate how the transition will occur. Organizations using Microsoft System Center and Azure can take advantage of AppController, an application used to manage and deploy services across private and public clouds based on System Center and Azure.

Independent of technology and type of cloud services being used, the following considerations must always be taken into account when transitioning to a live environment:

Internet bandwidth Applications that were once accessed in the local network are now hosted in a public cloud, accessed over the Internet. It is necessary to ensure that the organization has enough bandwidth to guarantee user access to the applications. Some organizations consider changing Internet service providers to be on the same network as the vendor used to host their cloud services, decreasing the number of hops between the organization and the vendor.

Prioritizing applications Some routers and firewalls can use technologies—such as Wide Area Application Services (WAAS) from Cisco—that allow rules to be created to prioritize bandwidth usage based on the application being accessed.

WAN design Smaller offices that are connected via WAN links to a central office and access the Internet from the central office may work better with a direct connection to the Internet. Depending on cost analysis, the WAN design of an organization might have to change to accommodate the traffic going over the Internet.

Preparing for Incident Management

The Information Technology Infrastructure Library (ITIL) defines *incident* as "Any event which is not part of the standard operation of a service and which causes, or may cause, an interruption to or a reduction in, the quality of that service." The stated ITIL objective when dealing with incidents is to "restore normal operations as quickly as possible with the least possible impact on either the business or the user, at a cost-effective price."

Incident management is a core process of every organization that relies on IT services to maintain its business. This process is owned and operated by the Service Desk function in ITIL. No matter how complex an organization's enterprise architecture is, all incident management processes can be simplified, as displayed in Figure 9.3.

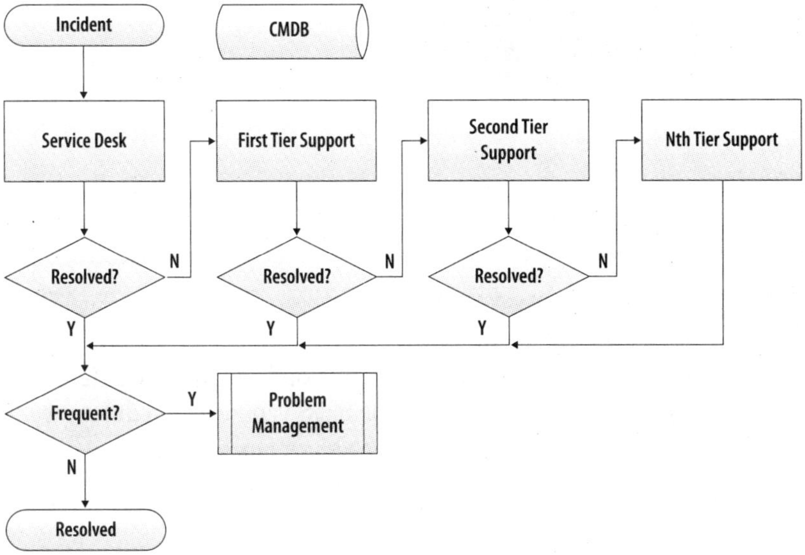

FIGURE 9.3 Incident management process

There are dozens of applications that can be used to implement the simplified incident management process shown in Figure 9.3. However, when you're moving applications to the cloud, incident management becomes a lot more complex. This complexity comes about due to several factors:

Different incident management processes and software Each cloud vendor might have its own process for incident management and use different systems to track incidents. Organizations must consider whether or not their incident management software must interoperate with the incident management system used by the vendor.

Lack of transparency Not only may the process and software used for incident management be different for each vendor, most organizations are not privy to the details of how incident management works for vendors, creating a black box.

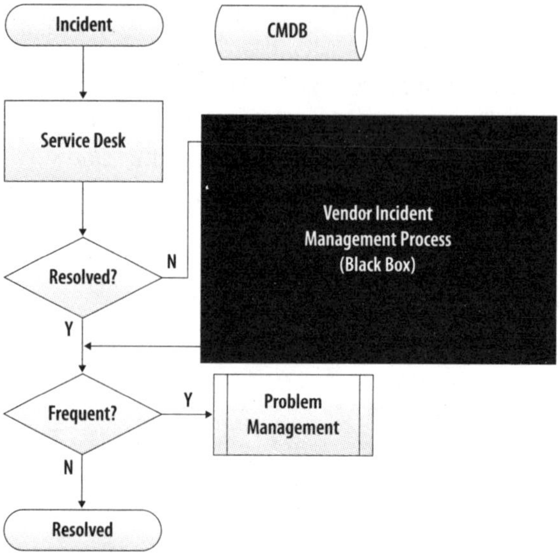

FIGURE 9.4 Incident management process black box

Multiple vendors Most organizations use different cloud vendors for different services. It is very common to use more than one SaaS vendor and a different vendor for PaaS or IaaS. This further escalates the black box issue because each vendor might have its own process, as shown in Figure 9.5.

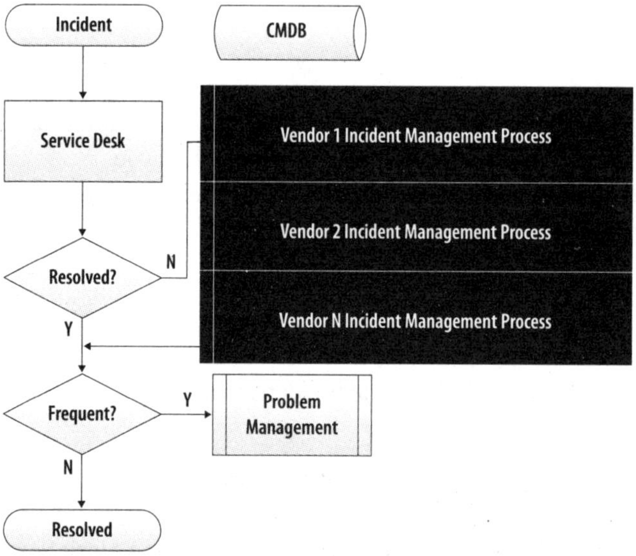

FIGURE 9.5 Incident management process black box

To better prepare for incident management in a cloud environment using different vendors, it is important to define clearly the service description, service-level agreement (SLA), and support agreement maintained with each vendor.

The service description must be detailed and specify the service being provided by the vendor in clear and concise language to ensure that both the organization and the vendor understand what is being provided.

The service-level agreement must specify the availability of the service being contracted in the service description and account for penalties if the SLA is not met as well as contain all assurances needed by the customer as discussed earlier in this chapter.

The support agreement must specify who is responsible for each line of support and how data is to be integrated between the disparate systems.

The organization and each individual vendor agrees upon each of these elements. It is important for the organization to integrate the processes provided by each vendor with its internal incident management process to allow better control of incident management as a whole.

The Essentials and Beyond

This chapter illustrates the roles of vendors and organizations on the rollout of a cloud-based solution, whether the solution is SaaS, PaaS, or IaaS. It also describes the challenges found with incident management processes when deploying solution hosted by a vendor.

Additional Exercises

- Identify an application that can be migrated from on-premises to a SaaS solution. Discuss the challenges an organization would face to execute the migration, and the skills necessary to make the transition.
- Identify an application that can be migrated from on-premises to an IaaS solution. Discuss the challenges an organization would face to execute the migration, and the skills necessary to make the transition.

To compare your answer to the author's, please visit www.sybex.com/go/cloudessentials.

Review Questions

1. What does a service-level agreement guarantee?

   A. Service availability

   B. Service security

   C. Service interoperability

   D. Service support

(Continues)

The Essentials and Beyond *(Continued)*

2. Which of the following are important factors that must be negotiated with a SaaS vendor? (Choose all that apply.)

   A. Contract renewals
   B. Data ownership
   C. Programming language
   D. Server operating system

3. Which is the following services requires a broader capacity of technical skills owned by the organization contracting a cloud service vendor?

   A. SaaS
   B. PaaS
   C. IaaS

4. Which of the following organizational skills are important skills to have when moving applications to the cloud? (Choose all that apply.)

   A. Vendor management
   B. Desktop security
   C. Data integration
   D. Customer management

5. What application can be used to move a service from an on-premises test environment to the public cloud in a hybrid cloud environment using Microsoft System Center and Azure?

   A. Operations Manager
   B. Configuration Manager
   C. AppController
   D. Virtual Machine Manager

6. Which of the following are important factors to consider when transitioning from an on-premises application to an SaaS application? (Choose all that apply.)

   A. Internet bandwidth
   B. Processor architecture
   C. WAN design
   D. Programming language

7. Which of the following elements must be defined to ensure that an organization is well prepared for incident management for cloud-based services? (Choose all that apply.)

   A. Service description
   B. Service-level agreement
   C. Support agreement
   D. Contract renewal agreement

(Continues)

THE ESSENTIALS AND BEYOND *(Continued)*

8. True or false? An organization contracting a vendor to provide a SaaS application must have the necessary technical skills to maintain and operate the application being hosted on the cloud.

   A. True B. False

9. True or false? An organization contracting a vendor to provide IaaS on a public cloud is responsible for maintaining the operating system used by the virtual machines hosted in the IaaS environment.

   A. True B. False

10. True or false? An organization contracting a vendor to provide PaaS on a public cloud is responsible for deciding what programming language to use when developing cloud-based applications.

    A. True B. False

CHAPTER 10

Cloud Service-Level Management

Service-level management processes are used to provide a framework that allows you to define services, agree upon the necessary service level required to support business processes, develop the service-level agreements (SLAs) and operational-level agreements (OLAs) to satisfy these requirements, and specify the costs of services.

In this chapter we will cover the different components of the Information Technology Infrastructure Library, or ITIL, and dive into one of these components, Service Level Management, to see how it can be applied to cloud computing.

- **Understanding ITIL service management**
- **Applying ITIL to cloud computing**
- **Developing and utilizing performance metrics**
- **Implementing continual service improvement**

Understanding ITIL Service Management

The Information Technology Infrastructure Library (ITIL) is a technology agnostic, vendor-neutral framework of structured, scalable, best practice processes that organizations can adopt and adapt to fit their own environments. It was created by the Central Computer and Telecommunications Agency (CCTA) of the UK government in the '80s in an attempt to better manage IT processes across government agencies by using proven best practices used by large organizations across the globe. It is, indeed, a library, initially comprising over 30 books. Its latest release, from 2011, groups the body of knowledge into five volumes, as seen in Figure 10.1.

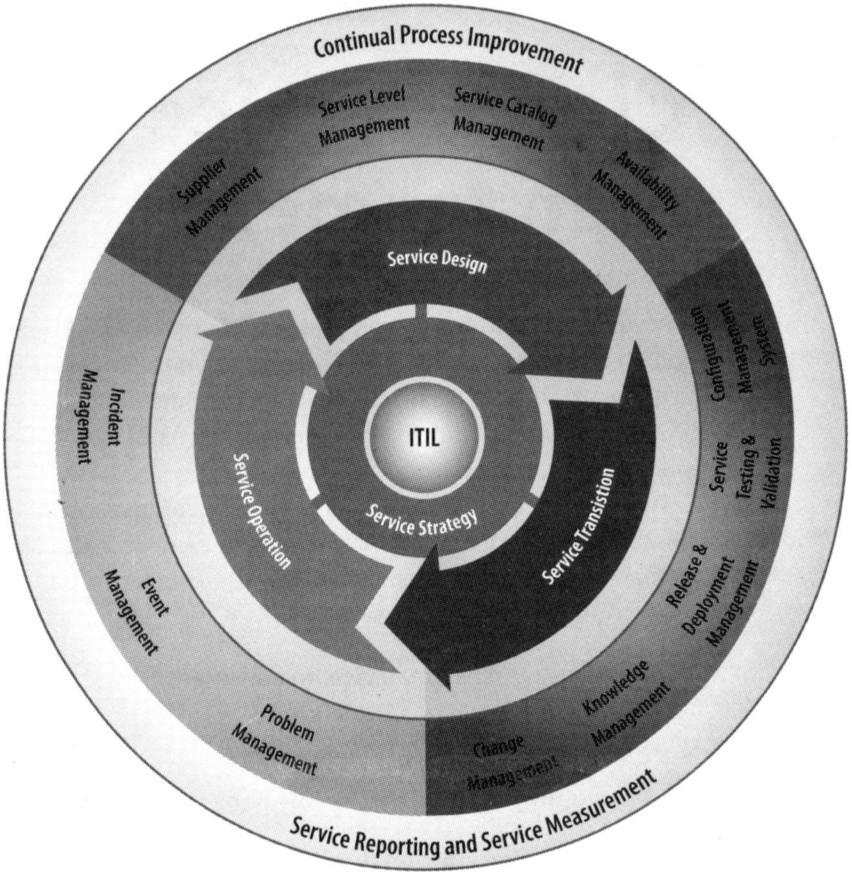

FIGURE 10.1 ITIL life cycle

ITIL Overview

The latest version of ITIL, ITIL 2011, provides a holistic perspective on the life cycle of services, encompassing the whole IT organization and every supporting component used to deliver services to the organization. There are 26 different processes identified in ITIL 2011, grouped into five distinguished volumes:

- Service Strategy
- Service Design
- Service Transition
- Service Operation
- Continual Process Improvement

Service Strategy

The ITIL Service Strategy volume provides guidance on classification of service provider investments in services. The most important topics covered in service strategy are service value definition, service assets, market analysis, business case development, and service provider types. The following processes are covered in Service Strategy:

- Strategy management
- Demand management
- Service portfolio management
- Financial management
- Business relationship management

Service Design

ITIL Service Design provides guidance on the design of IT services, processes, and service management. Design in ITIL focuses more specifically on services provided to the organization instead of individual technologies. The following processes are covered in Service Design:

- Design coordination
- Service management catalog
- Service level management
- Availability management
- Capacity management
- IT service continuity management
- Information security management
- Supplier management

Figure 10.2 shows the different processes covered by ITIL Service Design.

Service Transition

ITIL Service Transition provides guidance on the deployment of services required by an organization into a production environment. The following processes are covered in Service Transition:

- Transition planning and support
- Change management

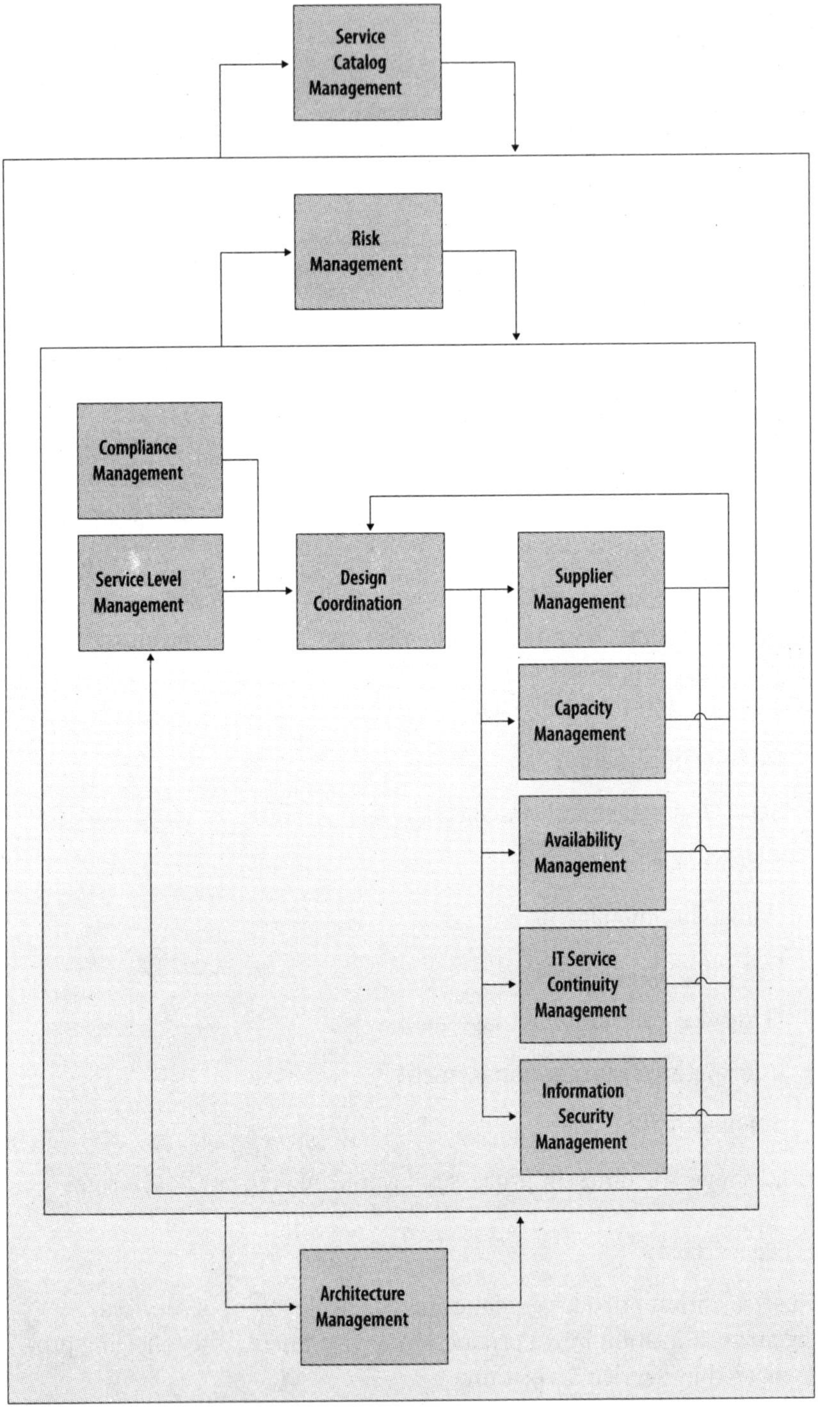

FIGURE 10.2 ITIL Service Design processes

- Service asset and configuration management
- Release and deployment management
- Service validation and testing
- Change evaluation
- Knowledge management

Figure 10.3 shows the different processes covered by ITIL Service Transition.

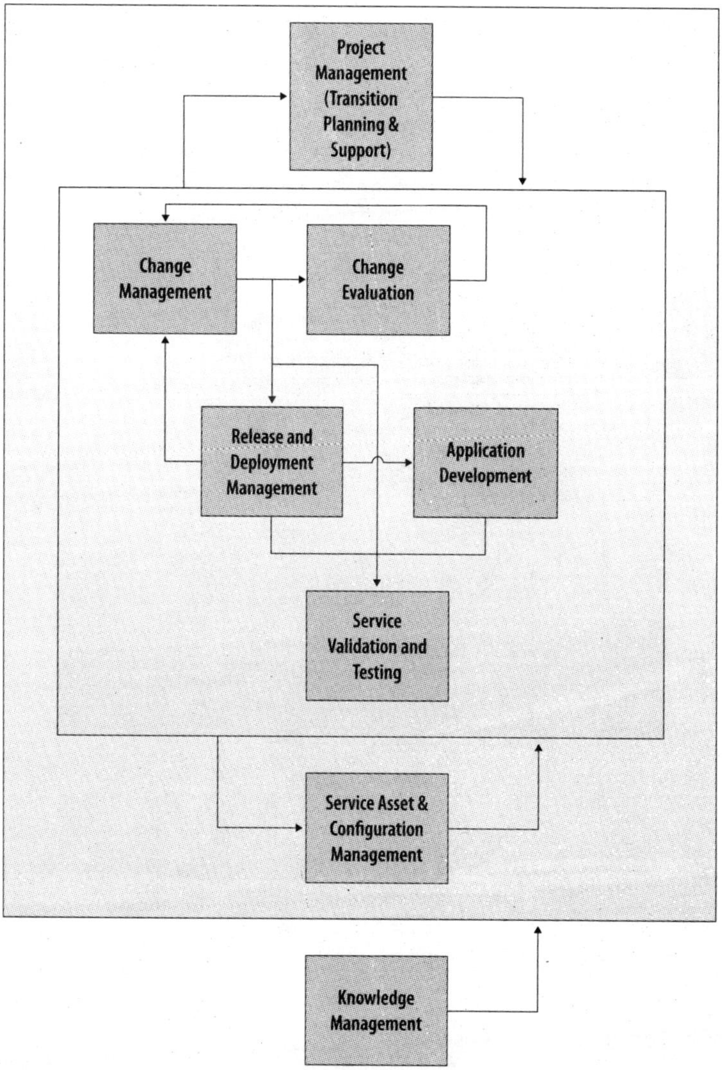

FIGURE 10.3 ITIL Service Transition processes

Service Operation

ITIL Service Operation provides guidance on achieving the delivery of agreed levels of service to end users and the organization. The following processes are covered in Service Operation:

- Event management
- Incident management
- Problem management
- Request fulfillment
- Access management

Figure 10.4 shows the different processes covered by ITIL Service Operation.

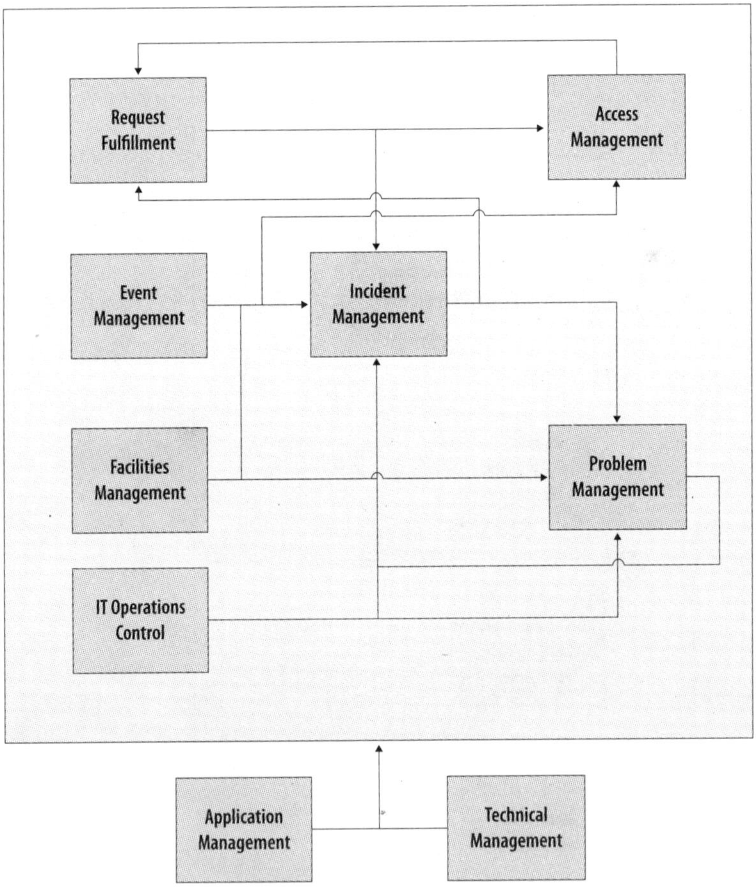

FIGURE 10.4 ITIL Service Operation processes

Continual Process Improvement

ITIL Continual Process Improvement provides guidance on aligning and realigning IT services to changing business needs by identifying and implementing improvements to the IT services used to support the business. Continual Process Improvement needs to be planned and scheduled as a process with well-defined activities, inputs, outputs, and roles.

Figure 10.5 shows the ITIL Continual Process Improvement processes.

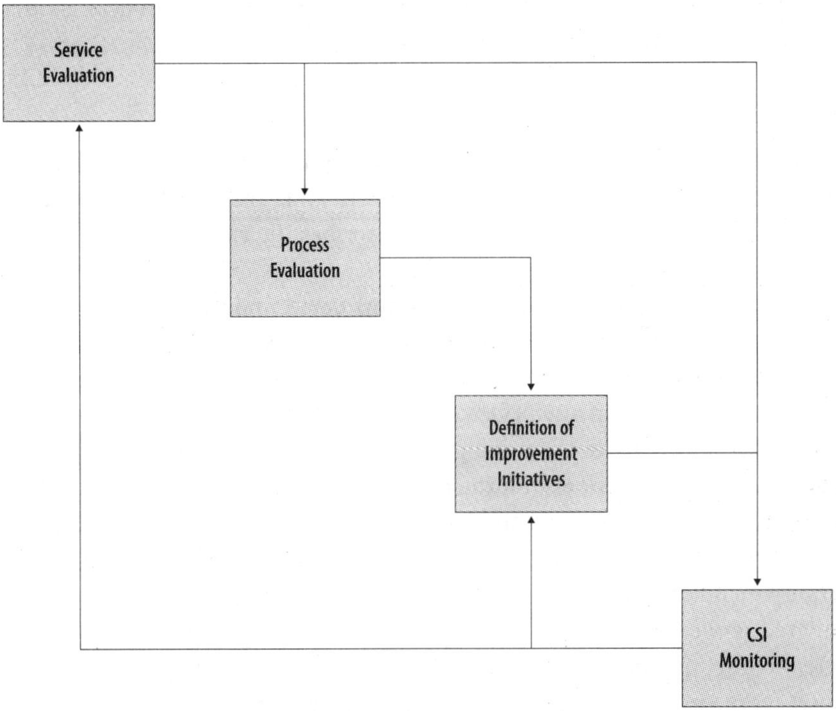

FIGURE 10.5 ITIL Continual Process Improvement processes

Applying ITIL to Cloud Computing

The objective of this book is not to cover ITIL in its entirety because, as you have seen, ITIL is a full library with five different volumes grouping several processes. There are several books in the market today covering ITIL and its many processes and functions. What you will learn here, however, is how to apply some of the concepts prescribed in ITIL to cloud computing.

Planning the Service Strategy

You now know that service strategy is composed of five individual processes: strategy management, demand management, service portfolio management, financial management, and business relationship management.

Strategy Management

The strategy management process is at the center of the ITIL Service Strategy, holding all other processes together. The strategy management plan details how to turn ideas into useful, cost-effective services.

Demand Management

A demand management process is used to understand, anticipate, and influence customer demand for services. Customers come to an IT organization to request services that add value to the business. ITIL describes the value of a service in terms of utility and warranty.

Utility includes functionality, increased performance, and the removal of constraints. For instance, a cloud-based accounting service may provide the same functionality as an accounting service hosted on premises, but it may also allow the user to work from any device connected to the Internet, removing the constraint of connectivity to the corporate network and increasing performance by allowing the user to work even if the corporate network is unavailable. In this scenario, the cloud-based service provides more value, or at least more utility, than the same service hosted on premises.

Warranty includes availability, capacity, continuity, and security of a service. Cloud-based services tend to have a better availability because they are not restricted to a set of hardware; better capacity because they can be scaled out by adding more virtual machines; better continuity because if a data center is down, the services can be provided from a different data center; and the same degree of security as an on-premises service, given the right security measures.

Demand managers must be able to analyze customer requests, capacity data, and business trends to determine what new services are needed by the business. One of the inputs for this analysis is the actual service portfolio maintained by the organization.

Service Portfolio Management

In real life, organizations manage a large array of services that might be composed of traditional multitiered applications and cloud-based services hosted on a private cloud, a public cloud, or a hybrid cloud. A well-defined portfolio management process will allow you to keep track of the existing services and relate events and performance monitoring back to each service in your configuration management database (CMDB).

Configuration Management Database (CMDB)

A configuration management database, or CMDB, is a centralized database that contains information about the entire enterprise architecture, including its services, hardware, settings, performance data, users, and processes. Each entry in a CMDB is referred to as a configuration item, or CI.

One of the biggest challenges of maintaining a CMDB for cloud-based services is that hardware is virtualized and to a certain extent not important. After all, if a virtual machine fails, there is another VM in place to take its load, and you can even automatically create a brand-new VM to take its place. We will discuss this shift of paradigm better later on in this chapter, in the section "Developing and Utilizing Performance Metrics."

Service portfolio management must include financial data related to the services maintained by the IT organization.

Financial Management

Financial management processes should be in place to manage service costs and report them back to the organization along with service value information that can be used to track the return on investment (ROI) of the service.

In a cloud computing environment, the financial analysis and reporting process can be used to charge the organization back for time used by cloud services.

Business Relationship Management

The business relationship management processes are put in place to manage the relationship between the IT organization and the customer by monitoring customer complaints, conducting customer satisfaction surveys, identifying service requirements, and signing up customers to services.

By providing these processes, an IT organization can effectively measure the efficiency of services migrated to the cloud and compare them to the traditional services they replaced. This monitoring is also a key input into Continual Process Improvement.

Planning a Service Desk Operation

In ITIL, the service desk is defined as the single point of contact to meet the communication needs of users and the IT organization. It serves as an interface between the service providers and users or customers.

Users and Customers

In ITIL, users are the actual people who consume a service to execute their day-to-day tasks, whereas customers are those paying for the service provided to the users. In a lot of cases, a customer can also be a user.

When considering providing cloud-based service to users, you must define how the service desk is going to handle requests and incidents for the cloud-based services. In a SaaS scenario, for instance, the vendor contracted to provide the SaaS service usually handles incidents and requests for change. However, you do not want to expose the users to two different service desks. Instead, your service desk must be prepared to handle the calls and act as an interface between the SaaS provider and the user.

Similar action must be taken in relation to PaaS and IaaS services. In this case, the service desk must be able to identify that the service the user is calling about is a cloud service, and if the incident is related to availability issues, the service desk must be able to identify who to contact, problem management staff at the organization, or vendor support. Once again, the service desk is the interface between the user and the actual support.

In any case, the user should not have to worry, or even know, about how the service is hosted. If they have an issue to be dealt with, the service desk is the place to go to.

To plan for a service desk that includes managing requests and incidents for cloud-based services, consider the following:

- Document each service available to users in the service portfolio.
- For each service, identify the type of application (traditional vs. cloud based) and hosting environment (on premises, data center, or hybrid).
- For each service, identify the vendor responsible for handling requests.

Developing and Utilizing Performance Metrics

Maintaining a cloud operation requires a different set of performance metrics depending on whether you are the cloud provider, cloud consumer, or both.

Running a Cloud Service Operation

With the change of paradigm to cloud computing, we see several software companies delivering complete cloud operations management suites. BMC, VMware, and Microsoft currently have their own systems to manage the end-to-end delivery of cloud services from both a private and a public cloud perspective. Independent of the system you use, you need to understand how to monitor cloud services and what performance metrics to look for.

We have discussed service-level agreements before, and you should be familiar with the idea of a five 9s availability (or four 9s, three 9s, etc.). The way we measure availability for traditional computing environments is very straightforward. We look at each component of a service and determine its availability. For instance, a service might be composed of a front-end web server and a backend database server. By looking at the mean time between failures (MTBF) of each component on each server, you can determine the overall availability of the system. You also need to take into account power management and network devices. But let's make it easy for now. Imagine that after looking at each individual server you conclude that the availability of the web server is 99.9 percent and the availability of the database server is also 99.9%. The overall availability of the service would be 99.9% × 99.9%, which is 99.8%. That goes to show how hard it is to obtain a five 9s availability.

Taking the same example, we can cluster the database server, increasing the availability to 99.999%, and add another server to the front end in load balancing, increasing the availability of the front end to 99.999%. Once again, the overall availability would be 99.998%. Still *not* five 9s!

All these examples are taking into account traditional applications, not cloud computing. By switching to a cloud computing environment and providing highly available virtual machines, these numbers can increase substantially. But it is one thing to estimate availability and a completely different beast to monitor and maintain it. That is where some of the operations management systems available in the market today come into place.

General Performance Metrics

Before you can monitor a cloud environment, you need to know what metrics must be used. The metrics used depend directly on the type of cloud services being provided or consumed. For instance, if you are an IaaS provider, you will be interested in monitoring your virtualization infrastructure and metering the VMs used by your customer for billing purposes. If you are a PaaS provider, you will monitor not only your virtualization infrastructure but also the operating system on each individual VM provided to your customers, along with metering on the same VMs for billing purposes. For a better understanding of some of the elements monitored for each type of service, refer to Table 10.1.

TABLE 10.1 Elements monitored for specific types of services

Service	Role	Elements Monitored
IaaS	Provider	Virtualization hosts Network fabric Storage fabric Consumer VMs (if required by SLA) Consumer VM metering (for billing purposes)
	Consumer	Operating system for VMs Services on VMs Connectivity to services
PaaS	Provider	Virtualization hosts Network fabric Storage fabric Operating system on consumer VMs Platform components (application servers, database servers)
	Consumer	Services on VMs Connectivity to services

SaaS	Provider	Virtualization hosts
		Network fabric
		Storage fabric
		Operating system for consumer VMs
		Platform components (application servers, database servers)
		Operating system on VMs
		Services on VMs
	Consumer	Connectivity to services

Let's concentrate on the consumer side of the business and move from SaaS up to IaaS.

Software as a Service (SaaS) Performance Metrics

When monitoring a SaaS application as a consumer, you focus on two simple questions:

- Can I access the service?
- Does the service perform as expected?

These questions can be answered by using a synthetic transaction. Synthetic transactions are prerecorded actions taken on a service that mimic a user accessing the service and executing regular tasks. They are executed from locations where a user would normally connect to the service. That way, you are able to tell if the service is available to the user at a given facility and, if it's available, how long it takes to execute predefined actions.

For instance, imagine that you contracted a SaaS vendor to provide access to a service that allows invoicing of customers. Your company has offices in New York and Miami. You want to ensure that users are able to access the service from both offices and place an order within 1 minute. To monitor that, you can create a synthetic transaction by recording an end user accessing the service and creating a mock order, then deleting it. Your synthetic transaction can be then configured to be executed from a machine in each office, which we refer to as a watcher node. The watcher node collects performance data from the calls made to the service and reports that data back to an operations management application. This process can be scheduled to occur every few hours, minutes, or seconds. And the operations management application can have rules defined to raise an alert if your metrics are not met and calculate the overall availability of the service by taking into account data from both New York and Miami.

In this scenario, the performance metrics were overall availability of the service from Miami and New York (as a percentage of time) and time to create an order (in seconds).

Platform as a Service (PaaS) Performance Metrics

PaaS performance metrics include connectivity to services (as discussed in the preceding section, on SaaS performance metrics) along with service monitoring for the services being provided by the VMs. Depending on how the PaaS provider works, VMs can be automatically spawned in case one fails or in case your application sends a request to the PaaS platform. For instance, you can create a rule that says a new VM must be spawned in the front-end farm for every 1,000 users concurrently connected to the service.

However, this type of monitoring does not take into account the qualitative aspects of these VMs. The VMs are running one or more services that you designed and developed. You must monitor those services to ensure that they are working correctly and, if they are not, restart them or kill the VM and spawn a new one.

Monitoring the availability of a service on a given operating system is usually a very straightforward task that all operations management applications are able to handle. If your solution is composed of multiple services, the operations management application should be able to combine these services into a distributed application to calculate the overall availability of the service and ensure that it complies with the SLA or OLA being provided.

The biggest problem occurs when your service contains custom code you built. In this scenario, if you want to monitor performance for the service, you might have to rely on calls to a monitoring API provided by the PaaS provider. Check with your provider to understand how you can monitor services you develop in its platform.

If you consider just individual services on VMs being hosted by your PaaS provider, you should be able to monitor the availability of those services over a period of time and configure your operations management application to calculate the overall availability of the service as a distributed application. Operations management applications can also be used to execute tasks in case a certain condition is met. For instance, if you are monitoring a front-end web server, you can create a rule to restart the web server service once the service stops, and if it stops again, you can execute a task to spawn a new VM and shut down the current one.

In this scenario, your performance metrics, beyond service availability to users, are the availability of each service hosted by your VMs over time.

Infrastructure as a Service (IaaS) Performance Metrics

In an IaaS consumer environment, you must monitor all the metrics established for PaaS and the operating system on the virtual machines. Since you are responsible for the OS, you must maintain the VM OS by monitoring and applying updates and monitor the necessary services on the VMs to ensure that they are operational. At this level, you are responsible for monitoring memory, processor, disk, and network usage as you would with a physical computer. Bottlenecks can be solved by allocating more memory, processor, disk, or network bandwidth for VMs or scaling out the application tier by spawning more VMs. Make sure you are monitoring not only the resources consumed by the VMs but also the number of users connected to each VM. That way you can better determine if a spike in resource consumption is related to a growing number of users or application issues.

Tools

There are several tools, from different vendors, that you can use to better monitor and manage a cloud computing environment. Microsoft has its own private/public cloud management suite: System Center 2012. BMC has its Cloud Operations Management suite. And VMware has VMware Cloud Management. Covering each of these products (or better, each suite of products) would require a volume of books all by itself. System Center 2012 alone is composed of seven individual products. To better understand these products, visit the sites listed in Table 10.2.

TABLE 10.2 Tool URLs

Product	URL
BMC Cloud Operations Management	`www.bmc.com/solutions/cloudops`
Microsoft System Center 2012	`www.microsoft.com/en-us/server-cloud/system-center/datacenter-management-capabilities.aspx`
VMware Cloud Management	`www.vmware.com/solutions/datacenter/virtualization-management/overview.html`

Implementing Continual Process Improvement

According to ITIL 2011, the overall Continual Process Improvement processes can be resumed as shown in Figure 10.6.

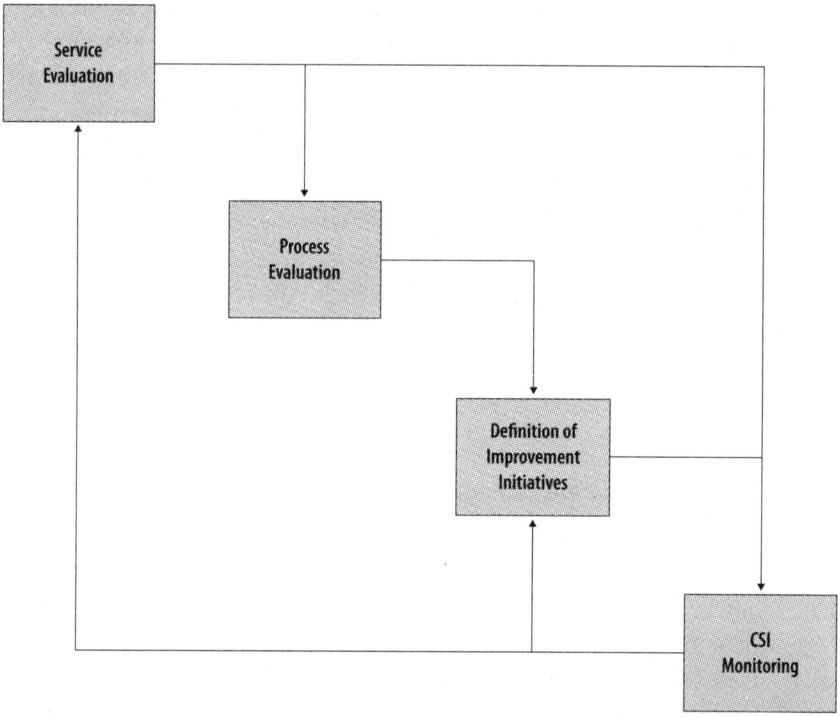

FIGURE 10.6 ITIL Continual Process Improvement processes

Each individual process can be further detailed according to the following topics.

Service Evaluation

The objective of the service evaluation process is to review business services and infrastructure services continuously, with a predefined schedule. The main goal of this periodic review is to identify more efficient and economical ways of providing each one of the services being maintained.

Process Evaluation

The objective of the process evaluation process is to review the processes currently in place to manage an IT infrastructure periodically. Just as with the service evaluation process, the process evaluation process aims at identifying changes to the current processes to make them more efficient and cost effective.

Definition of Improvement Initiatives

The definition of improvement initiatives process aims at taking the results from the service evaluation and process evaluation processes and transforming them into actionable items that make up their own improvement project. This project must be managed and implemented as any other project within an organization. Action items may be internal or require interaction with vendors and external consultants.

CSI Monitoring

Monitoring the CSI initiatives allows an organization to ensure that the action items identified in the definition of CSI activities process are being executed according to plan and gives them the opportunity to correct any of the action items as needed.

The Essentials and Beyond

This chapter illustrates the most commonly used ITIL processes and how they can applied to a cloud environment in a SaaS, PaaS, or IaaS scenario.

Additional Exercises

- Identify current ITIL processes in your organization.
- Identify how these processes must change to accommodate a cloud-based service.

To compare your answer to the author's, please visit `www.sybex.com/go/cloudessentials`.

Review Questions

1. True or false? ITIL is a collections of tools used to manage an IT infrastructure.

   A. True   B. False

(Continues)

THE ESSENTIALS AND BEYOND *(Continued)*

2. What are the five volumes in ITIL? (Choose five.)

   A. Service Design
   B. Service Development
   C. Service Strategy
   D. Service Transition
   E. Service Operation
   F. Service Analysis
   G. Continual Process Improvement

3. Which ITIL volume provides guidance on the deployment of services into a production environment?

   A. Service Strategy
   B. Service Design
   C. Service Transition
   D. Service Operation

4. Which ITIL volume provides guidance on incident and problem management?

   A. Service Strategy
   B. Service Design
   C. Service Transition
   D. Service Operation

5. What are some examples of utility value provided by a cloud-based service?

   A. Access from anywhere
   B. Higher availability
   C. Better security
   D. Business continuity

6. How do you calculate the overall availability of a service composed of two tiers, where each tier is 99.999% available?

   A. Multiply the availability values.
   B. Average the availability values.
   C. Subtract each value from 100%, add the results, and subtract that from 100%.
   D. Add the values, subtract from 200%, and subtract that from 100%.

7. Which of the following elements should be monitored by a consumer of a SaaS service?

   A. Network fabric
   B. Storage fabric
   C. Services on VMs
   D. Connectivity to service

8. Which of the following elements should be monitored by a consumer of a PaaS service?

   A. Network fabric
   B. Storage fabric
   C. Virtualization hosts
   D. Services on a VM

(Continues)

THE ESSENTIALS AND BEYOND *(Continued)*

9. True or false? A watcher node is responsible for measuring application performance of a cloud service.

   A. True
   B. False

10. What are synthetic transactions?

    A. Database transactions
    B. File system transactions
    C. Operations that mimic user interaction with a service
    D. . Operations that mimic a cloud service

CHAPTER 11

Security in the Cloud

Many security risks apply equally to traditional computing and cloud computing, but the relative immaturity and lack of standardization in cloud computing lead to security risks unique to that environment. This chapter provides a foundation for understanding security and risk and then applies those concepts to cloud security risks. Issues concerning privacy and compliance will be discussed in Chapter 12.

- **Understanding security and risk**
- **Reviewing security standards**
- **Exploring common security risks and mitigations**
- **Implementing an ISMS**
- **Responding to incidents**
- **Recognizing security benefits**

Understanding Security and Risk

Before discussing security risks specific to cloud computing, it is necessary to have a functional understanding of security and risk management. Although there are numerous types of security risks related to business, this chapter focuses on information security.

Key Principles of Information Security

At its core, the goal of information security is to protect the confidentiality, integrity, and availability of an organization's data. Together, these are often referred to as the *CIA triad*, as illustrated in Figure 11.1.

Confidentiality Confidentiality refers to the sensitivity of data. Confidential data needs to be protected from unauthorized access, use, or disclosure. Examples of confidential information include personnel files, personal health information, financial records, and trade secrets.

Integrity Integrity refers to the reliability of data. To have integrity, data needs to be protected from unauthorized modification.

Availability Availability refers to the accessibility of data. To be available, data needs to be protected from disruption of service.

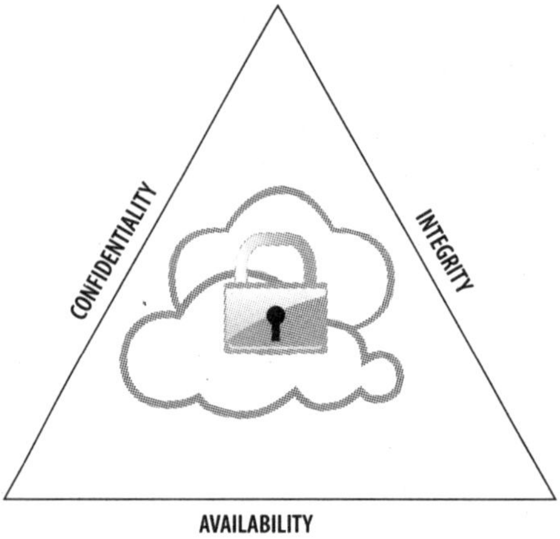

FIGURE 11.1 The CIA triad

Security Controls

The goal of protecting the confidentiality, integrity, and availability of an organization's data is achieved through application of security controls, which are measures designed to prevent, detect, and minimize the impact of security incidents. Security controls can be categorized as management, technical, or operational, and all three categories of controls are necessary to implement a successful information security management system (ISMS), which is discussed in more detail later in this chapter. The three security control categories are as follows:

Management Management controls include guidelines, standards, and policies. They align with an organization's goals and regulatory requirements and provide a framework for operational procedures.

Technical Technical controls are those applied directly to and executed by information technology resources. Examples include access control, authentication, firewalls, and encryption.

Operational Operational controls generally involve processes and procedures enacted by individuals. They are based on management controls and incorporate technical controls. Examples include disaster recovery planning, configuration management, incident response, and physical security.

Also necessary, even critical, is the support of upper management. Although technical controls can be put into place by IT staff and supervisors can implement operational controls, management controls must come from an organization's upper and executive management. It is their responsibility to set policy that supports business goals and to allocate resources in support of policy.

Defense in Depth

Another key concept of security is defense in depth. This refers to using a layered framework to implement security controls on computing facilities, network perimeters, hosts (servers, workstations, laptops, and so on), applications, and data. Defense in depth is often used in physical security, such as at a bank. Just as a bank would not protect its assets (and those of its customers) by just locking the doors, sensitive or critical data should not be protected only with a network firewall or only with a password. Figure 11.2 illustrates the concept of a layered security framework.

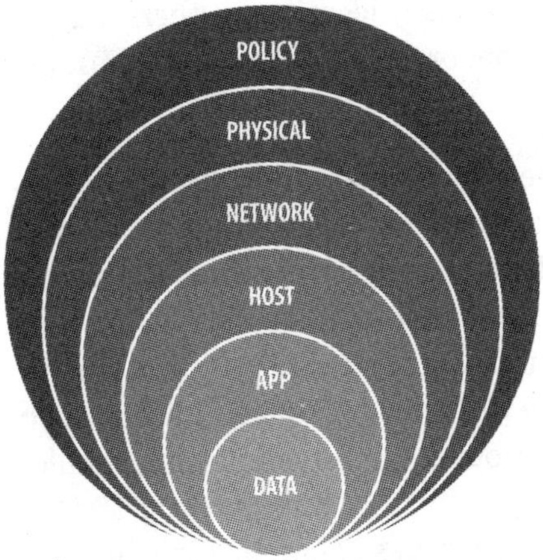

FIGURE 11.2 A layered security framework

Risk Management Basics

Risk is a factor of probability (likelihood) and impact (loss)—specifically, the probability that a particular incident will occur and the impact to the business when that happens. Incidents include, but are not limited to, theft or loss of equipment, unauthorized data access, denial of service, and unauthorized data manipulation. An in-depth discussion of risk management is outside the scope of this book, but a brief overview of the process follows:

Step 1: Identify and categorize assets. The first step is identification of assets, physical and logical. This includes hardware, software, data, virtual hosts, and any other information resources. The owners and custodians should be identified during the inventory process, and information systems and data should be categorized based on their level of sensitivity and criticality. This step may also involve determination of appropriate controls based on regulation and security policy.

Step 2: Identify threats and vulnerabilities. A threat is anything that has the potential to negatively impact information systems and consequently the business processes supported by them. Threats may be human, environmental (or natural), or electronic in nature. Human threats range from criminal hackers to employees sharing login credentials. Environmental threats include fire, water, power failure, and weather events. Electronic threats include malware, software defects, and automated attacks.

For every identified threat, there will be associated vulnerabilities. Some vulnerabilities, such as defects in software, may be easily identified. Others may be specific to a particular industry or organization, or even to a particular host or data set.

Step 3: Assess risk. Perform a risk assessment by evaluating the likelihood that a threat will turn into an actual security event and determining the impact should that occur. One way to estimate probability is by determining if the appropriate security controls are applied. For example, the likelihood of malware is significantly lessened if all hosts have antimalware software installed, the software is updated frequently, and scans are performed regularly. Impact, such as loss of reputation, funds, sales, employee productivity, or equipment, should be determined by management.

Both probability and impact are then assigned values of low, medium, or high and a risk rating is obtained by plugging those values into a risk matrix, as illustrated in Figure 11.3.

		Probability		
		Low	Medium	High
Impact	Low	Low	Low	Medium
	Medium	Low	Medium	High
	High	Medium	High	Critical

FIGURE 11.3 A simple low-medium-high risk matrix

Step 4: Address risk. Risks are typically addressed in order of priority, and an organization may choose to accept the risk and do nothing, avoid the risk by discontinuing the risky behavior, mitigate the risk by applying security controls, or transfer the risk such as through insurance or outsourcing. These decisions will be based on business needs and the organization's risk appetite, which is the amount of risk an organization is willing to accept.

Risk Transference

Although it is possible to transfer some risk through outsourcing, it may not be possible to transfer risk completely, and it is not possible to transfer legal liability. For example, an organization may choose to transfer the risk of theft of computing equipment by contracting with a third-party data center. If equipment is then stolen from the data center, the organization successfully avoided that risk. If, on the other hand, the theft of equipment led to a data breach that was in violation of the organization's contract or legal regulations, the organization retains that liability.

Step 5: Monitor Risk Monitoring is performed to ensure that mitigation (or other risk management decisions) is effective.

Organizations subject to legislation or industry regulation are generally required to engage in some type of risk management activities. Even those that do not have requirements can greatly benefit from it. More information on risk management can be found by reviewing recognized risk management standards such as the following:

- ISO/IEC 31000 Risk Management Standard
- NIST Special Publication 800-37, *Guide for Applying the Risk Management Framework to Federal Information Systems*
- COSO *Enterprise Risk Management Integrated Framework*

Reviewing Security Standards

Standards are, by definition, a set of established rules, principles, and requirements—an approved model. There are many recognized information security standards, some freely available and some commercial, but all have the benefit of being well researched and extensively reviewed. The information security standard an organization chooses to adopt may be determined by the organization's industry or sector or by business needs. Organizations should familiarize themselves with various standards when selecting a cloud services provider to ensure that the standards the provider follows align with those of the organization.

Statement on Auditing Standards No. 70

SAS 70 is an auditing standard that can include information technology controls and safeguards. It is important to note that passing an SAS 70 audit does not ensure that a cloud service provider is secure, only that is it complying with its identified controls.

The following are some of the more well-known information security standards:

COBIT 5 for Information Security COBIT is a framework for IT management and governance maintained by ISACA. Version 5 includes guidance on enterprise information security pulled from other ISACA frameworks such as the Val IT Framework, the Risk IT Framework, and the IT Assurance Framework.

ISO/IEC 27000 series This is a set of information security management standards published by the International Organization for Standardization (ISO) and the International Electrotechnical Commission (IEC).

NIST Special Publications – 800 series NIST has published a variety of robust information and computer security-related standards in its Special Publication 800 series. Although primarily intended for US government agencies, these standards (with some exceptions) are generally suitable for organizations with comparable security requirements and in some cases map directly to ISO/IEC standards.

NIST has three special publications relevant to cloud computing:

- SP 800-144: *Guidelines on Security and Privacy in Public Cloud Computing*
- SP 800-145: *The NIST Definition of Cloud Computing*
- SP 800-146: *Cloud Computing Synopsis and Recommendations*

Open Security Architecture (OSA) OSA is an open-source project that provides security standards in the form of patterns (in other words, diagrams and explanatory text), drawing from other recognized standards such as NIST SP 800-53, *Recommended Security Controls for Federal Information Systems and Organizations*. Its *Cloud Computing Pattern* (SP-011) identifies the key control areas and activities of cloud computing.

Payment Card Industry Data Security Standards (PCI-DSS) PCI-DSS is a security framework maintained by the PCI Security Standards Council and designed to protect cardholder data. It includes security requirements for networking, data protection, vulnerability management, access control, monitoring, and policy. It also includes specific requirements for shared hosting that apply to cloud computing:

- Data and process isolation
- Logging and audit trails
- Timely forensic investigation

A related standard, Payment Application Data Security Standard (PA-DSS) applies to software vendors that develop payment applications. Organizations seeking to use cloud-based payment applications should ensure that they are compliant with these standards.

Standard of Good Practice for Information Security This standard is maintained by the Information Security Forum (ISF) and aligns closely with other information security standards discussed in this section. It is updated annually, and the current version includes coverage of cloud computing.

Exploring Common Security Risks and Mitigations

The same basic risks associated with traditional computing also occur in cloud computing, but cloud computing has its own particular risks regardless of deployment model. Public and private clouds both require some type of security across boundaries, whether it be boundaries between customers in a public cloud or between an organization's divisions in a public cloud. Additionally, cloud computing operates on a shared responsibility model, with organizations and providers having their own security-related duties.

CSA Security, Trust & Assurance Registry

The Cloud Security Alliance (CSA) is a not-for-profit organization that promotes the use of security best practices in cloud computing. The CSA Security, Trust & Assurance Registry (STAR) is a registry of security controls provided by cloud computing providers that is designed to assist users of cloud services with security assessment and evaluation of current and potential providers.

Before looking at specific risks and mitigation techniques, there are some perimeter defenses that should be implemented in all cloud implementations, where applicable:

Firewalls A firewall is an appliance or application that inspects and regulates network traffic based on a set of configurable rules, such as allowing or blocking traffic on specific network ports or to/from specific hosts. It does this by examining data packets to identify the source, the destination, and sometimes the payload and then comparing this information to the rules. Firewall appliances for use in a cloud computing environment have the ability to scale as customer needs dictate, are highly reliable with redundant network connections and power, and are generally more robust than traditional firewalls. Figure 11.4 shows an example of a traditional firewall configuration.

STATEFUL PACKET FILTERING

The firewall analyzes inbound and outbound traffic based on its current rules. It also keeps track of session state, which allows it to ensure that inbound packets were requested from within the network.

STATELESS PACKET FILTERING

The firewall analyzes data packets and allows or denies them access to the network based on its current rules. Session state is not maintained, as with stateful packet filtering, making stateless packet filtering useful for controlling access to the network. Common examples include blocking incoming traffic on port 80 (HTTP) or port 21 (FTP).

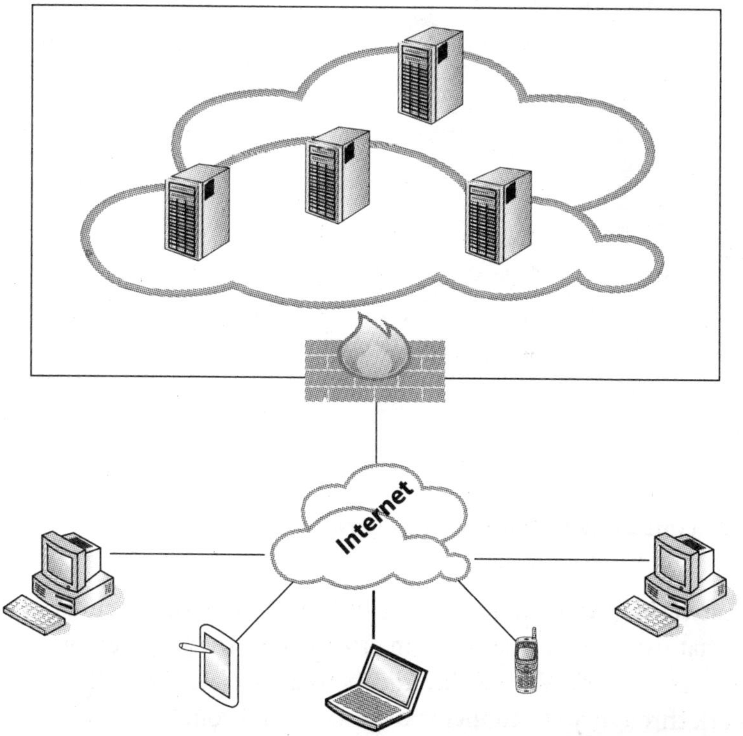

FIGURE 11.4 A traditional firewall configuration

Virtual firewalls A virtual firewall is designed specifically to protect virtual hosts and operates in different modes depending on how it is deployed. In bridge mode, the virtual firewall is deployed within the network infrastructure, where it acts like a traditional firewall. In hypervisor mode (as shown in Figure 11.5), the virtual firewall is not on the network at all but rather within the hypervisor environment in order to directly monitor virtual machine traffic.

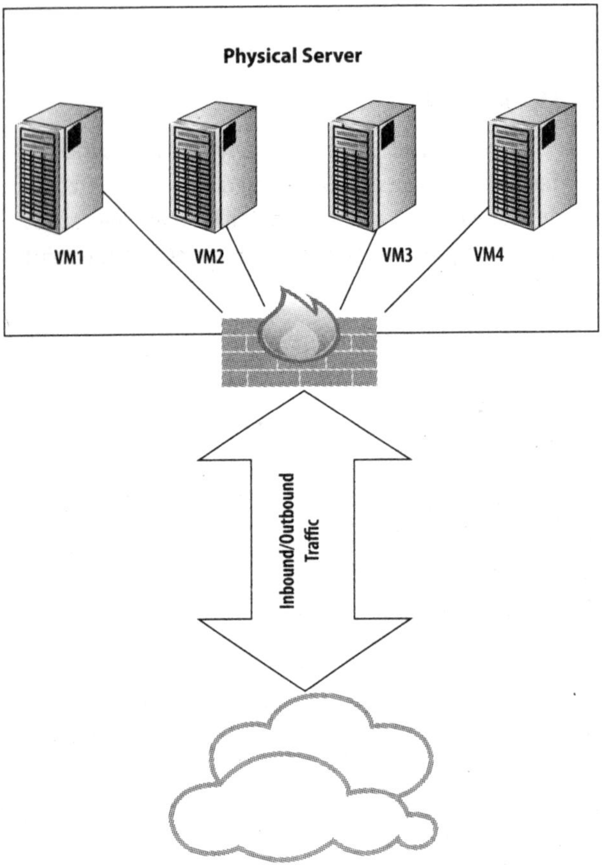

FIGURE 11.5 A virtual firewall configuration in hypervisor mode

Virtual private networks A virtual private network (VPN) is used a secure private network that uses a public network (in other words, the Internet) or another intermediate network. VPN communications are isolated from the rest of the network through an IP tunnel and are secured through encryption and authentication. In cloud computing, this allows end users to access cloud resources securely, regardless of their location, as long as they have the proper credentials and are using a device that can support the VPN client. When investigating VPN solutions, organizations should identify the devices in use to ensure compatibility.

Application Interface

Customers interact with cloud service providers through software known as application programming interfaces (APIs). If the APIs are not properly secured, it can impact all three elements of the CIA triad—data may be exposed or altered and services or accounts may be disabled or hijacked. APIs may be insecure due to weaknesses such as programming defects, transmission of data (including login credentials) in cleartext, or ineffective monitoring capabilities.

> As discussed in Chapter 8, "Applications in the Cloud," APIs are detailed road maps that show how to write applications or services at one level of the software stack that use applications and services at another level.

Mitigation

Mitigation against weak APIs is generally the responsibility of the provider and includes secure application development and testing. Adequate testing is particularly important when APIs interact with each other. Some responsibilities may be shared, such as authentication and access control (discussed in Chapter 12, "Privacy and Compliance") and the use of encryption for communications. If your organization has these requirements, they should be included in the SLA.

Shared Technology

One of the main benefits of cloud computing is economy of scale due to shared resources and multitenancy. Unfortunately, shared technology also leads to security risks. Availability may be impacted by performance issues caused by improper allocation of storage or memory or even by attacks against another customer in a multitenant environment. Confidentiality or integrity may be impacted by insufficient data isolation.

Mitigation

There are two main categories of mitigations for shared technology risk — operational security and incident response. Operational security processes include application of proper controls, timely testing and installation of security patches, and security monitoring. With regard to incident response, a provider should have a defined process for responding to security breaches and notifying customers.

Insider and Criminal Threats

As with any other industry, cloud service providers are not immune to inadvertently hiring unethical employees that may use their access to customer resources for malicious purposes. This is not a risk specific to cloud computing; however, these individuals (known as malicious insiders) may find employment with a cloud service provider more attractive.

Cloud computing can also be abused by individual criminals or criminal organizations, which target providers due to quick and easy registration and free trial periods. They may use cloud services to host malware, serve up spam, or create botnets to attack other networks. This poses a risk to legitimate customers because they may be sharing resources that could be blacklisted or involved in criminal investigation.

As mentioned earlier, accounts may be hijacked due to vulnerabilities in APIs. Accounts as well as network traffic and even the service itself may be compromised through hacking, phishing, password theft, and other criminal tactics.

Mitigation

Cloud service providers can mitigate the risk of malicious insiders doing damage by implementing HR processes such as background and reference checks as well as strong internal security policies and controls. For example, access for provider employees should follow the principle of least privilege and employee actions should be logged in audit trails.

Data Exposure and Loss

There are many ways in which data can be exposed in a cloud computing environment, some of which have already been discussed. Risks also include weak authentication and access control, insecure deletion of data, and jurisdictional issues. These risks are discussed in Chapter 12. Data loss can occur during normal operations as the result of a system failure or due to a security incident.

Mitigation

Encryption of data in storage and transmission is a powerful mitigation tool for reducing the risk of unauthorized data access. Encryption can also be used during user authentication to prove identity. Implementing encryption does provide some challenges, particularly with regard to key management. Key management encompasses the entire life cycle of a key, from initial generation to eventual revocation. It also includes processes to manage the secure exchange, storage, and replacement of keys. Lost keys can render data unreadable, and compromised keys may lead to loss of data confidentiality or integrity. Encryption can also be cumbersome and add overhead to data processing. An organization should perform a risk assessment to determine the most effective use of encryption.

TYPES OF ENCRYPTION

Encryption can be symmetric, asymmetric, or hybrid. Symmetric encryption involves a single shared key that is used to encrypt and decrypt data. Examples include AES, 3DES, and Blowfish. Asymmetric encryption uses a key pair consisting of a public and private key instead of a single shared key. The public key is published for general use, while the private key is kept secret. Data encrypted with a public key can be decrypted with only its companion private key. Examples include digital signatures and public key encryption. Asymmetric encryption can also be used to transmit a shared key, which is then used for symmetric encryption. Secure Sockets Layer (SSL), used for secure web communications, is an example of this type of hybrid encryption.

Other mitigations include strong authentication and access control (discussed in Chapter 12), periodic auditing, secure deletion of data, and appropriate disaster recovery planning.

Organizational Risks

The organization itself is also exposed to security risks by implementing cloud services. First and foremost is the loss of control, particularly when hybrid or public clouds are used. In all service models (e.g., IaaS, PaaS, SaaS), customers cede a significant amount of control to the cloud service provider, often with very little transparency with regard to security controls, hiring practices, location, and general business practices. This lack of transparency results in customers being unable to properly manage risk due to unknown risk exposure and potentially no guarantees that the provider is adequately managing risk.

Mitigation

Many organizational risks in cloud computing can be mitigated through the provider's SLA. The SLA should clearly define security responsibilities of both the organization and the service provider. Other elements addressable in the SLA include, but are not limited to, security incident notification procedures, recovery time, and the right to audit.

Other risks can be addressed through the organization's security policies. Once cloud services are adopted, security policies should be updated to reflect new processes and procedures associated with the cloud environment as well as acceptable use of cloud services. Once security policies have been developed and approved, organizational staff must be educated through a security awareness training program. In addition to being informed of the policies themselves, staff should also be educated on the motivating factors behind the policies.

Implementing an ISMS

As mentioned earlier in this chapter, threats to CIA are managed through an information security management system (ISMS), which is, generally speaking, a system of policies, processes, and controls. Be aware that it is not enough simply to apply security controls; an organization should develop a process for identifying, implementing, monitoring, and updating appropriate and cost-effective controls based on current business needs. ISMS implementations are based on the Plan-Do-Check-Act (PDCA) process. PDCA, as illustrated in Figure 11.6, is an iterative cyclical management process popularized by Edward Deming for quality control. Its applicability to ISMS is discussed next.

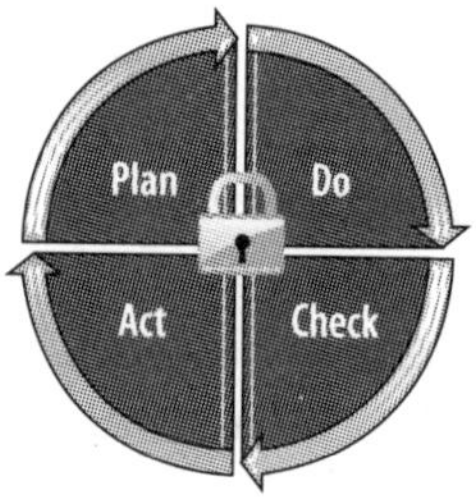

FIGURE 11.6 The PDCA cycle

Plan: Design the system. The organization identifies the security standards and policies that apply to its environment, defines security metrics, and uses risk assessment results to identify appropriate security controls.

Do: Implement the controls. The controls selected as a result of the risk assessment are implemented.

Check: Evaluate the system. The ISMS is evaluated for effectiveness. This includes, but is not limited to, monitoring logs, analyzing metrics, and reviewing assessment results.

Act: Change as necessary. Changes to the ISMS will need to be made periodically due to the identification of changes in regulation or security policy, changes to the computing environment, or identification of vulnerabilities and opportunities for improvement.

Remember, a strong ISMS is necessary for both organizations and cloud service providers due to shared responsibility for security management.

Responding to Incidents

Despite the best laid plans of administrators, incidents do happen. An incident is any event that impacts the confidentiality, integrity, or availability of an information system, including unplanned interruptions of service. Incidents are not limited to malicious attacks against a system. They also include events such as accidental information releases, power or network failures, and theft or loss of computing equipment.

Before further discussion, it is important to understand the following concepts:

Incident management The process of planning for, detecting, and responding to incidents. It may also be referred to as incident response. Organizations can prepare for incidents by developing an incident response plan that includes step-by-step instructions for the incident response process as well instructions for determining when to activate the incident response plan. Not all incidents trigger formal incident response—many events are simply handled as part of day-to-day operations, such as malware detection and removal.

Incident response team A trained group of individuals prepared and authorized to handle incidents. The team should include qualified technical personnel, upper management, and representatives from various organizational units such as human resources, legal, and public relations.

As with the ISMS, discussed in the preceding section, incident management responsibility is shared between the cloud service provider and the customer. As such, the cloud service provider and the customer must have clear understanding of the following:

- What constitutes an incident
- The cloud service provider's incident response capabilities
- Communication procedures between the customer's incident response team and the provider's incident response team
- Recovery requirements and capabilities
- Any legal considerations, particularly with regard to data ownership and jurisdiction

Organizations should not wait until an incident has occurred before discussing incident response with a cloud service provider. Incident response discussions should occur prior to vendor selection, and both customer and provider roles and responsibilities should be clearly outlined in the SLA.

Digital Forensics in the Cloud

In incidents involving criminal activity or malicious intrusion into an organization's network, it is often necessary to use specialized technical investigative techniques referred to as *digital forensics*. The forensic process involves acquiring the devices to be analyzed, performing the analysis on a forensic image of the device's media, and generating a report.

In traditional computing, if forensic analysis were required, the physical server would be seized. In a public cloud computing environment, everything is virtualized and evidence can reside on multiple virtual and physical servers, none of which are owned by the data owner and all of which have multiple tenants whose privacy must be respected. Additional complications occur if the cloud service provider's network crosses geopolitical boundaries. (This is discussed in more detail in Chapter 12.)

Organizations that are concerned about being able to successfully perform digital forensic investigations should investigate using cloud service providers that have adequate tools and procedures available to support investigation and are willing to provide access to such via the SLA. Organizations would also be wise to consider the number of dependencies involved because cloud service providers often purchase services from other cloud service providers and each dependency adds additional complexity.

Recognizing Security Benefits

It would be remiss to end this chapter without discussing the security benefits of cloud computing, most of which are related to scale. Cloud service providers have the ability to take advantage of economy of scale, just as organizations do, and can potentially provide a greater level of security than an organization could on its own by spreading the cost out across its customer base. This includes the following benefits:

- Increased availability and improved disaster recovery through redundancy and multiple locations
- Security specialists
- 24/7 staffing and monitoring

Not every cloud service provider will have these capabilities, just as not every organization is incapable of having its own highly effective security measures. When evaluating cloud services, as well as individual providers, an organization must take into account the security capabilities of the provider versus its own security capabilities.

THE ESSENTIALS AND BEYOND

There is a recognized need for cloud computing standards, and governments, service providers, industry organizations, subject matter experts, and standards organizations are working toward this goal. There seems to be a general consensus on cloud security standards, fortunately, with organizations such as NIST publishing security guidelines and other standards being updated to include cloud computing.

ADDITIONAL EXERCISES

- **Identify cloud computing security recommendations from organizations such as NIST, the European Network and Information Security Agency (ENISA), and CSA. How are they similar? How are they different?**
- **Select an industry with which you are familiar (e.g., education, financial, manufacturing) and search for industry-specific guidelines for cloud computing security. If none exist, are existing guidelines sufficient? If guidelines do exist, how mature are they?**

To compare your answer to the author's, please visit `www.sybex.com/go/cloudessentials`.

(Continues)

The Essentials and Beyond *(Continued)*

Review Questions

1. Which of the following is not an appropriate mitigation to protect against malicious insiders?

   A. Employee background checks
   B. Security policies
   C. Timely installation of security patches
   D. Logging

2. Which security measures can be used to secure communications between cloud services and end users?

   A. VPN
   B. SSL
   C. Firewall
   D. Both A and B.

3. True or false? There are no significant security benefits to using cloud services.

   A. True
   B. False

4. Regarding information security management systems, in what phase of the Plan-Do-Check-Act cycle does metrics analysis occur?

   A. Plan
   B. Do
   C. Check
   D. Act

5. Encryption is not an appropriate mitigation technique for which of the following security risks?

   A. Unauthorized access to confidential data
   B. Loss of organizational control
   C. Cleartext password transmission
   D. Weak data destruction processes

6. Which of the following is not an appropriate mitigation technique against data exposure?

   A. Audit
   B. Recovery
   C. Data isolation
   D. Encryption

7. Which of the following does not impact data confidentiality?

   A. Man-in-the-middle (MitM)
   B. Cross-site scripting (XSS)
   C. Denial of service (DoS)
   D. Password theft

(Continues)

The Essentials and Beyond *(Continued)*

8. True or false? If the cloud service provider has a strong information security management system (ISMS), the customer does not have to have one as well.

    A. True

    B. False

9. With regard to security, the service-level agreement should clearly outline ____________________.

    A. The security management responsibilities of the cloud service provider

    B. The security responsibilities of the customer

    C. The provider's security incident notification procedures

    D. All of the above

10. Risk is a factor of ____________________.

    A. Threats and vulnerabilities

    B. Probability and impact

    C. Vulnerabilities and exploits

    D. Probability and vulnerability

CHAPTER 12

Privacy and Compliance

Many (perhaps most) organizations are subject to various legal requirements that govern how data is collected, stored, processed, and shared. Organizations considering adopting cloud services should identify applicable legal requirements and consider the effects of cloud services on compliance. This chapter provides an overview of common legal and compliance risks.

- **Identifying legal risks**
- **Identifying privacy risks**
- **Managing identity in the cloud**

Identifying Legal Risks

An organization cannot simply rely upon the cloud service provider to ensure compliance with laws and regulations. Although the provider may have some responsibility as a data controller or custodian (depending upon the provider's role in processing data), at the end of the day the responsibility and legal liability lies with the organization or individual owning the data.

The following legal risks should be considered by organizations considering adopting cloud services:

Data location and jurisdiction Data in the cloud may be stored or processed in multiple data centers located anywhere in the world. Figure 12.1 illustrates a hypothetical situation in which the customer is located in North America, the cloud provider in Europe, and the provider's data centers in various locations around the world.

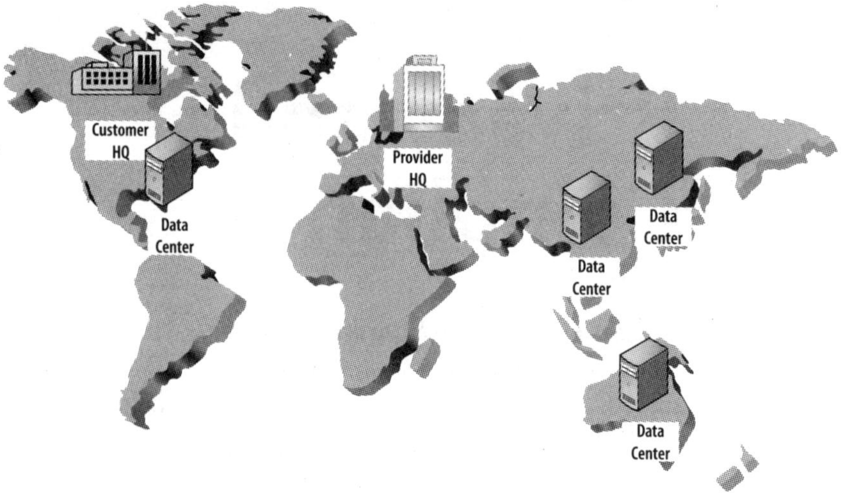

FIGURE 12.1 A map showing potential differences in geographic locations among customers, providers, and data centers

While having data in multiple locations has obvious benefits for disaster recovery, it can also raise some significant legal concerns. For example, data may be subject to export restrictions, and some laws have facility requirements.

Because the world's laws have generally not kept up with advances in technology and are not often aligned, jurisdiction becomes a risk. Data in the cloud could potentially be subject to the laws of the following locations:

- The location of the physical servers
- The location of the service provider's headquarters
- The location of the data owner
- The locations the data passes through between the provider's servers

The risk can be mitigated by contractually obligating the service provider to keep data within appropriate geographic locations.

Data isolation Data isolation may be required by regulations that address data security. In traditional computing, data can be isolated physically (e.g., a separate server) or logically (e.g., a separate virtual server, file store, or database). In the cloud, multitenancy is common, and it may be more difficult to ensure that compliance with data isolation requirements is achieved. In a multitenant cloud environment, isolation is logical. It can occur at the hypervisor level, by isolating virtual machines, or at the database level, which may involve the following:

- Isolation at the row level in a shared database is accomplished by uniquely identifying each tenant and associating each row with the owner's unique key.
- Isolation at the schema level is implemented by using a shared database with separate tables for each tenant.
- The greatest level of isolation occurs by providing tenants with individual databases, although this leads to increased costs.

Data destruction It is important to consider what happens to data in the cloud after the contract between an organization and cloud service provider expires or is terminated. The organization must have assurances (via contract or terms of service) that its data will be deleted from all servers, including archives, so that it cannot be recovered.

Bankruptcy

If a cloud service provider files for bankruptcy, there is a risk that data may be exposed during the disposition of assets. In fact, data may even be considered a corporate asset and sold, depending upon the provider's terms of service.

Terms of Service

Cloud service providers do not always individually contract with customers. They may have published terms of services and privacy policies that apply to all customers. These terms and policies must be carefully reviewed prior to provider selection. Even if the terms appear to be compatible with the data owner's needs, there is always the risk that the provider will change the terms of service, possibly without sufficient notification. This may result in civil or even criminal liability for the data owner.

Additionally, certain categories of information have specific legal requirements that may impact the use of cloud services. Here are several examples:

Health information In the United States, the privacy and security of health records is governed by the Health Insurance Portability and Accountability Act (HIPAA). HIPAA primarily affects health care providers and health plans (covered entities); however, compliance is also required of business associates that have access to electronic protected health information (EPHI). This would include cloud service providers. The covered entity and the cloud service provider are required to enter into a business associate agreement that defines the compliance obligations of each party.

Privileged information Certain professionals, such as doctors and lawyers, have legal obligations to keep client information confidential, although laws vary by state and country. Provider terms of service must be carefully reviewed to avoid undermining legal privilege.

Personally identifiable information (PII) This type of information can be used to uniquely identify an individual. The types of data categorized as PII depend upon the jurisdiction, as do the security requirements and limits on use. Examples of PII include contact information, financial information, online account usernames, government-issued identity documents (e.g., SSN, passport), and biometric data.

We discuss specific risks associated with privacy in the section "Identifying Privacy Risks" later in this chapter.

Records Management

Both public and private sector organizations can be subject to records retention requirements. Prior to moving to the cloud, organizations should determine what their record retention requirements are based on business, legal, and regulatory needs; ensure that their internal policies are compliant; and then ensure that compliance can be retained in the cloud.

The following conditions related to records management and retention can lead to risk:

- Original metadata being associated with archived records
- Provider-based record retention periods shorter than those required by the organization
- Destruction of records after retention expires

The following risks are related to records production:

Lawful access and compelled disclosure Government agencies seeking information may choose to compel disclosure of information from service providers instead of directly from the data owners. This is detrimental to data owners because neither the provider nor the government is required to notify them. In fact, some countries have gag orders that prevent service providers from providing any notification at all. See Table 12.1 for examples of laws regulating governmental access.

TABLE 12.1 Examples of laws regulating governmental access

Law	Jurisdiction
Anti-Terrorism Act of 2001	Canada
Directive 2006/24/EC	European Union
USA PATRIOT Act	United States
Electronic Communications Privacy Act	United States
Convention on Cybercrime	International
Mutual legal assistance treaties	Various

Private litigation Information may also be compelled from service providers in private litigation. This carries similar risk but adds the additional risk of impacting compliance. While a data owner may be able to successfully resist or quash a subpoena, the service provider may have no obligation to try.

Electronic discovery (e-discovery) Electronically stored information (ESI) is subject to production in the discovery phase of litigation. In addition to data files and records, metadata is considered to be ESI and subject to discovery. Organizations should consider the likelihood of litigation when selecting a cloud service provider to ensure that the provider's technical and business processes would not negatively impact the organization. For example, a cloud provider's archival process may not maintain the original metadata.

Mitigations for these risks include due diligence on the part of the organization and a service-level agreement (SLA) that takes the organization's compliance requirements into account. Additionally, organizations concerned with records retention should consider using records or document management software in the cloud instead of a more traditional file system.

Software Licensing

Maintaining software license compliance in the cloud can be challenging. Traditional models of software licensing are not always compatible with cloud computing, and vendors may be slow to move to more cloud-friendly licensing models. The three traditional software licensing models are as follows:

Per user In this licensing model, each user is granted a license. Because cloud computing can be used to facilitate a highly mobile or distributed workforce, this licensing model may prove costly for organizations with a global workforce with low concurrent logins.

Per device Each device (or each processor in a device) is granted a license in this model. This works well for physical hardware but not as well in a dynamic virtualized environment in which the number of machines and processors is unlikely to remain constant. Some software vendors that use per-device license models may consider virtual servers to be the equivalent of physical servers, but this does not solve the licensing problems that arise due to dynamic scaling.

Enterprise The organization is granted a license, regardless of number of users or devices. This type of licensing is often the most cost effective, particularly for large organizations, but these licenses may not translate to the cloud. For example, even if an organization has an enterprise license for a database product, a cloud service provider may still charge per instance for hosting the database.

Using the Right Cloud Services Provider

Some software licensing risks can be eliminated by using the appropriate vendor. Software vendors that are also cloud service providers may have simplified licensing for customers that use their software in their cloud. Additionally, some service providers, such as Amazon, have partnered with major software vendors such as Adobe, Citrix, Microsoft, SUSE, and Oracle to provide a clear licensing structure to their customers.

The consequences of being out of compliance depend on software license agreements and applicable laws and regulations. An application with built-in antipiracy protections may simply stop working if the maximum number of licenses is reached. Generally, underlicensing software is considered the same as piracy, as far as copyright law is concerned. Many major software vendors are members of the Business Software Alliance (BSA), an antipiracy watchdog group. Should a BSA software audit uncover licensing violations, an organization's liability could be up to US$150,000 per title plus additional fines.

Software Licensing and the Sarbanes-Oxley Act

The Sarbanes-Oxley Act (SOX) requires that publicly traded US companies have adequate internal controls that ensure reliable financial reporting. Because violations in software licensing can lead to large fines that can negatively impact financial statements, companies subject to SOX may have additional risk when moving to the cloud due to software license complexity.

Where possible, investigate using cloud-friendly software licensing that supports the following:

Concurrency Licensing based on the number of users allowed to use the software at once can be more cost effective for organizations in which many users need access to an application but are unlikely to need to use it at the same time.

Mobility In the cloud, applications and operating systems move between virtual environments, such as from host to host, data center to data center, and even from cloud to cloud.

Flexibility Subscription or pay-as-you-go license models may be attractive for organizations using public cloud services that are not heavily invested in traditional software licenses, particularly for IaaS services.

Auto-scaling The number of servers may increase or decrease dynamically to provide sufficient quality of service and may overrun per-device or per-processor licenses.

Audit

Most regulations impacting data security and privacy require periodic auditing for compliance and security. Organizations may also choose to schedule their own internal audits based on risk. They should ensure that SLAs support these audit requirements and also must be diligent in monitoring and enforcing SLAs to avoid falling out of compliance.

Organizations subject to audit should consider the following questions:

- How will accounts for auditors be provisioned?
- Will appropriate audit logs be available? How long can they be retained and how are they secured?
- What are the cloud service provider's policies on vulnerability management and security monitoring?
- Has the cloud service provider undergone an independent audit?

Identifying Privacy Risks

Privacy requirements vary between geographic locations, not only from country to country but even from state to state. As we discussed in "Identifying Legal Risks" earlier in this chapter, data may become subject to the laws of countries in which the service provider or data center is located. Table 12.2 shows examples of privacy legislation in several countries. Please note that this is just a small sampling of laws and organizations should always consult with appropriate legal services prior to placing data outside their geopolitical borders.

TABLE 12.2 Examples of privacy legislation

Law	Jurisdiction	Applicability
Personal Information Protection and Electronic Documents Act (PIPEDA)	Canada	Protection of PII in commercial activities
EU Data Protection Directive	European Union	Processing of PII and movement of data between member states
UK Data Protection Act	United Kingdom	Protection of PII
Children's Online Privacy Protection Act (COPPA)	United States	Collection and use of children's personal information
Family Educational Rights and Privacy Act (FERPA)	United States	Student educational records
Gramm-Leach-Bliley Financial Services Modernization Act (GLBA)	United States	Consumer data related to financial products and services
Privacy Act of 1974	United States	Collection and use of PII by federal agencies

Law	Jurisdiction	Applicability
Video Privacy Protection Act	United States	Use of PII associated with video rentals
Swiss Federal Act on Data Protection	Switzerland	Processing of PII by private individuals and federal authorities

Because of the global nature of commerce, some efforts have been made to facilitate the transfer of data between countries. One such effort is the US-EU Safe Harbor Framework.

Safe Harbor

The US-EU Safe Harbor Framework was created to allow the transfer of personal data between resources in the United States and the European Union, which have different restrictions on privacy. It allows individual US organizations to comply with the EU Directive on Data Protection. A similar framework exists between the United States and Switzerland to facilitate compliance with the Swiss Federal Act on Data Protection. According to the US Department of Commerce, in order to participate, US organizations must comply with the seven Safe Harbor principles:

Notice Individuals must be notified about the information collected, used, and disclosed

Choice Individuals must be provided with the opportunity to opt out of having their personal information disclosed to a third party.

Transfer to third parties Organizations must ensure that the third party subscribes to the Safe Harbor principles or is compliant with the EU Directive on Data Protection.

Access With some exceptions, individuals must be allowed to access and manage their personal information.

Security Reasonable protections must be implemented to protect personal information.

Data integrity Data must be reliable and accurate.

Enforcement Certification must be maintained annually to remain in the program, and there must be mechanisms in place both to effectively handle complaints and violations and to verify compliance.

Managing Identity in the Cloud

The purpose of identity management is to manage the life cycle of users and other entities that need trusted access to organizational resources. Identity management also goes hand in hand with privacy, and identity records for users generally contain PII that may be subject to privacy regulations. Prior to discussing the characteristics of identity management systems, it is necessary to understand the three main elements of identity and access control:

Authentication Authentication is the process of verifying an entity's identity by validating one or more factors: something you know, something you have, or something you are. A user ID–password combination (something you know) is currently the most widely used form of authentication. Other forms include security tokens or smart cards (something you have) and biometrics (something you are).

Authorization Authorization is the process of determining whether an entity is allowed to access a resource and with what level of permissions based on access control lists.

Role-Based Access Control

Using role-based access control (RBAC) is an effective way of managing access for a large number of users. Instead of being assigned permissions directly, users are assigned to role-based groups and permissions are managed at the group level.

Authentication, authorization, and accounting are often referred to as AAA, Triple-A, or the AAA protocol.

Accounting Accounting is the process of tracking resource usage for operational, security, and compliance purposes. Operationally, accounting can be used for capacity monitoring and billing. Monitoring of access logs and the ability to generate audit trails are often required by security policy and regulation.

An organization should consider its security, privacy, and compliance needs when evaluating an identity management system. One of the primary characteristics a system should support is the ability to assign users to roles to support separation of duties, association of users with business roles, and role-based access controls. Additionally, organizations should consider requirements such as self-service functions (e.g., password reset, user data update) and access to user data.

Managing identity in the cloud presents some risks and challenges, particularly with regard to complexity and interoperability:

Identity provisioning Identity provisioning is the process of creating and deactivating user accounts (deactivation may also be called deprovisioning). In IaaS and SaaS deployments, service providers may have proprietary provisioning processes that may add complexity to business processes, particularly if each offering an organization uses has different methods of provisioning.

Credential management Many security standards and data protection laws have requirements for credential management, particularly user accounts and passwords. An organization must ensure that its compliance needs are met for requirements such as secure transmission of passwords, strong password policies, password storage, and self-service password reset.

Complexity may be reduced through the use of federated identity management and single sign-on (SSO). When choosing a cloud service provider, organizations should consider their existing environment and standards supported by potential vendors.

Federated Identity Management

In discussing federation, we refer to service providers and identity providers. A service provider is an application or service, and an identity provider is an authentication authority. An organization may be its own identity provider (e.g., via the organization's directory services) or it may use an external source (e.g., OpenID, Google, Microsoft Windows Live ID).

Federation allows users in different security domains to share services without having identities in each domain. Identity providers provide information (i.e., identity attributes) to service providers, taking the burden of authentication off of individual service providers and placing it with a trusted identity provider. It also allows an organization to take advantage of single sign-on (SSO).

Single Sign-On

Implementing SSO allows an organization's users to authenticate once and access multiple applications, as shown in Figure 12.2. This improves efficiency by streamlining the authentication process, reduces IT overhead by reducing account administration duties, and improves security by requiring the user to remember only one password. (Increasing the number of passwords a user must remember increases the likelihood that the user will write them down.) SSO can be configured using Kerberos in both Windows and Unix/Linux environments, using smart cards, and through standards such as OpenID, Security Assertion Markup Language (SAML), and Web Services Federation Language (WS-Federation).

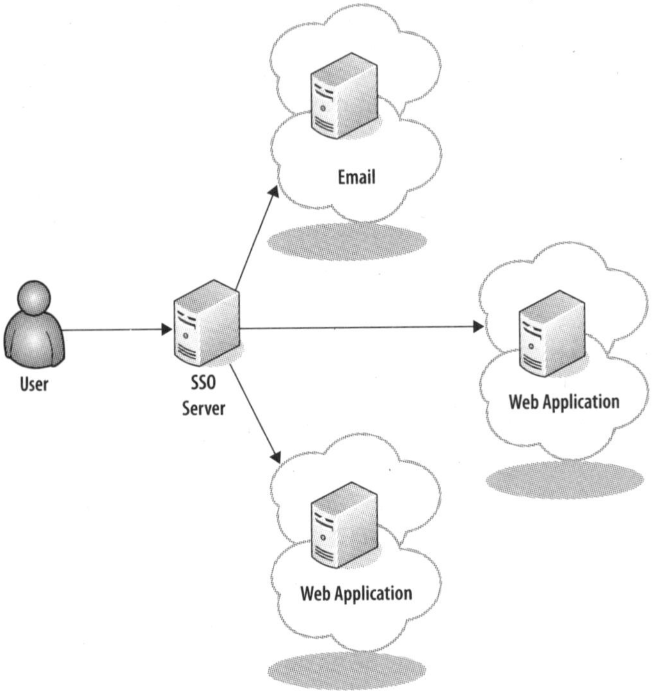

FIGURE 12.2 Simple SSO diagram showing a user authenticating to a SSO server and accessing both email and web applications

The Essentials and Beyond

Cloud computing is being adopted at a rapid pace, and current industry forecasts indicate a steady growth over the next five to eight years. In response, the Open Data Center Alliance, the Distributed Management Task Force, and other standards organizations are working to establish a common set of cloud computing standards. World governments are also taking a closer look at cloud computing, including both private and public sector use, which should result in new and updated legislation.

Additional Exercises

- Identify proposed cloud-related legislation in your country.
- Compare and contrast proposed cloud computing standards.

To compare your answer to the author's, please visit `www.sybex.com/go/cloudessentials`.

(Continues)

The Essentials and Beyond (Continued)

Review Questions

1. What is the process of verifying a user's identity?

   A. Authorization
   B. Authentication
   C. Logging in
   D. Access control

2. Which countries could claim jurisdiction over data in the cloud?

   A. The country in which physical servers storing data reside
   B. The countries that data passes through between the provider's servers
   C. The country in which the data owner resides
   D. All of the above

3. True or false? Dynamic scaling of resources in the cloud may lead to noncompliance with software licenses.

   A. True
   B. False

4. An organization can address regulatory compliance risks in the cloud in all the following ways except which one?

   A. Its own security policies
   B. Periodic audits
   C. Service-level agreements with cloud providers
   D. Delegation of full responsibility for compliance to the cloud service provider

5. True or false? Government agencies must always notify a data owner when they compel disclosure of information from a cloud service provider as part of lawful access.

   A. True
   B. False

6. Which of the following actions would not lead to risks related to records retention in the cloud?

   A. Secure destruction of records on schedule
   B. Restrictions on archived storage
   C. Difficulties associating metadata with archived records
   D. Unauthorized access

(Continues)

The Essentials and Beyond *(Continued)*

7. Authentication to multiple services in the cloud can be streamlined by adopting which of the following identity management mechanisms?

   A. Kerberos

   B. Integrated Windows authentication

   C. Single sign-on

   D. Authorization

8. True or false? The United States and the European Union have compatible data privacy laws.

   A. True

   B. False

9. Which of the following is not a legal risk associated with cloud computing?

   A. Data isolation

   B. Jurisdiction

   C. Cost

   D. Electronic discovery

10. The identity management process of allowing users in different security domains to share services without having identities in each domain is called what?

    A. Single-sign on

    B. Federated

    C. Authentication

    D. Authorization

APPENDIX A

Future of the Cloud

Now that you understand the concepts behind cloud computing and are able to identify what applications would benefit from it, how to maintain cloud services either privately or in a public cloud, and how to manage the transition from a standard data center to a cloud-based data center, it is time to look ahead and understand how hardware is changing to provide more reliable cloud-based environments and how data center infrastructures are being re-created from scratch to adapt to this world. This appendix provides an overview of the future of cloud computing.

- **Exploring hardware developments**
- **Exploring smart cities**
- **Automated data centers**

Exploring Hardware Developments

When you look at how a cloud infrastructure is built, you can separate the resources used into three categories: compute, storage, and network. Independent of what operating system and management tools are used to manage a cloud infrastructure, those components, often referred to as *fabric*, must be present. After all, cloud computing is all about sharing compute, storage, and network resources among several virtual machines.

Therefore, you can say that to build a private cloud, all you need in terms of hardware are servers, switches, and hard drives. The main idea here is that virtual machines can be created quickly (where "quick" means 15 minutes or less) and moved from one server to another in case of failure so they are highly available. You can achieve this goal in different ways. Just as an illustration, in February 2013, a group of Microsoft employees put together a private cloud infrastructure by using four Surface Pro devices. You can find their experiment at the following location:

```
http://blogs.technet.com/b/building_clouds/archive/2013/02/21/
surface-pro-hijinks-video.aspx
```

Of course, large organizations require a lot more power than a few cores, 32 GB of RAM and more than 400 GB of storage space, and a wireless network to maintain a private cloud. But what these Microsoft employees showed us is that there is not that much mystery in building a private cloud infrastructure. You need servers that are capable of using virtualization technology, a network, virtualization software, and technical skills.

Although it is perfectly acceptable to build your own cloud infrastructure by combining the necessary hardware that make up your fabric, a lot of hardware companies are now offering, or developing, what they call a *cloud-in-a-box solution*. The idea here is to bring all the fabric into a single, manageable rack that uses virtualization technology to create and manage cloud-based services. This new hardware tendency has been spreading throughout all major hardware and software vendors since 2010 and does not seem to be slowing down at all.

One of the main advantages of this approach is that organizations do not need to configure the fabric for their private clouds. You save time and money by not having to integrate disparate hardware systems from different vendors. Instead, you concentrate your efforts on managing this new hardware that contains all you need to run a private cloud.

Other hardware companies are taking a different approach and providing services to create a private cloud with their existing hardware solutions. Some of them are doing that while working with their research and development teams to build their own flavor of a cloud-in-a-box approach. The only concern about these solutions is the fact that cloud services must be *elastic*. Elasticity is provided by these systems but there are limitations. For example, some of these systems cannot be connected to each other, limiting the number of virtual machines supported. Other systems have a limit on the number of "boxes" you can connect. But all provide a quicker road to a private cloud infrastructure than building your own.

Elasticity

The term *elasticity*, in cloud computing, refers to the ability of a service to scale in and out depending on demand. For example, a web site might be hosted on a single virtual machine, and as more users connect to the website, one or more virtual machines can be automatically brought online to handle the load. The number of virtual machines used to host the site decreases as the number of users declines.

Here's a list of different companies providing some type of cloud-in-a-box solution as of February 2013:

Dell Dell works in partnership with both Microsoft and VMware on its vStart series. Dell vStart is a preconfigured rack that uses Dell PowerEdge servers, network switches, and storage in conjunction with either Microsoft Hyper-V or VMware vSphere to provide a scalable private cloud infrastructure. The top-of-the-line model, as of writing, was the Dell vStart 1000, which uses Dell PowerEdge blades, Dell Compellent Fibre Channel storage, and Dell Force10 networking with 8, 16, 24, or 32 blades. The Microsoft Hyper-V solution uses System Center 2012 to manage the private cloud.

`www.dell.com/Learn/us/en/555/by-need-it-productivity-deploy-systems-faster-dell-vstart?c=us&l=en&s=biz`

Fujitsu Fujitsu created its NuVola Private Cloud Platform by combining its ETERNUS storage system and PRIMERGY servers with either VMware or Microsoft Hyper-V. This solution is similar to Dell's, and you can find more information about its appliances at

`www.fujitsu.com/us/services/infrastructure/nuvola/`

Hitachi Similar to Dell and Fujitsu, Hitachi provides a private cloud solution by combining its Hitachi Compute Blade 2000 servers with the Hitachi Virtual Storage Platform. They support from 450 to 10,000 virtual machines depending on the number of blades being used. You can find more information at

`www.hds.com/solutions/it-strategies/cloud`

HP HP offers a cloud-in-a-box solution named CloudSystem Matrix. HP describes it as an IaaS for private and hybrid cloud environments. Its system uses a self-service portal for quick auto-provisioning along with tools to manage the entire cloud environment. You can find out more at

`http://h18004.www1.hp.com/products/blades/components/matrix/index.html`

IBM Similar to HP, IBM offers a cloud-in-a-box solution it calls PureFlex System. You can find more information at

`www-03.ibm.com/systems/pureflex/express/index.html`

Oracle Similar to HP and IBM, Oracle offers a cloud-in-a-box solution called Exalogic Elastic Cloud. You can find more information about their offering at

`www.oracle.com/us/products/middleware/exalogic/overview/index.html`

Automated Data Centers

Although the cloud-in-a-box solutions discussed in the previous section provide a great way to start a private cloud, what we see happening at data centers all across the world is very different. More and more, data centers use commodity servers in large scales with easy-to-find, cheaper components. Investments in automation and modularity are the current norm.

The reason behind this trend is directly linked to providing the availability, scalability, and reliability that a cloud service requires. High-performance servers and data centers are built with state-of-the-art fault-tolerant and reliable technologies. Yet, failures happen daily at any data center. It is a matter of simple probability. If you have the same level of availability across thousands of servers, the chance that some server in the farm will become unavailable at any given point increases dramatically. This is a great example of Murphy's Law ("Anything that can go wrong, will go wrong."), and it's what a lot of companies today realize. Companies are now building data centers expecting hardware to fail and providing redundancy by using larger amounts of commodity servers instead of more robust fault-tolerant technologies. They create their fault tolerance based on automation.

One of the most interesting examples of this change in the way data centers are built is found at the newer Microsoft data centers. Microsoft used shipping containers housing hundreds of servers that are directly plugged into water, power, and network sources. These containers are easy to transport, use commodity servers and storage solutions, and maintain redundant copies of the data being used. As servers and hard drives fail within the container, copies of the data are used from other sources and more redundant copies made. Virtual machines are failed over to other nodes within the container, or to another container. Data is also copied across containers, so once most of the hardware fails within a container, you can simply disconnect the container and its load will fail over to other containers. The failed container is substituted by a brand-new container, and the old container is serviced. This approach reduces the amount of man-hours spent fixing hardware issues. You expect hardware to fail, it fails, and you do not service it until you completely replace it. There is a lot more to the new Microsoft data centers than automation. You can learn more at `www.globalfoundationservices.com`.

This level of automation requires sophisticated management systems. Data protection and virtual machine management are some of the key components in this type of environment, along with monitoring systems. Microsoft provides a management suite called System Center 2012 that contains all of these management components, among others. You can learn more about System Center 2012 at:

`www.microsoft.com/en-us/server-cloud/system-center/default.aspx`

Exploring Smart Cities

The concept of a smart city has been around for a few decades. Different terms have been used to describe it in the past, such as *digital city* or *intelligent city*. Whatever terminology is used, smart cities are often measured along six different areas:

- Smart environment
- Smart governance
- Smart economy
- Smart mobility
- Smart people
- Smart living

Whichever area you concentrate on, the main focus is on information and communication technologies (ICT). A smart city is created by using a wireless sensor network that makes up a distributed network of intelligent sensor nodes that measure different parameters to guide the management of the city.

Smart cities use technology to increase local prosperity, competitiveness, and social sustainability.

However, the mere presence of investment in ICT alone does not define a smart city. Investments in human capital are also required. A more educated workforce, currently referred to as the "creative class," is often associated with urban development.

There are currently more than a dozen projects in different countries working to implement the concept of smart cities. Some of the most popular ones are the Amsterdam Smart City, SmartCity Kochi, SmartCity Malta, and Living PlanIT Portugal.

Amsterdam Smart City The Amsterdam Smart City (ASC) is a partnership between businesses, authorities, research institutions, and the people of Amsterdam that focuses on five themes associated with smart cities: living, working, mobility, public facilities, and open data. The ASC has identified three areas within the Amsterdam Metropolitan Area to use as urban living labs where new products and services can be tested and demonstrated. They currently have 32 projects that vary from smart power management to smart sports parks. For more information on the Amsterdam Smart City, visit `http://amsterdamsmartcity.com`.

SmartCity Kochi Kochi, Kerala, India, is home to SmartCity Kochi, a smart city project that has been delayed several times after being inaugurated in October 2011. In January 2013, SmartCity Dubai (the company heading the project) and the Kerala government agreed on terms to move the project forward. The first phase of the project is scheduled to be ready in 18 months and consists of a 3.5 million square foot building.

SmartCity Malta SmartCity Malta is another project headed by SmartCity Dubai. The geographical location of Malta, in the Mediterranean with easy access to Europe, North Africa, and the Middle East, has transformed the island into an investment center for foreign companies. The island was ranked second place in promoting ICT by the World Economic Forum in 2007, which makes it a perfect target for a smart city. For more information on SmartCity Malta, visit `http://malta.smartcity.ae`.

Living PlanIT Portugal Living PlanIT is a technology company that is working in conjunction with the municipality of Paredes in Portugal to build a smart city called PlanIT Valley that will combine intelligent buildings with connected vehicles, providing its citizens with a higher level of information about their built environment. Its efficiency will extend into the optimum control of peak electricity demand, adapted traffic management for enhanced mobility, assisted parking, and emergency services with the capacity to have priority when needed in the flow of traffic. For more information on PlanIT Valley, visit `http://living-planit.com/planit_valley.htm`.

APPENDIX B

Answers to Review Questions

Chapter 1

1. **B** The cloud is a symbol used to represent the Internet in network diagrams, adopted to represent a "location" for cloud services.
2. **A** Self-serve management of resource allocation reduces IT administrative overhead, while automated resource allocation reduces administrative overhead for business and IT operations.
3. **B** Although cloud computing utilized virtualization extensively, virtual hosting services predate cloud computing solutions and lack the flexibility of resource assignment possible in the cloud.
4. **B** A thin client system does not have a hard drive or flash drive for storage, so it relies on remote applications to operate.
5. **B** Flexible resource assignment allows the cloud service provider to share resources across multiple customers, reducing active server count, power load, and cooling requirements. The sustainable nature of cloud services includes the mobility of data and service operations as well as the potential for green cooling options.
6. **A** Cloud computing allows flexibility in applications by including XML technologies for distributed application design and high-performance computing models.
7. **C** Cloud computing is a flexible self-service and network-accessible pool of computing resources; it is rapidly transforming the modern enterprise network environment by moving on-premises services to remote cloud service providers.
8. **B** Although cloud computing can provide opportunities for reduced environmental impact through transparent migration to optimal locations and by leveraging economies of scale, it still relies on the same basic components found in a traditional data center.

9. **D** Being "in the cloud" means only that a service, application, or other component of technology infrastructure is being supported within a cloud computing flexible resource pool environment. There is no specific location that can be pointed to as "the cloud" in general.

10. **C** System virtualization allows a single powerful host computer's resources to support multiple virtualized machines at once, allowing full utilization of available resources and reduced power consumption needed during "idle" times.

Chapter 2

1. **D** Cloud-bursting supports private cloud capacity overruns by failing over to public cloud resources in a compatible hybrid cloud configuration.

2. **D** The cloud service manager will be responsible for financial management, including pricing, service levels, and service classes that will factor into cloud hosting contracts and billing policies.

3. **B** Although the spectrum of virtualization begins with the transfer of traditional servers to virtualized hosting in the data center and ends with the fully virtualized public cloud, organizations can take advantage of any level of virtualization without any of the others. This spectrum presentation is merely a mechanism for aligning the various types of virtualized computing.

4. **A** The traditional data center's server costs tend to be capital expenses because the burden for change and update lies solely with the organization.

5. **B** Private clouds are constructed atop local data center resources. Hybrid clouds can blend two or more cloud types including public, private, or other hybrid clouds, while community clouds might be located in one community member's data center but would be remote for all other members.

6. **C** NIST specifies the four types of clouds as public, hybrid, private, and community. Community clouds operate as private for the related community of organizations or as a secured partition of a public cloud for all others. A partitioned public cloud is an example of a community cloud that does not reside within the data center of any of the partner consuming organizations.

7. **C** Like the current distributed electrical power grid, public clouds provide resources to clients based on utility and consumption. Costs are operational for planning and vary based on level of use.

8. **A** Because a private cloud resides on resources controlled or managed by an organization, it is preferable to other forms of clouds when accountability for data access, location, and other factors are mandated, such as in the case of Health Insurance Portability and Accountability Act (HIPPA) or Sarbanes-Oxley data control requirements.

9. **B** A community cloud may be resident on one organization's data center resources but shared with partner organizations as a remote community cloud service. Community clouds may also reside outside of all organizational cloud hosting and be accessed remotely by all partners in the community, as in the case of a partitioned public community cloud service.

10. **D** Although both Google Docs and Microsoft's Azure platform are individually examples of public clouds, integration between these services would be considered a public/public hybrid solution.

Chapter 3

1. **A** Because Software as a Service cloud applications are entirely controlled by their provider, this type of cloud service is the most common and numerous today.

2. **B** Although the proprietary language options available to a particular PaaS development environment present the most obvious form of vendor lock-in potential, standards do not yet exist across all SaaS or even all IaaS providers' options, leading to some concerns that an early move into the cloud could create additional costs later for switching to an alternate service.

3. **A** The cloud service provider manages resource allocation provisioned for its customers using a subscription or utility-like fee schedule across all types of cloud services. Consumers of SaaS cloud services do not need to interact directly with the platform or infrastructure itself, allowing the provider to manage updates and patches behind the scenes. PaaS consumers similarly do not need to know the infrastructural components behind their application development

environment, and even IaaS consumers do not need to worry about the hardware-level support tasks anymore.

4. **E** NIST defines cloud computing service models for applications (SaaS), platforms (PaaS), and infrastructures (IaaS). Hardware as a Service is just an alternate way to refer to IaaS. Everything as a Service (XaaS) is simply a general term reflecting the evolution of traditional data center models into integrated flexible and adaptable alternatives integrating elements of cloud computing. Industry giants like Google, HP, and Microsoft are starting to use the XaaS designation, but it does not align to a formal category of cloud services.

5. **C** SaaS options offer almost no application development, while PaaS application development is tied to a provider's selection of available languages—sometimes even using proprietary versions of common languages to lock clients into their services. IaaS allows the greatest flexibility because an organization can deploy its own resources from the operating system up.

6. **B** Because the organization is no longer involved in acquisition, installation, and maintenance upgrades, software management life cycles can be shortened and costs reduced through cloud service integration.

7. **C** Borrowing from cloud computing's distributed computing origins, very large or complex databases can be broken up, or sharded, for simultaneous processing across multiple cloud resource pools.

8. **C** Of the three NIST models, IaaS allows the greatest flexibility from the operating system up.

9. **B** Of the three NIST models, PaaS presents the greatest limitation on cloud application design that could lead to an organization's "lock in" to a particular cloud vendor's services. Each vendor's PaaS services (such as Google Apps, Microsoft Azure, and Amazon Elastic Cloud) offer a limited spectrum of application development languages, often involving proprietary variations even when using standard language bases. Movement to another cloud service provider will involve rewriting many application functions or applications in their entirety.

10. **B** Although most cloud "as a Service" products can be aligned within the NIST definitions, many cloud services blend varying levels of the NIST models. The common Dropbox service, for example, includes both SaaS (web client for accessing files) and IaaS (cloud file storage) elements into its particular product.

Chapter 4

1. **A** Because SaaS cloud applications are entirely controlled by their provider, this type of cloud service is the most common and numerous today.
2. **B** Although the proprietary language options available to a particular PaaS development environment present the most obvious form of vendor lock-in potential, standards do not yet exist across all SaaS or even all IaaS providers' options, leading to some concerns that an early move into the cloud could create additional costs later for switching to an alternate service.
3. **D** Mobile devices are able to access cloud services not only through their web browsers but also through applications loaded onto the devices.
4. **E** NIST defines cloud computing service models for applications (SaaS), platforms (PaaS), and infrastructures (IaaS). Hardware as a Service is just an alternate way to refer to IaaS. Everything as a Service (XaaS) is simply a general term reflecting the evolution of traditional data center models into integrated flexible and adaptable alternatives integrating elements of cloud computing. Industry giants like Google, HP, and Microsoft are starting to use the XaaS designation, but it does not align to a formal category of cloud services.
5. **A** SaaS options offer almost no application development, while PaaS application development is tied to a provider's selection of available languages—sometimes even using proprietary versions of common languages to lock clients into its services. IaaS allows the greatest flexibility because an organization can deploy its own resources from the operating system up.
6. **B** Because the organization is no longer involved in acquisition, the software management life cycles for installation and maintenance upgrades can be shortened and costs reduced through cloud service integration.
7. **B** IaaS represents cloud resources provided at the lowest level—storage, databases, network interconnections, and similar functions. This is the most flexible level of cloud service but requires the most management and planning of the consuming organization. Platform as a Service represents cloud resources provided at the development level for custom application development and hosting. Public and hybrid clouds are deployment models, not service models.

8. **C** Network communication is defined by the Open Systems Interconnection (OSI) model, in which data is passed through a series of layers comprising similar communication functionality. Hypertext Transfer Protocol (HTTP) and Simple Mail Transfer Protocol (SMTP) are high-level application protocols that run over Transport Control Protocol (TCP), a low-level data delivery protocol.
9. **B** In client/server architecture, thin clients are unable to perform their own processing and rely upon server-based applications and services. Thick clients, on the other hand, have enough processing and storage resources to perform local processing. Desktops and mobile devices are examples of thin or thick clients.
10. **D** The development of customized and personalized applications is a function of PaaS. With PaaS, applications are developed, deployed, updated, and maintained by an organization's own development staff, as opposed to SaaS, in which the cloud service provider performs those functions. Aggregation of data is generally considered to be a benefit of enterprise SaaS, while the ability to run applications without them being installed on individual machines is an advantage of both enterprise and personal SaaS.

Chapter 5

1. **C** Computers, servers, and other physical devices are fixed assets and therefore, capital expenses. Operating expenses are those associated with ordinary business operations. A cost is considered direct or indirect based on whether it can be assigned to a single process, product, or service or to multiple ones, so more information would be required for option B or option C to be correct.
2. **B** Vertical scaling, or scaling up, involves adding resources to a single node or host. Horizontal scaling, or scaling out, involves adding additional nodes to a distributed system, while diagonal scaling is a combination of the two. Load balancing is a process associated with scaling application services.
3. **B** This is referred to as vendor-lock in and can be problematic when the organization wants to switch to a different cloud service provider.
4. **D** Increasing capital expenses is not a business driver for cloud computing. Businesses looking to adopt cloud computing are seeking to decrease capital expenses (e.g., hardware costs) by shifting the cost to operations.

5. **B** Organizational agility is the ability to rapidly adapt to market changes. It is similar to strategic flexibility, but strategic flexibility involves anticipating and preparing for uncertainty. Utility and process transformation are levels of maturity identifying how an organization can leverage cloud services.

6. **B** Pay-as-you-go billing allows for rapid development without being limited by the cost of computing hardware or being stalled by procurement times. Economies of scale is a tool for cost reduction. Mobility and improved disaster recovery are cloud computing benefits, but they do not directly relate to time to market.

7. **A** Some managers prefer to "see" what they are paying for, even if it is otherwise unnecessary. A more appropriate reason for keeping control over the hardware would be if it is required for legal or regulatory compliance. Additionally, organizations that have significant IT investment, particularly recent investment, may not be able to justify disposing of infrastructure, and sufficient Internet connectivity is required for public cloud implementations.

8. **B** An organization with a geographically distributed workforce is an ideal candidate for using a public cloud solution.

9. **C** A hybrid cloud is the best solution for organizations with appropriate infrastructure and compelling reasons to implement a private cloud solution but that also have periods of high demand that make bursting into the public cloud much more cost effective than purchasing additional infrastructure. Moving everything to the public cloud or trying to utilize a community cloud would not align with the mandate of leveraging existing internal resources.

10. **D** Compliance is the responsibility of the organization, not the cloud service provider. Software license management, backups, and patch management duties may all be transferred to a cloud service provider to reduce administrative overhead.

Chapter 6

1. **C** Although throughput and resiliency address the ability to transport ever-larger volumes of data that must remain available, scalability addresses the ability to expand both network and system resources to meet expanding variable data consumption in a cloud service environment.

2. **A** Virtual Extensible Local Area Network (VXLAN) services provide virtual Layer 2 (Data-Link) network tunnels between Layer 3 (Network) subnets.

3. **A** The primary cause of network congestion is oversubscription of devices on the network segment, which depends on the number of devices and the bandwidth available to each.

4. **D** Resource pooling makes it possible for automated cloud provisioning systems to allow computing resources such as storage, memory, network bandwidth, virtual servers, and processing power to be assigned dynamically or upon request.

5. **B** Federated cloud services can provide interconnections between clouds, allowing multiple clouds to be managed as a single cloud resource pool in private/private, private/public, and public/public configurations.

6. **D** Network congestion can be addressed by expanding the available bandwidth (upgrading the network) or by segmenting subnetworks to limit collisions between devices on the same subnet.

7. **C** Availability in automated cloud self-service makes it possible to manage resource allocation and provisioning even during off-hours, weekends, and holidays when the IT staff is otherwise engaged. Concealing complexity from operators eases development and resource access at all times, so it would not be associated with holidays in particular.

8. **B** The storage gateway can store regularly accessed data in its cache to improve response time in comparison to repeated access against the original storage server.

9. **C** A cloud orchestration layer provides the ability to arrange, organize, integrate, and manage multiple cloud services, facilitating cloud interoperability if it is not already present.

10. **A** The Cloud Security Alliance (CSA) is a group that focuses on audit and security standards for cloud computing.

Chapter 7

1. **D** The cost of technical support escalations, although monetary, is an element of IT service management. Changes in software licensing and the shifting of technology from CAPEX to OPEX are likely to require significant changes to an organization's budgeting process.

2. **B** A successful pilot indicates an organization's readiness, and identification of regulatory requirements is necessary to determine both the business needs and the appropriate service provider. Executive management support, as well as that of key stakeholders, is necessary due to the changes in organizational cultural, domain management, and business processes that will occur. A fully staffed help desk may be of little consequence if help desk functionality is transferred to the cloud service provider.

3. **C** A service-level agreement (SLA) acts as an intermediary between the customer and the provider, and one of its functions is to document the roles and responsibilities of both the customer and the provider so that there are no surprises. A service-level objective is a quality of service measurement. Web hosting and software license agreements are also contracts between customers and providers; however, they may not contain all the necessary elements of an SLA.

4. **A** While personnel from multiple business units may participate in negotiation, review of the SLA, and management of cultural change, a successful pilot program requires representatives from all business elements in order to accurately identify potential issues.

5. **C** CompTIA and EXIN differ on vendor selection with regard to standards. EXIN does not indicate a preference in technology (e.g., Java), while CompTIA does. As such, whether or not the provider uses Java-based standards may not be a critical success factor, but the other options certainly are.

6. **B** Prior to identification of services, deployment models, and vendors, the organization must identify its business processes and their technical dependencies. After all this is done, the organization can implement its pilot program.

7. **A** The type of service provider (Infrastructure, Software, or Platform as a Service) is a prerequisite for embarking on a pilot program.

8. **C** Organizations considering using cloud services for mission-critical services or data should be very concerned with both availability and performance because deficiencies in either could negatively impact business. The other options are all standard elements of SLAs.

9. **D** It requires both business and technical staff to accurately identify business processes, their technological dependencies, and the impact of change to both. The organization's infrastructure, however, is generally the domain of technical staff.

10. **A** Any consideration of cloud service adoption should be based on business needs. Regulatory requirements, security requirements, and cost control are all examples of specific business needs.

Chapter 8

1. **A, B, D** The three tiers of a distributed application are the presentation tier (user interface), application tier (business logic), and data tier (data storage).
2. **D** Desktop applications can use all the power available in a desktop to allow for security, reliability and manageability but cannot scale out to use other computers.
3. **B** Distributed applications do not require the use of a web server and can have any type of user interface.
4. **A, B** You can make a web-based distributed application highly available by providing several web servers and scalable by adding servers as needed based on usage. Security and reliability are no different than with a regular distributed application, although some people might argue that you can easily enable SSL to encrypt data transmission in a web application yet the same can be used for a regular distributed application.
5. **C** The four design patterns of cloud-based applications are predictable burst; unpredictable burst; start small, grow fast; and periodic processing.
6. **B** Stateful objects should be avoided at all times because calls from the client can reach different servers at any time, and code should be optimized for multicore use.
7. **C** IaaS offerings are the most expensive of the three main XaaS offerings and require the customer to handle operating system maintenance. However, they allow for minimal changes to the existing code because you are basically moving your servers to a virtualized cloud environment.
8. **D** Although some cloud service providers provide only proprietary development tools, most providers allow the use of commonly used tools such as Visual Studio and programming languages such as C# and Java.

9. **B** Big data applications are I/O bound, which may result in large costs for transferring data over the Internet.

10. **C** DDOS attacks can cause new instances of a presentation layer server to be added automatically, increasing the compute cost of the application.

Chapter 9

1. **A** A service-level agreement specifies how frequently a service is available for use. This is usually a percentage value, like 99.9%, which specifies that the service is down for no more than 8.76 hours a year for a service expected to run 24 hours a day every day of the year.

2. **A, B** SaaS vendors tend to have an automatic contract renewal clause and policies on data ownership and deletion. It is necessary to understand and negotiate those with vendors. The programming language used by a SaaS vendor cannot be changed by a customer because the SaaS vendor owns the application and develops its code; the same goes for the operating system running on the servers.

3. **C** When using an IaaS vendor, the customer is responsible for managing everything on the virtual servers, from the operating system to the application.

4. **A, C** Cloud service vendors must be managed closely since the daily operations of the organization now relies on the availability of services provided by the vendor. Integration of data maintained on premises and on the cloud is needed to provide a more accurate picture of the business and facilitate business decisions. Desktop security does not affect cloud services because data is stored and changed in the cloud. Customer management does not affect cloud systems.

5. **C** AppController can be used to manage and create services on a private or public cloud using Microsoft System Center and Azure.

6. **A, C** Internet bandwidth is the main factor that must be taken into account when moving to a SaaS model because all calls that used to be made to an on-premises application are now directed to the Internet. Because connectivity to the Internet is required, the WAN design of the organization must be looked into to ensure that remote offices have the necessary connectivity to run the SaaS applications.

7. **A, B, C** A service description details what is offered by the vendor, a service-level agreement specifies the availability of the service offered, and the support agreement details how incidents are handled by the vendor.

8. **B** SaaS vendors are responsible for code maintenance and operation of applications they host.

9. **A** IaaS is viewed as hardware as a service. The vendor manages the connectivity and storage but not the individual virtual machines.

10. **B** PaaS vendors have a predefined set of programming languages that can be used in their platform.

Chapter 10

1. **B** ITIL is a collection of best practices on how to manage an IT infrastructure. The best practices prescribed by ITIL are technology agnostic.

2. **A, C, D, E, G** ITIL is composed of five distinguished volumes: Service Design, Service Strategy, Service Transition, Service Operation, and Continual Process Improvement.

3. **C** ITIL Service Transition provides guidance on the deployment of services required by an organization into a production environment.

4. **D** ITIL Service Operation provides guidance on achieving the delivery of agreed levels of service to end users and the organization, including event management, incident management, problem management, request fulfillment, and access management.

5. **A** Utility includes functionality, increased performance, and the removal of constraints. For instance, a cloud-based accounting service may provide the same functionality as an accounting service hosted on premises, but it may also allow the user to work from any device connected to the Internet, removing the constraint of connectivity to the corporate network and increasing performance by allowing the user to work even if the corporate network is unavailable.

6. **A** Availability values are similar to probabilities. It is probable that a five 9s service will be available 99.999% of the time. To determine overall availability of independent events, you need to multiply the individual probabilities. For instance, the probability of getting a 6 from rolling a die is 1/6, the probability of rolling a 6 twice in a row is $1/6 \times 1/6$, or 1/36.

7. **D** SaaS consumers do not have access to the underlying platform. They can only, and should always, monitor access to the services being consumed.

8. **C** PaaS consumers do not have access to the underlying fabric of a cloud solution, but they are responsible for developing and deploying services to the VM. They can, and should, monitor these services.

9. **A** A watcher node is a computer located at a user facility that connects to a service and performs operations to measure response time and connectivity to the service.

10. **C** A synthetic transaction is a set of prerecorded operations that mimic how a user operates a given service. Synthetic transactions are used to verify if a service is available from a specific location and the performance of said service.

Chapter 11

1. **C** While timely installation of security patches is a security control, it does not apply to malicious insiders. Employee background checks, strong security policies, and logging employee actions are appropriate mitigations because they reduce the risk of malicious employees being hired, limit the access they may have to customer data, and provide an audit trail to aid in incident response.

2. **D** Firewalls manage network traffic but do not, on their own, secure communications. Virtual private networking (VPN) creates a private network over an intermediate network such as the Internet through tunneling, isolating communications. Secure Sockets Layer (SSL) is a type of encryption used to secure web communications.

3. **B** Although there are numerous risks, there are also significant benefits related to scale. Cloud service providers often take advantages of economy of scale to provide security services many organizations would be unlikely to afford on their own.

4. **C** Metrics analysis is part of the Check phase, in which the ISMS is evaluated for effectiveness. Metrics are identified in the Plan phase and implemented in the Do phase. Changes to metrics are made in the Act phase.

5. **B** Loss of organizational control is a problem when an organization is unable to properly manage risk due to unknown exposure. This risk is mitigated by clearly defining security responsibilities and requirements in the service-level agreement (SLA). Encryption is an appropriate mitigation technique against the risk of unauthorized access to confidential data and weak data destruction procedures because even if unauthorized individuals did gain access to encrypted files, they would be unreadable without the key (or a great deal of computing power to dedicate to breaking the encryption). Encryption also protects against the danger of password compromise in transmission.

6. **B** Recovery is part of incident management and takes place after a security incident has occurred, such as restoring from backup after data loss. It does not prevent data exposure from occurring. An audit can be used to test whether or not appropriate controls are in place. Data isolation reduces the risk of data exposure in a multitenant environment. Encryption renders data unreadable without the appropriate key.

7. **C** DoS is an attack against availability. MitM attacks involve eavesdropping on encrypted communications. XSS involves injecting malicious code into hyperlinks with the goal of intercepting data. Password theft leads to unauthorized access of confidential data.

8. **B** A strong ISMS is necessary for both organizations and cloud service providers due to shared responsibility for security management.

9. **D** Security management responsibilities of both the provider and the customer should be defined in the SLA to ensure that proper controls are applied and monitored. The provider's security incident notification procedures should be defined in the SLA to ensure that they meet the business needs and regulatory requirements of the customer.

10. **B** Risk is a factor of probability (likelihood) and impact (loss)—specifically, the probability that a particular incident will occur and the impact to the business when that happens. Threats, vulnerabilities, and successful exploits have the potential to negatively impact an organization but do not in and of themselves define risk.

Chapter 12

1. **B** Authentication is the process of verifying an entity's identity by validating one or more factors against a trusted identity provider. Authorization is the process of determining whether a user has

permission to access a resource and is similar to access control. Logging in is the process of presenting credentials for authentication.

2. **D** Data in the cloud may be subject to multiple jurisdictions, based on the laws of the countries in which the data resides or passes through as well as the country of residence of the data owner and cloud service provider.

3. **A** The number of servers an organization needs may increase or decrease dynamically to provide sufficient quality of service and may overrun per-device or per-processor licenses.

4. **D** Although the organization can delegate operational duties to a cloud service provider and in some cases the cloud service provider may share responsibility with the organization, an organization cannot delegate responsibility for compliance or liability. Options A, B, and C are all examples of appropriate mitigations against noncompliance.

5. **B** Not only are government agencies not required to notify data owners, certain countries have gag orders that prevent the service providers from providing notification to the data owners.

6. **D** Unauthorized access is a security and privacy risk and is not directly related to records retention. Secure destruction of records on schedule, provider restrictions on archived storage, and difficulties associating metadata with archived records are all records retention risks that should be addressed prior to moving records subject to retention into the cloud.

7. **C** Implementing single sign-on allows an organization's users to authenticate once and pass identity attributes on to multiple applications. Kerberos is a secure authentication protocol that can be used in single sign-on. Integrated Windows authentication refers to Microsoft products authenticating against a domain login. Authorization occurs after authentication and involves determining proper permissions.

8. **B** The United States and the European Union have taken different approaches toward privacy, and US organizations that are compliant with US privacy laws may not be compliant with stricter EU laws. This has resulted in the Safe Harbor Framework, which allows organizations to certify that they are compliant with EU privacy laws so that they may handle EU data.

9. **C** Cost is a business risk, not a legal risk. Data isolation, jurisdiction (in reference to data location), and electronic discovery are all legal risks.

10. **B** In federated identity management, identity information is passed from identity providers to service providers (e.g., cloud services), allowing an organization to take advantage of single sign-on. Authentication refers to validating an entity's identity, and authorization is the process of determining whether an entity has permission to access a resource.

CompTIA's Certification Program

CompTIA, an ANSI-accredited certifier (0731), offers vendor-neutral certifications that cover a wide spectrum of topics related to information technology. CompTIA's certifications can help companies verify the skills of prospective employees and contractors, without focusing on a particular vendor's product suite.

CompTIA began with its industry-standard Professional certifications like the A+, Network+, Security+ and Project+. Many of these have since been recognized as requirements for employment in industry and governmental settings. Expanding to meet increasing demands for vendor-neutral topical expertise certification in rising areas, CompTIA has a Basic series that includes the Strata IT Fundamentals certification as well as its first Mastery certification: the CompTIA Advanced Security Practitioner (CASP). Finally, CompTIA also has a number of Specialty certifications in multiple niche areas, including cloud computing.

CompTIA Cloud Essentials The CompTIA Cloud Essentials certification is an entry-level coverage of cloud computing concepts from both technical and business perspectives. You must take and pass one exam to earn the CompTIA Cloud Essentials certification.

CompTIA Green IT The CompTIA Green IT certification is an entry-level certification covering strategies and knowledge needed to conduct environmentally friendly techniques within an organization's information technology infrastructure and data centers. You must take and pass one exam to earn the CompTIA Green IT certification.

CompTIA HealthCare IT Technician The CompTIA HealthCare IT Technician certification covers knowledge specific to implementing, deploying, and supporting information technology in various clinical health care settings. You must take and pass one exam to earn the CompTIA HealthCare IT Technician certification.

CompTIA IT for Sales The CompTIA IT for Sales certification is an entry-level certification that covers professional knowledge of technology basics necessary to support or complete sales activities with customers in technical markets. You must take and pass one exam to earn the CompTIA IT for Sales certification.

Social Media Security Professional The Social Media Security Professional certification covers knowledge and skill areas needed to mitigate business risk posed by social media networking channels.

Certification Objectives Map

Table C.1 provides objective mappings for the CompTIA Cloud Essentials exam (CLO-001), which is intended for individuals with at least six months working in an environment that relies on IT services. This table identifies the chapters and sections where the CLO-011 exam objectives are covered.

TABLE C.1 CompTIA Cloud Essentials (CLO-001) Exam objectives map

Objectives	Chapter and Section
Characteristics of Cloud Services from a Business Perspective	Chapters 1, 2, 3, 5
1.1 Understand common terms and definitions of cloud computing and provide examples.	Chapter 1, Defining Cloud Computing, Understanding Cloud Computing Technologies
1.2 Describe the relationship between cloud computing and virtualization.	Chapter 2, Evolving from Virtualization to the Cloud
1.3 Name early examples of cloud computing.	Chapter 1, Understanding Resource Management Automation, Understanding Virtualized Computing Environments
1.4 Understand several common definitions of cloud computing and their commonalities/ differences.	Chapter 2, Identifying Cloud Deployment Models and Scope Modifiers
1.5 Recognize what types of organizations might benefit from cloud computing.	Chapter 5, Identifying Value Now and in the Future, Choosing the Appropriate Cloud Model, Making the Right Decision

1.6 Recognize what types of organizations might not benefit from cloud computing.	Chapter 5, Making the Right Decision
1.7 Distinguish between the different types of clouds, including SaaS, IaaS, PaaS, and give examples of them.	Chapter 3, Categorizing Cloud Services, Examining Software as a Service, Examining Platform as a Service, Examining Infrastructure as a Service
Cloud Computing and Business Value	**Chapters 5, 11**
2.1 Recognize the similarities and differences between cloud computing and outsourcing.	Chapter 5, Identifying Business Drivers for Cloud Computing
2.2 Understand the following characteristics of clouds and cloud services from a business perspective: ▶ Scalability ▶ Security ▶ Hardware independence ▶ Variable costs ▶ Time to market ▶ Distribution over the Internet	Chapter 5, Identifying Business Drivers for Cloud Computing , Examining the Business Impact Chapter 11, Understanding Security and Risk, Exploring Common Security Risks and Mitigations, Recognizing Security Benefits
2.3 Demonstrate how the characteristics of cloud computing enhance business value.	Chapter 5, Identifying Business Drivers for Cloud Computing , Examining the Business Impact, Identifying Value Now and in the Future
Technical Perspectives/Cloud Types	**Chapters 2, 6, 8, 11**
3.1 Understand the difference between private and public types of clouds from a technical perspective and provide examples.	Chapter 2, Identifying Cloud Deployment Models and Scope Modifiers Chapter 6, Achieving Interoperability

(Continues)

TABLE C.1 *(Continued)*

3.2 Understand at a high level the following important techniques and methods for cloud computing deployment: ▶ Networking ▶ Automation and Self-service ▶ Federation ▶ The role of standardization	Chapter 6, Leveraging Automation and Self-Service, Understanding Federated Cloud Services Chapter 8, Understanding the Role of Standard Applications
3.3 Explain technical challenges and risks for cloud computing and methods to mitigate them for: ▶ Cloud storage ▶ Application performance ▶ Data integration ▶ Security	Chapter 6, Understanding Cloud Networks, Achieving Interoperability Chapter 8, Preparing for Technical Challenges Chapter 11, Exploring Common Security Risks and Mitigations
3.4 Describe the impact of cloud computing on application architecture and the application-development process.	Chapter 8, Developing Cloud-Ready Applications
Steps to Successful Adoption of Cloud	**Chapters 7, 8, 9**
4.1 Explain typical steps that lead to a successful adoption of cloud computing services: ▶ Understand selection criteria for a pilot ▶ Relate SaaS, PaaS, IaaS deployment to organizational goals	Chapter 7, Aligning Cloud Deployments with Organizational Goals, Identifying the Impact of Cloud Adoption to Business Processes
4.2 Understand the roles and capabilities of cloud computing vendors and dependencies on the vendors.	Chapter 7, Aligning Cloud Deployments with Organizational Goals Chapter 9, Identifying Vendor Roles and Responsibilities

4.3 Understand the following organizational capabilities that are relevant for realizing cloud benefits: ▶ Skills that are required in an organization adopting cloud computing ▶ Critical success factors	Chapter 9, Identifying Organizational Skill Requirements
4.4 Describe multiple approaches for migrating applications.	Chapter 8, Migrating Applications to the Cloud
Impact and Changes of Cloud Computing on IT Service Management	**Chapters 7, 8, 9, 10, 11**
5.1 Understand the impact and changes of cloud computing on IT service management in a typical organization: ▶ Service Strategy ▶ Service Design ▶ Service Operation ▶ Service Transition	Chapter 10, Understanding ITIL Service Management, Applying ITIL to Cloud Computing
5.2 Use a structured approach based on ITIL to explore the potential impact of cloud computing in your organization.	Chapter 7, Understanding the Importance of Service-Level Agreements Chapter 8, Identifying and Mitigating Risks Chapter 9, Preparing for Incident Management Chapter 10, Applying ITIL to Cloud Computing, Developing and Utilizing Performance Metrics, Implementing Continual Service Improvement Chapter 11, Implementing an ISMS, Responding to Incidents

(Continues)

TABLE C.1 *(Continued)*

Risks and Consequences of Cloud Computing	Chapters 5, 11, 12
6.1 Explain and identify the issues associated with integrating cloud computing into an organization's existing compliance risk and regulatory framework: ▶ Security, Legal, Compliance, Privacy risks	Chapter 11, Reviewing Security Standards, Exploring Common Security Risks and Mitigations Chapter 12, Identifying Legal Risks, Identifying Privacy Risks, Managing Identity in the Cloud
6.2 Explain the implications for direct cost and cost allocations.	Chapter 5, Examining the Business Impact
6.3 Understand how to maintain strategic flexibility.	Chapter 5, Examining the Business Impact

NOTE Exam objectives are subject to change at any time without prior notice and at CompTIA's sole discretion. Please visit the CompTIA website (`www.comptia.org`) for the latest information on the Cloud Essentials exam.

EXIN's Certification Program

EXIN's original purpose in support of the European Ministry of Economic Affairs has been expanded to provide internally recognized certifications for information technology, with ISO certification (ISO 9001:2008). EXIN's certifications can help companies verify the skills of prospective employees and contractors, particularly those operating within or as partners of European markets.

EXIN began development of IT standards, including the well-known ITIL certification. Their certifications have expanded to meet changes in the information technology arena and the European Economic Union's efforts toward modernization of business processes.

EXIN Cloud The EXIN Cloud Computing Foundation certification reflects strategies and knowledge needed to implement and integrate cloud computing components within an organizational enterprise network. You must take and pass one exam to earn the EXIN Cloud Computing Foundation certification.

EXIN Green IT The EXIN Green IT certification is an entry-level certification covering strategies and knowledge needed to conduct environmentally friendly techniques within an organization's information technology infrastructure and data centers, in support of GREEN ICT and SMART initiatives within the European market. You must take and pass one exam for each of the two EXIN Green IT certificates: Foundation and Citizen.

EXIN ITSM based on ISO/IEC 20000 The EXIN IT Service Management certificate based on ISO/IEC 20000 compliance focuses on management and auditing of service management practices in accordance with ISO/IEC 20000 requirements. You must take and pass two exams to earn the ITSM Foundation and Foundation Bridge certificates, with nine additional focused certificates expanding this achievement across three functional areas—professional, manager/executive, and auditor—with a requirement of one additional exam per focus certificate.

ITIL The IT Infrastructure Library (ITIL) is the current gold standard for IT Service Management, representing knowledge of implementation, maintenance, and management of IT services and IT product delivery. You must take and pass one exam to earn the ITIL Foundation Certificate in Service Management, with 10 additional intermediate certificates expanding this achievement across specific functional areas, with a requirement of one additional exam per intermediate certificate.

Certification Objectives Map

Table D.1 provides objective mappings for the EXIN Cloud Computing Fundamentals exam (EX0-116), which is intended to provide a foundation for IT managers, IT professionals, business managers and procurement specialists involved with cloud computing initiatives. This table identifies the chapters and sections where the exam objectives are covered.

TABLE D.1 Cloud Computing Foundation exam objectives map

Objectives	Chapter and Section
The Principles of Cloud Computing	**Chapters 1, 2, 3, 4, 5, 6**
1.1.1 Explain what Cloud computing is.	Chapter 1, Defining Cloud Computing, Understanding Resource Management Automation
1.1.2 Compare the four main Deployment Models for Cloud computing (Private, Public, Community and Hybrid cloud).	Chapter 2, Identifying Cloud Deployment Models and Scope Modifiers
1.1.3 Describe the three main Service Models for Cloud computing (SaaS, PaaS and IaaS).	Chapter 3, Categorizing Cloud Services, Examining Software as a Service, Examining Platform as a Service, Examining Infrastructure as a Service
1.2.1 Describe the main concepts from which Cloud computing developed.	Chapter 1, Understanding Distributed Application Design, Understanding Virtualized Computing Environments, Understanding High-Performance Computing Models Chapter 2, Evolving from Virtualization to the Cloud

1.2.2 Explain the role of network and servers in Cloud computing.	Chapter 1, Understanding Cloud Computing Technologies Chapter 4, Accessing the Cloud Chapter 6, Understanding Cloud Networks
1.2.3 Describe the role of the Internet in Cloud computing.	Chapter 1, Defining Cloud Computing
1.2.4 Explain the role of Virtualization in Cloud computing.	Chapter 1, Understanding Virtualized Computing Environments
1.2.5 Describe the role of managed services in Cloud computing.	Chapter 1, Defining Cloud Computing
1.3.1 Explain the difference between a single purpose and multipurpose architecture.	Chapter 3, Examining Infrastructure as a Service
1.3.2 Describe the service-oriented architechture.	Chapter 3, Categorizing Cloud Services
1.4.1 Identify the main drivers for Cloud computing.	Chapter 5, Identifying Business Drivers for Cloud Computing
1.4.2 Identify the main limitations of Cloud computing.	Chapter 5, Examining the Business Impact
Implementing and Managing Cloud Computing	**Chapters 7, 8, 9, 10, 11, Online Appendix**
2.1.1 Describe the main components of a local cloud environment and how they are interconnected.	Online Appendix
2.1.2 Describe the use of Virtual Private Network access to a Local Area Network.	Chapter 11, Exploring Common Security Risks and Mitigations Online Appendix
2.1.3 Describe the risks of connecting a local cloud network to the public internet.	Online Appendix
2.2.1 Describe the use of IT Service Management principles in a Cloud environment.	Chapter 8, Identifying and Mitigating Risks Chapter 9, Preparing for Incident Management Chapter 10, Understanding ITIL Service Management, Applying ITIL to Cloud Computing

(Continues)

TABLE D.1 *(Continued)*

2.2.2 Explain the management of service levels in a Cloud environment.	Chapter 7, Understanding the Importance of Service-Level Agreements Chapter 10, Developing and Utilizing Performance Metrics, Implementing Continual Service Improvement
Using the Cloud	**Chapters 1, 4, 5, 7, 8, 9, 11**
3.1.1 Describe how to access Web Applications through a Web Browser.	Chapter 4, Accessing the Cloud
3.1.2 Describe the Cloud Web Access Architecture.	Chapter 4, Accessing the Cloud
3.1.3 Describe the use of a Thin Client.	Chapter 1, Understanding Cloud Computing Technologies Chapter 4, Accessing the Cloud
3.1.4 Describe the use of mobile devices in accessing the cloud.	Chapter 1, Understanding Cloud Computing Technologies Chapter 4, Empowering Mobile Computing
3.2.1 Identify the impact of Cloud computing on the primary processes of an organization.	Chapter 7, Identifying the Impact of Cloud Adoption to Business Processes
3.2.2 Describe the role of standard applications in collaboration.	Chapter 8, Understanding the Role of Standard Applications
3.3.1 Explain how using Cloud computing changes the relation between vendors and customers.	Chapter 9, Identifying Vendor Roles and Responsibilities
3.3.2 Identify benefits and risks of providing cloud-based services.	Chapter 5, Identifying Business Drivers for Cloud Computing Chapter 11, Recognizing Security Benefits
Security and Compliance	**Chapters 11, 12**
4.1.1 Describe the security risks in the cloud.	Chapter 11, Exploring Common Security Risks and Mitigations
4.1.2 Describe measures mitigating security risks.	Chapter 11, Exploring Common Security Risks and Mitigations

4.2.1 Describe the main aspects of Identity management.	Chapter 12, Managing Identity in the Cloud
4.2.2 Describe privacy and compliance issues and safeguards in Cloud computing.	Chapter 12, Identifying Legal Risks, Identifying Privacy Risks
Evaluation of Cloud Computing	**Chapters 5, 7, 10**
5.1.1 Describe the costs and possible savings of Cloud computing.	Chapter 5, Examining the Business Impact
5.1.2 Describe the main operational and staffing benefits of Cloud computing.	Chapter 5, Identifying Business Drivers for Cloud Computing
5.2.1 Describe the evaluation of performance factors, management requirements and satisfaction factors.	Chapter 10, Developing and Utilizing Performance Metrics, Implementing Continual Service Improvement
5.2.2 Describe the evaluation of service providers and their services in Cloud computing.	Chapter 7, Aligning Cloud Deployments with Organizational Goals Chapter 10, Developing and Utilizing Performance Metrics

NOTE Exam objectives are subject to change at any time without prior notice and at EXIN's sole discretion. Please visit the EXIN website (`www.exin.com`) for the latest information on the EXIN Cloud Computing Foundation exam.

Glossary

123D Catch

An SaaS photogrammetry cloud service provided by Autodesk.

accounting

The process of tracking resource usage for operational, security, and compliance purposes.

application programming interface (API)

An interface design specification that allows software-to-software communication at the code level. Later service-oriented architecture (SOA) allowed dissimilar technologies to interoperate at the interface level even if their APIs are incompatible by using an SOA "wrapper" to intercept access requests and reformat data as needed.

audit

The methodical examination and evaluation of something (e.g., account, system, process, organization, person, or project) for the purpose of ascertaining its validity, reliability, quality, security, and/or compliance with regulations.

authentication

The process of verifying an entity's identity by validating one or more factors: something you know, something you have, or something you are.

authorization

The process of determining whether an entity is allowed to access a resource and with what level of permissions.

availability

Refers to the accessibility of data. To be available, data needs to be protected against disruption of service.

Aviary

An SaaS audio/video production suite of applications.

botnet

A group of computers under the control of a "bot herder." Supporters of the Anonymous hacktivist organization downloaded the Low-Orbit Ion Cannon (LOIC) utility to lend their computers to denial of service attacks conducted by the group, but most botnets comprise individual computers infected with malware.

business model innovation level

The level of maturity at which an organization is able to leverage cloud services to change its business model or key business processes through innovation.

capital expense (CAPEX)

As opposed to OPEX, a capital expense is one intended to create future benefits to an organization, typically by procurement of fixed assets or upgrades. Capital expenses involve property that extends beyond the current tax year so must then be amortized or depreciated over succeeding tax years.

CCTA

The Central Computer and Telecommunications Agency of the UK government was responsible for the creation of the first version of Information Technology Infrastructure Library (ITIL) in the 1980s.

client access license (CAL)

Client access licensing models are employed by proprietary software companies, controlling client access to server software and server software services. Most client access licenses are per-user or per-device licenses or they limit the number of concurrent users that may access server hosted software at one time.

cloud bursting

Cloud bursting is a hybrid cloud implementation used when the demand for local private cloud resources exceeds local resources, at which point the app "bursts" out of the private cloud into designated public cloud resources to manage the overrun.

cloud computing stack

The term *cloud computing stack* refers to the integration of all three primary cloud service models defined by NIST—Software as a Service (SaaS), Platform as a Service (PaaS), and Infrastructure as a Service (IaaS).

Cloud Data Management Interface (CDMI)

A standard that defines administration and access for managing content and security over cloud resources.

Cloud Security Alliance (CSA)

A group that focuses on cloud audit and security standards.

Cloud Standards Customer Council (CSCC)

A group that influences standards based on cloud user requirements.

community cloud

Community clouds are provisioned for use by a group of related organizations with shared concerns, often hosted locally (private) by one or more members but otherwise operating as remote (public) clouds for the other members of the community.

compliance

Adherence to regulations, policies, standards, and other requirements.

confidentiality

Refers to the sensitivity of data. Confidential data needs to be protected from unauthorized access, use, or disclosure.

congestion

A state in the network when there are too many devices in a particular network segment and they are interfering with one another.

Continual Process Improvement

ITIL Continual Process Improvement provides guidance on aligning and realigning IT services to changing business needs by identifying and implementing improvements to the IT services used to support the business. Continual Process Improvement needs to be planned and scheduled as a process with well-defined activities, inputs, outputs, and roles.

cross-site scripting (XSS)

A web-based exploit in which an attacker injects malicious code into a hyperlink and steals information or credentials when the user clicks it.

customer relationship management (CRM)

Customer relationship management software solutions bridge sales, marketing, customer service, and support services to manage an organization's interactions with existing and future customers. Salesforce is a dominant cloud CRM provider in the current market.

Database as a Service (DBaaS)

Database as a Service represents an element of Infrastructure as a Service (IaaS) implementation, providing for the storage and processing of extremely large data sets using cloud resource scalability.

DDOS attack

Distributed denial of service attacks are engineered to use a botnet, which is a group of computers under the control of a "bot herder," to flood a server with requests.

denial of service (DoS) attack

An attack against availability in which an attacker disrupts service for a user or an organization using various flood-type techniques.

direct cost

A cost that can be directly attributed to a product, process, or service, such as the cost for materials or labor.

distributed denial of service (DDOS)

A denial of service (DoS) attack that is carried out against a service from many compromised computers in a coordinated manner.

Distributed Management Task Force (DMTF)

A collection of groups developing standards for cloud management interfaces, audit data, interoperability, software license management, and virtualization.

Dropbox

An SaaS file storage application.

economic denial of sustainability (EDoS) attack

An attack in which the attacker takes advantage of use-based cloud pricing models to drive up an organization's usage costs to unsustainable levels.

encryption

A method of protecting data confidentiality by transforming readable data into unreadable data through the use of an algorithm and key.

enterprise resource planning (ERP)

Enterprise resource planning software solutions bridge accounts receivable, accounts payable, manufacturing, and CRM functions within an organization to manage information interchange between business elements and external partner organizations.

Everything as a Service (XaaS)

Everything as a Service represents the continued expansion of cloud-service-level combinations and integration between cloud and traditional services. This is not a clearly defined term but a living reference used to describe whatever the current level of integration provides.

fabric

Underlying infrastructure used for cloud computing. For instance, storage fabric is used to represent all storage available to provision VMs on a cloud; network fabric represents the physical network used by virtualization hosts in a cloud environment.

failover clustering

A failover cluster is a group of servers that work together to maintain high availability of applications and services. If one of the servers, or nodes, fails, another node in the cluster can take over its workload without any downtime (this process is known as failover).

federated cloud

A collection of cloud services using technology that allows them to be managed as a single integrate cloud.

federated identity management

The identity management process of allowing users in different security domains to share services without having identities in each domain.

financial management

The process by which an organization's financial resources are directed, monitored, and controlled.

firewall

An appliance or application that inspects and regulates network traffic based on a set of configurable rules, such as allowing or blocking traffic on specific network ports or to/from specific hosts.

Force.com

A PaaS application development platform hosted by SalesForce.

GoGrid

An IaaS service hosting provider.

Google Apps

A PaaS application development platform hosted by Google.

Google Drive

An IaaS file storage application hosted by Google.

high-performance computing (HPC)

Powerful specialized or grid-based computing that distributes simultaneous analysis or problem solving across many nodes to complete data processing tasks very rapidly. HPC systems may be called supercomputers, but this is a term that applies to the top HPC systems at the time—a group that is always changing as new, faster machines are created.

horizontal hybrid cloud

Horizontal hybrid cloud models provide services to different access groups.

horizontal scaling

Adding more nodes (i.e., physical or virtual network devices) to a distributed system. Also referred to as scale out.

hybrid cloud

Hybrid clouds are provisioned using two or more components of private, community, or public clouds. They require more maintenance than the other models but offer greater flexibility for the organization in return. Hybrids can be constructed as collections of other clouds, vertical hybrids, horizontal hybrids, or a mixture of the various types as needed by a particular organization.

Hyper-V

Hyper-V is a hypervisor technology owned by Microsoft and available with the Windows Server operating systems.

identity

A set of attributes that distinguishes one individual or entity from others.

identity management

The process of identifying individuals and other entities needing access to data or other information resources and managing their life cycle.

IEEE Standards Association (IEEE-SA)

A group within the IEEE focusing on standards covering cloud portability, interoperability, and federation.

incident

An unplanned interruption of service; an event that impacts the confidentiality, integrity, or availability of an information system.

incident management

The process of planning for, detecting, and responding to incidents.

indirect cost

A cost that is not associated with a single process, product, or service, such as the cost for administrative staff, utilities, or rent.

information leak

A vulnerability in which system information is revealed to an attacker. This information may then be used to plan an attack.

information security management

The activities and controls taken to protect information and information systems.

information security management system (ISMS)

A system of policies, processes, and controls used to identify, implement, monitor, and update appropriate and cost-effective security measures based on current business needs.

Information Technology Infrastructure Library (ITIL)

The Information Technology Infrastructure Library is a collection of industry-proven best practices on how to operate an IT infrastructure within a large organization by aligning IT with business needs. ITIL provides prescriptive guidance on the different processes relate to planning, deploying, and operating an IT infrastructure.

Infrastructure as a Service (IaaS)

Infrastructure as a Service represents cloud resources provided at the lowest level—storage, databases, network interconnections, and similar functions. This is the most flexible level of cloud service but requires the most management and planning of the consuming organization.

integrity

Integrity represents the reliability of data. To have integrity, data needs to be protected from unauthorized modification or deletion.

Java

Java is a general-purpose object-oriented programming language intended for use across all platforms, making it ideal for use in web-based applications. Java is currently owned and supported by Oracle but regularly falls victim to exploitation of newly identified vulnerabilities by hackers. CompTIA considers Java-based cloud hosting and development to be a positive for the purposes of the Cloud Essentials exam.

Low-Orbit Ion Cannon (LOIC)

A net stress test tool sometimes used to conduct DDoS attacks.

man-in-the-middle (MitM) attack

A man-in-the-middle attack leverages a third system that intercepts data between two end points for inspection or manipulation, causing the end point systems to operate normally because each identifies the eavesdropping system as the legitimate opposite end point. Message authentication packets integrated within tunneling encryption like SSL help protect against this type of interception attack.

Microsoft Office

A traditional user productivity suite from Microsoft.

mobility

The ability to access information resources from any device, anywhere, and at any time.

multitenancy

Multitenancy refers to workloads from multiple clients, virtual machines, or services being shared by a hosting server and separated only by logical access policies.

National Institute of Standards and Technology (NIST)

A group responsible for standards defining cloud types, cloud security, and audit practices.

NetSuite

An SaaS enterprise management suite.

Office 365

A SaaS cloud-based user productivity suite from Microsoft.

Open Security Architecture (OSA)

An open-source project that provides security standards in the form of patterns (in other words, diagrams and explanatory text), drawing from other recognized standards such as NIST Special Publication 800-53, *Recommended Security Controls for Federal Information Systems and Organizations*.

operating expense (OPEX)

As opposed to CAPEX, operating expenses represent the day-to-day "cost of doing business," typically including utilities and consumables whose costs can be deducted in the current tax year in net profit calculations. Operating expenses reflect level of consumption and use and so are well aligned with cloud service cost models.

operational-level agreement (OLA)

A formal, negotiated document that defines (or attempts to define) in quantitative (and perhaps qualitative) terms the service being offered to an internal customer, such as a different department in your organization. Similar to a SLA.

Organization for the Advancement of Structured Information Standards (OASIS)

A group developing standards for cloud identity management, data sharing, privacy, and portability.

pay-as-you-go model

A variable cost model in which a customer pays only for the services used.

Payment Card Industry Data Security Standards (PCI-DSS)

A security framework that is maintained by the PCI Security Standards Council and designed to protect cardholder data. It includes security requirements for networking, data protection, vulnerability management, access control, monitoring, and policy.

personally identifiable information (PII)

Information that can be used to uniquely identify an individual. Examples of PII include contact information, financial information, online account usernames, government-issued identity documents (e.g., SSN, passport), and biometric data.

photogrammetry

A CPU-intensive way to create a 3D model using multiple photos of the object from different angles.

Pixlr

A SaaS image-editing application.

Plan-Do-Check-Act (PDCA)

Plan-Do-Check-Act, also termed the Deming cycle, is an iterative cyclical management process popularized by Edward Deming for quality control. PDCA encompasses planning, implementation, evaluation, and change and is used in project management, continuous improvement efforts, and quality management.

Platform as a Service (PaaS)

Platform as a Service represents cloud resources provided at the development level for custom application development and hosting. Consuming organizations have no concern over infrastructural decisions but may be limited by the available languages supported by their PaaS provider. Many providers at this level implement proprietary versions of languages to prevent customers from easy migration to other alternatives.

privacy

The condition of secrecy or seclusion. With regard to data, it refers to the expectation of secrecy when personal information is collected or shared.

private cloud

A private cloud is owned, managed, and operated by an organization and often resides on equipment shared by traditional data center configurations that are local to the organization.

process transformation level

The maturity level at which an organization is able to leverage cloud computing to improve its business processes.

profiling

Database profiling is a process of analysis of data organization and data use to identify potential issues so that alternative application procedures can be put in place to protect data against undesired modification or loss.

public cloud

Public cloud services represent the most thoroughly virtualized cloud infrastructural design, removing data center resources partially or completely from the organization's data center. Public clouds may be configured for access by an organization or partitioned group (community) or for the general public.

Rackspace

An IaaS service hosting provider.

return on investment (ROI)

Return on investment (ROI) is a performance measure used to evaluate the efficiency of an investment or to compare the efficiency of a number of different investments.

Salesforce

A SaaS vendor that expanded its original Human Resources application to include the Force.com PaaS platform.

scalability

The capability to increase or decrease resources based on need.

scale out

Adding more nodes (i.e., physical or virtual network devices) to a distributed system. Also referred to as horizontal scaling.

scale up

Adding resources to a single node, such as memory, processing power, or redundant components. Also referred to as vertical scaling.

Secure Sockets Layer (SSL)

Encryption for secure web communications that uses a strong asymmetric key to establish a connection and a lighter-weight symmetric key for the session, creating an encrypted tunnel between a web client and web application through which data can be transmitted over public networks. Message authentication codes negotiated by the protocols protect message integrity during transmission.

security

Policies, processes and measures implemented to protect the confidentiality, integrity, and availability of information systems. Security includes management, technical, and operational controls to protect information services and data resources.

Service Design

Information Technology Infrastructure Library (ITIL) Service Design provides guidance on the design of IT services, processes, and service management. Design in ITIL focuses more specifically on services provided to the organization instead of individual technologies.

service desk

ITIL defines the service desk as the central point of contact between users and service providers. It is also the main point for reporting incidents.

service-level agreement (SLA)

A service-level agreement is a contract between customers and service vendors that defines the levels of service and service characteristics that the customer can demand and the vendor is responsible for fulfilling.

Service Operation

ITIL Service Operation provides guidance on achieving the delivery of agreed levels of service to end users and the organization.

service-oriented architecture (SOA)

A set of interface programming standards that allow software-to-software interoperability between applications written using differing API standards.

Service Strategy

The ITIL Service Strategy volume provides guidance on classification of service provider investments in services. The most important topics covered in Service Strategy are service value definition, service assets, market analysis, business case development, and service provider types.

Service Transition

ITIL Service Transition provides guidance on the deployment of services required by an organization into a production environment.

sharding

Database sharding involves the separation of large or complex data sets into smaller shards for simultaneous processing or analysis across distributed cloud resources.

Shazam

A SaaS application that can identify an overhead song.

single sign-on

A mechanism that allows an organization's users to authenticate once and access multiple applications.

SkyDrive

An IaaS file storage service by Microsoft.

Software as a Service (SaaS)

Software as a Service represents cloud resources provided as prebuilt applications accessible over the Internet. Consuming organizations have limited or no control over feature additions or application changes. They are limited to the provided functions of the application. SaaS is the most common form of cloud service in today's enterprise networks because it does not require software installation and applications can run within cloud clients such as web browsers or thin client terminals. All support for SaaS offerings is left to the provider, reducing local support requirements.

staffing benefit

The ability to reduce or retask staff due to improvements in efficiency.

stateful objects

A stateful object is an instance of a class that may morph itself into various states. For example, an object can be created but not initialized, later be initialized and made ready for use, and at the end be disposed of (but still remain accessible in memory).

stateless objects

A stateless object represents just one state for its whole life cycle. Modeling this as an immutable object, whose fields are initialized only once during construction and then remain unchanged, seems to be the most straightforward design technique.

Statement on Auditing Standards (SAS)

Auditing and reporting guidelines for external auditors based on accepted standards.

storage area network (SAN)

A SAN is a flexible dedicated network connecting computers and storage devices virtually rather than connecting drives directly to individual computers.

Storage Networking Industries Association (SNIA)

Organization whose Cloud Storage Initiative is developed the Cloud Data Management Interface (CDMI) standard for assigning metadata that defines required services.

synthetic transaction

Set of prerecorded operations that mimic an end user accessing a service remotely.

System Center

System Center is a suite of products sold by Microsoft to manage private clouds and networks.

thick client

A thick client, often termed a workstation, is an access device that has powerful CPUs, local application storage, and display and input device connections. Thick clients can run applications locally, accessing remote cloud services as needed.

thin client

A thin client is an access device with minimal local processing power and display and input device connections but lacking local storage for applications. Thin clients require remote services to provide application functions and processing power.

time to market

The amount of time from product conception to release.

total cost of ownership (TCO)

The complete cost of an object or service throughout its lifetime, from purchase to disposal, including both direct and indirect costs.

Ubuntu One

An IaaS file storage service that also offers SaaS integration with music players on multiple platforms.

use case

A use case is the smallest unit of activity that is meaningful to the user. A use case must be self-contained and leave the business of the application in a consistent state.

utility

Utility, as defined by ITIL, measures the functionality, performance, and removal of constraints of a service.

utility level

The level of maturity at which an organization experiences immediate usefulness from cloud computing, such as reduction in costs.

vendor lock-in

Vendor lock-in, or proprietary lock-in, is a situation in which an organization must continue to use a specific set of technologies or products from a specific vendor to avoid significant costs for transferring to alternative equivalents.

vertical hybrid cloud

Vertical hybrid models bring together all services required for a particular task.

vertical scaling

Adding resources to a single node, such as memory, processing power, or redundant components. Also referred to as scale up.

virtual firewall

A firewall designed specifically to protect virtual hosts, operating in different modes depending on deployment. In bridge mode, the virtual firewall is deployed within the network infrastructure like a traditional firewall. In hypervisor mode, the virtual firewall is within the hypervisor environment and directly monitors virtual machine traffic.

virtual private network (VPN)

A secure private network interconnected securely over a public network (in other words, the Internet) or another intermediate network. VPN communications are isolated from the rest of the network through an IP tunnel and are secured through encryption and authentication.

VMware vCloud

VMware vCloud is a VMware suite of products used to manage private clouds.

warranty

Warranty, as defined by ITIL, measures the availability, capacity, continuity, and security of a service.

watcher node

A watcher node is a computer running a synthetic transaction and reporting its results to an operations management application.

web service

Developed for SOA over web connectivity, web services implement software-to-software interoperability using the XML language and the Web Services Description Language (WSDL) standard.

Words With Friends

A SaaS multiplatform cloud crossword game application.

Zoho Docs

A SaaS user productivity suite that includes features like macros.

INDEX

D

N

O

P

S

T

U